AMERICA'S
TEST KITCHEN

also by america's test kitchen

Umma
When Southern Women Cook
Cocktails Illustrated
Food Gifts
America's Test Kitchen 25th Anniversary Cookbook
A Very Chinese Cookbook
Boards
Gatherings

The Sheet Pan
The Skillet
Cook It in Your Dutch Oven
Cook It in Cast Iron
Ultimate Air Fryer Perfection
Kitchen Gear

Baking for Two
Everyday Bread
The Cook's Illustrated Baking Book
The Perfect Cookie
The Perfect Pie
The Perfect Cake

The Science of Good Cooking
Cook's Science
The New Cooking School Cookbook: Fundamentals
The New Cooking School Cookbook: Advanced Fundamentals

Mostly Meatless
Vegan for Everybody
Vegan Cooking for Two
Vegetables Illustrated
How Can It Be Gluten Free Cookbook Collection

The Complete Anti-Inflammatory Cookbook
The Complete Plant-Based Cookbook
The Complete Beans and Grains Cookbook
The Complete Mediterranean Cookbook
The Complete Cooking for Two Cookbook, 10th Anniversary Edition
The Complete Diabetes Cookbook
The Complete Vegetarian Cookbook
The Complete One Pot
The Complete Autumn and Winter Cookbook
The Complete Summer Cookbook
The Complete Modern Pantry
The Complete Salad Cookbook

The Complete America's Test Kitchen TV Show Cookbook
The Complete Cook's Country TV Show Cookbook

For a full listing of all our books:
CooksIllustrated.com
AmericasTestKitchen.com

praise for america's test kitchen titles

"The book is a treasure for its endless kitchen wisdom, heart-filled recipes, and deep-rooted respect for all generations that came before. It showcases home cooking at its best, ranging from sauces, banchan (side dishes), and a slew of kimchi, to gurgling stews, tantalizing meats, and not-too-sweet fare."

Epicurious on *Umma: A Korean Mom's Kitchen Wisdom & 100 Family Recipes*

A Best Cookbook of 2024

Los Angeles Times* on *When Southern Women Cook

"This 'very' Chinese cookbook from a father-son duo is a keeper. The book—ATK's first devoted to Chinese cooking—proves that you can teach and entertain in the same volume . . . All in all, it's one of the most charming works I've seen in years, and I already want to get a second copy."

Washington Post* on *A Very Chinese Cookbook

"An exhaustive but approachable primer for those looking for a 'flexible' diet. Chock-full of tips, you can dive into the science of plant-based cooking or just sit back and enjoy the 500 recipes."

Minneapolis Star Tribune* on *The Complete Plant-Based Cookbook

"This comprehensive guide is packed with delicious recipes and fun menu ideas but its unique draw is the personal narrative and knowledge-sharing of each ATK chef, which will make this a hit."

Booklist* on *Gatherings

"True to its name, this smart and endlessly enlightening cookbook is about as definitive as it's possible to get in the modern vegetarian realm."

Men's Journal* on *The Complete Vegetarian Cookbook

"A mood board for one's food board is served up in this excellent guide . . . This has instant classic written all over it."

Publishers Weekly* (starred review) on *Boards: Stylish Spreads for Casual Gatherings

"Reassuringly hefty and comprehensive, ***The Complete Autumn and Winter Cookbook*** by America's Test Kitchen has you covered with a seemingly endless array of seasonal fare . . . This overstuffed compendium is guaranteed to warm you from the inside out."

NPR on *The Complete Autumn and Winter Cookbook*

"If you're one of the 30 million Americans with diabetes, ***The Complete Diabetes Cookbook*** by America's Test Kitchen belongs on your kitchen shelf."

Parade.com on *The Complete Diabetes Cookbook*

"Another flawless entry in the America's Test Kitchen canon, *Bowls* guides readers of all culinary skill levels in composing one-bowl meals from a variety of cuisines."

BuzzFeed Books on *Bowls*

"***The Perfect Cookie*** . . . is, in a word, perfect. This is an important and substantial cookbook . . . If you love cookies, but have been a tad shy to bake on your own, all your fears will be dissipated. This is one book you can use for years with magnificently happy results."

HuffPost on *The Perfect Cookie*

"The book offers an impressive education for curious cake makers, new and experienced alike. A summation of 25 years of cake making at ATK, there are cakes for every taste."

Wall Street Journal* on *The Perfect Cake

"The go-to gift book for newlyweds, small families, or empty nesters."

Orlando Sentinel* on *The Complete Cooking for Two Cookbook

DINNER TONIGHT

200 QUICK RECIPES

FOR INSPIRED
WEEKNIGHT COOKING

AMERICA'S TEST KITCHEN

Library of Congress CIP data has been applied for.

ISBN 978-1-966027-00-3

America's Test Kitchen

21 Drydock Avenue, Boston, MA 02210

Printed in Canada

10 9 8 7 6 5 4 3 2

Distributed by Penguin Random House Publisher Services

Tel: 800-733-3000

Pictured on front cover: Bucatini with Charred Zucchini, Mint, and Lemon (page 252)

Pictured on back cover (clockwise from top): Thai-Style Hot and Soup Soup with Shrimp and Noodles (page 311), Chickpea Shakshuka (page 235), Maple-Soy Salmon Bowls with Quinoa and Brussels Sprouts (page 136)

Editorial Director, Books: Adam Kowit
Executive Food Editor: Dan Zuccarello
Deputy Food Editor: Stephanie Pixley
Executive Managing Editor: Debra Hudak
Project Editor: Jack Bishop
Senior Editors: Camila Chaparro, Joe Gitter, Sara Mayer, and Valerie Cimino
Associate Editor: Claudia Catalano
Senior Photo Test Cook: José Maldonado
Test Cooks: Malcolm Jackson, Hannah Smokelin, and Stephanie Winter
Kitchen Interns: Abby Kolosowsky and Lillian Morrison
Assistant Editor: Julia Arwine
Creative Director, Editorial: Lindsey Timko Chandler
Associate Art Director and Designer: Rose Flynn
VP of Imagery: Casey Stenger
Senior Photography Producer: Meredith Mulcahy
Senior Staff Photographers: Steve Klise and Daniel J. van Ackere
Staff Photographers: Kritsada Panichgul and Kevin White
Additional Photography: Beth Fuller, Nina Gallant, Joseph Keller, and Carl Tremblay
Senior Food Stylist: Christine Tobin
Food Styling: Julia Heffelfinger, Joy Howard, Sheila Jarnes, Catrine Kelty, Chantal Lambeth, Gina McCreadie, Kendra McKnight, Ashley Moore, Christie Morrison, Marie Piraino, Elle Simone Scott, Kendra Smith, Sally Staub, and Janette Zepeda
Project Manager, Books: Kelly Gauthier
Senior Print Production Specialist: Lauren Robbins
Production and Imaging Coordinator: Amanda Yong
Production and Imaging Specialist: Tricia Neumyer
Production and Imaging Assistant: Chloe Petraske
Copy Editor: Deri Reed
Proofreader: Lauren Purcell
Indexer: Elizabeth Parson

Chief Executive Officer: Daniel Suratt
Chief Content Officer: Dan Souza
Senior Content Adviser: Jack Bishop
Executive Editorial Directors: Julia Collin Davison and Bridget Lancaster
Senior Director, Book Sales: Emily Logan

Edited by Jack Bishop

Jack has written five cookbooks and edited dozens more. He's been teaching television viewers how to shop for ingredients since the premiere of *America's Test Kitchen* in 2001. Jack has mediocre knife skills and avoids recipes that require fussy prep.

contents

AMERICA'S
TEST KITCHEN
TEST KITCHEN

AMERICA'S
TEST KITCHEN

KITCHEN

NO-BROIL
BROIL

welcome to america's test kitchen

This book has been tested, written, and edited by the folks at America's Test Kitchen, where curious home cooks become confident cooks. Located in Boston's Seaport District in the historic Innovation and Design Building, it features 15,000 square feet of kitchen space including multiple photography and video studios. It is the home of *Cook's Illustrated* magazine and is the workday destination for more than 60 test cooks, editors, and cookware specialists. Our mission is to empower and inspire confidence, community, and creativity in the kitchen.

We start the process of testing a recipe with a complete lack of preconceptions, which means that we accept no claim, no technique, and no recipe at face value. We simply assemble as many variations as possible, test a half dozen of the most promising, and taste the results blind. We then construct our own recipe and continue to test it, varying ingredients, techniques, and cooking times until we reach a consensus. As we like to say in the test kitchen, "We make the mistakes so you don't have to." The result is our best version of every recipe. We use the same rigorous approach when we test equipment and taste ingredients.

All of this would not be possible without a belief that good cooking, much like good music, is based on a foundation of objective technique. Some people like spicy foods and others don't, but there is a right way to sauté, there is a best way to cook a pot roast, and there are measurable scientific principles involved in producing perfectly beaten, stable egg whites. Our ultimate goal is to investigate thefundamental principles of cooking to give you the techniques, tools, and ingredients you need to become a better cook. It is as simple as that.

Founded in 1992, ATK is the leading multimedia cooking resource serving millions of cooks like you with our trusted expertise. Come inside our kitchens on public television's most-watched cooking shows, *America's Test Kitchen* and *Cook's Country*. Watch every season and our original streaming series on your favorite streaming platforms.

We invite you to explore our app and website for access to thousands of rigorously tested recipes, unbiased product reviews, classes, videos, and more in one easy-to-use, ad-free digital experience.

Download the five-star-rated ATK app today.
cooks.io/subscribe

Plus, stay inspired with our Dinner Tonight newsletter—new recipes, tips, and weeknight meal ideas from Jack Bishop, delivered straight to your inbox. **cooks.io/dinnertonight**

Follow us on Social

 @TestKitchen  @AmericasTestKitchen

 @TestKitchen  @AmericasTestKitchen

a highly opinionated guide to weeknight cooking *by Jack Bishop*

what i've learned from cooking 10,000 dinners

I've been making dinner for 49 years. I started as a young teenager. My mother would call from work and talk me through a recipe. Yes, I learned to cook from a harvest-gold wall phone.

Since then, I've cooked in a bare-bones college apartment for friends, made leisurely dinners with my girlfriend (then wife) in our various apartments, and prepared suppers for our two daughters (often a slog, but sometimes a joyous surprise). Lauren and I are now happy empty nesters cooking dinner together almost every night.

While preparing more than 10,000 dinners (that's the math!), I've learned what works (a well-stocked pantry and flexible recipes) and what doesn't (anything that requires too many pots, pans, and bowls). For the past year, I've also been writing a twice-a-week newsletter, Dinner Tonight, about making dinner and received invaluable feedback from home cooks like yourself. Thank you for all those emails.

Many readers tell me they want one-dish meals, although there's still a strong contingent that prefers the meat-starch-veg approach. From both camps, I hear over and over that you want something new. And many seem to want my blessing about changing up our kitchen-tested recipes. Permission granted, in perpetuity!

This collection of easy recipes—all on the table in 45 minutes or less—strikes the right balance between achievable and exciting. I've worked with food editors on our book team to select tried-and-true recipes my newsletter readers have praised (see page 17 for a list of their all-time favorites). My colleagues in the test kitchen have also developed dozens of new recipes that align with feedback from readers—more vegetables, beans, and grains; less meat; bolder flavors; faster prep; and fewer items to wash.

Sheet-Pan Jerk Chicken with Sweet Potatoes and Crisp Collard Greens (page 40) has just five ingredients (plus salt and oil), and cleanup is a breeze. Cacio e Pepe Beans with Squash, Sage, and Walnuts (page 228) is a wild mash-up of several Italian dishes that's totally unexpected and utterly delicious. There are 198 more similarly inventive but doable recipes in this book.

As the team has been testing recipes, I've been cooking along and helping to write up the suggestions you will find throughout the book. Pay close attention to Notes (essential info for all cooks) and the Kitchen Improv ideas (designed for cooks who like to experiment with tested recipes).

However you make dinner, I encourage and applaud your efforts. Creating something with your hands is immensely pleasurable. Let's make dinner tonight!

Jack Bishop

tips from your cooking coach

Half of cooking success happens in your head, and half in your hands. Making good decisions is just as important as good technique. Here's what I've learned over the years.

simplify meal planning

There are three basic steps you can take to make meal planning easier.

Build a good pantry.

I typically have to pick up only two or three ingredients to make dinner. That's because I have a well-stocked pantry. And if you make cooking a habit, your pantry will follow. You don't need hundreds of ingredients to cook well. Focus on always keeping workhorses such as chickpeas, soy sauce, and tahini on hand (see page 6). Also, get comfortable making smart substitutions (see page 9).

Organize your recipes.

This book is a great start. My wife likes to download recipes and saves all those PDFs in neat folders on her computer. I use the Favorites function on the ATK website and app. Whatever your system, have one. If you can easily browse trusted recipes, you are much more likely to cook.

Memorize a few side dish recipes.

I have a half dozen hands-off sides that I can make from memory. Throughout this book, there are spreads with super-simple sides. Find several you like, make them a couple times, and you'll have them down pat.

invest in your repertoire

A solid repertoire is the key to successful weeknight cooking. You get good at making these dishes, and you have the necessary ingredients on hand. An alternating mix of favorite recipes also eliminates the "decision fatigue" many cooks face. You're picking a dish from your favorites list, rather than combing through hundreds of internet recipes.

Your repertoire should change with the seasons and evolve as your cooking style or interests change. Here's the structure my wife and I have been using for decades, and I can't stress enough how well this approach has served us. If you cook less often, adjust these numbers.

Rely on a varied playlist.

Every month, we make six to eight trusted recipes two or three times each. We have all the necessary pantry staples for these dishes, and the recipe details stay fresh in my memory. There's usually a pasta or two on this list, a taco, a chicken dish, a big salad or two, and something with seafood.

Don't forget your old loves.

During any given month, my wife and I cook two or three long-time favorites, such as Spaghetti al Tonno (page 260) and Chipotle Mushroom and Cauliflower Tacos (page 398), one time each. This frequency keeps these recipes on the playlist but with less repetition.

Mix it up with something new.

Every month, we cook three or four tryouts. We save these new recipes for nights when we know we will have more time to focus. The winners are added to the playlist.

MY FEBRUARY MEAL PLAN

PASTA E FAGIOLI	WINE CLUB PARTY	SESAME GLAZED MEATBALLS	CACIO E PEPE BEANS	NORTH FORK TABLE W/ KIDS	SPAGHETTI AL TONNO	SPICY POLENTA W/ BEANS + KALE
CHICKEN TINGA TACOS	FRIED RICE W/ SHRIMP + LIME	SESAME GLAZED MEATBALLS	SWORDFISH W/ CHARRED ORANGE	CHANA MASALA	CHILI CRISP NOODLES	SUE + JON FOR DINNER
PASTA E FAGIOLI	COCONUT CURRY W/ TOFU	CHICKEN TINGA TACOS	SPICY POLENTA W/ BEANS + KALE	CRISPY ZA'ATAR CHICKEN	SWORDFISH W/ CHARRED ORANGE	SAMOSA GNOCCHI CHAAT
DINNER AT NANCY + JAKE'S	SESAME GLAZED MEATBALLS	PASTA E FAGIOLI	BUTTER CHICKEN	CHILI CRISP NOODLES	PIZZA AT BRIX + RYE	CACIO E PEPE BEANS

CURRENT FAVORITES

OLD FAVORITES

WANT TO TRY

CURRENT FAVORITES

Recipes I make often, with pantry items already on hand

OLD FAVORITES

Stand-out recipes I don't want to forget

WANT TO TRY

New recipes for when I have a bit more time

team up to cook faster

Two people cooking together can get dinner on the table more quickly. It's also a nice way to connect after a day apart. My wife and I have been a kitchen duo for 40+ years and we follow one of these two modes for working together. Two adults can follow these guidelines, as can one adult and a capable child.

Designate a lead cook and prep cook.

One of us makes dinner while the other assists. The lead cook has chosen the recipe(s) and created a shopping list. (Either one of us has done the shopping.) At game time, the lead cook is in charge of timing and making sure dinner is a success, directing the prep cook to wash and chop veggies or measure ingredients into prep bowls. The prep cook can also make a simple side dish.

Have a solo cook and a non-cook partner.

One of us makes dinner while the other focuses on other essential household tasks such as loading or unloading the dishwasher, washing pots and pans, helping the kids with homework, walking the dog, tidying up, setting the table, and getting everyone their favorite beverage.

keep the kids happy

Our daughters are now 30 and 26 and are both adventurous eaters. But that wasn't always the case. Here are some strategies that worked well for our family.

Involve kids in menu planning.

We often would ask at breakfast whether our kids would prefer recipe A, B, or C. This encouraged compromise and taking turns and gave them a stake in the process. Do the same thing with side dishes. Do you want crispy broccolini or olive oil green beans?

Give kids age-appropriate tasks.

Start with setting the table and move on to measuring ingredients and whisking and stirring. A size-appropriate apron can be surprisingly helpful—many kids love anything that involves dress-up.

Whenever possible, serve garnishes and sauces on the side.

This lets kids avoid things they don't like, and it gives them the opportunity to customize their dinner plate. Put a bowl of flake sea salt on the table too. Even if kids are just seasoning their own food, giving them the ability to "finish" their dinner can be helpful. See the list of Assemble-Your-Own Dinners on page 16.

Find plain side dishes your kids enjoy and serve them often.

If your kids aren't wild about tonight's dinner, it's good to know there's something else they will eat. Draw inspiration from the 20 side dish recipes scattered across the book. Also, flatbreads stashed in the freezer and easily reheated in the oven are helpful on nights when your kids are mostly eating the side dish for dinner.

rethink make-ahead

I admire folks who can cook a week of food on Sunday afternoon. I'm not one of those people. However, I do have simple ways to get ahead on dinner prep.

Prep an ingredient or component in advance.

For example, if I need some Parmesan on Monday, I often grate some extra to use in a recipe later in the week. Likewise, many sauces are fine made a day or two in advance. I might tackle that task on the weekend, or even after dinner during the week, so that things go faster another night.

Take 5 minutes to get organized in the morning.

Move anything that needs to be defrosted to the fridge. Double check that the parsley in the crisper drawer still looks fine. Put canned goods on the counter so you don't need to hunt around for them when you get home.

If you work at home, spend 10 minutes at lunch or during a midafternoon break organizing dinner.

This can be as simple as draining and rinsing a can of chickpeas, washing salad greens or herbs, or measuring out ingredients.

know what you can change in a recipe, and what you can't

Customizing recipes is highly personal but there are some strategies that increase the odds of success.

Make recipes as written, at least once.

When trying a new recipe, I might change an herb or spice, but otherwise I'm following the script.

Figure out the formula.

Every recipe has a basic structure, core technique, or ratio of ingredients that makes the dish unique. Don't tamper with these. But you can try a different protein or grain, switch up the seasonings, or use an analogous cooking method (many grill recipes work perfectly fine under the broiler).

stay engaged

Seasoned cooks get bored. It happens. Over the years, I've followed two approaches to keep up my interest in cooking. In both cases, it's about building your pantry, which I find makes it easier to cook new dishes.

Explore a new cuisine.

My wife and I have learned about so many cuisines based on travel, favorite restaurants, and reading novels set abroad. Once you start buying pantry staples for a few Spanish or Indian recipes, for example, the shopping for future recipes from that cuisine becomes progressively easier.

Discover a new ingredient.

I'm currently obsessed with chili crisp and use it as a garnish with both noodles and proteins. I've had similar infatuations with tahini, preserved lemons, za'atar, and high-end canned tuna packed in olive oil. Find an ingredient you love and that will shape new recipes you decide to test out.

invest in your pantry

your pantry is a work in progress

Think of the pantry like retirement savings. The goal is to set aside something every month—not to go out and shop for 100 ingredients today. Here are some very basic (and highly opinionated) guidelines to get you thinking. In the end, build the pantry that works for the types of recipes you like to cook.

PASTA

Have one stubby and one strand pasta on hand. I like either penne or orecchiette and linguine.

RICE & GRAINS

White rice is essential, and why not buy flavorful basmati rather than "regular" white rice? Quinoa and bulgur are useful because they cook so quickly, and farro is foolproof (it boils like pasta) and hearty.

BEANS

Because of their mild flavor, chickpeas and cannellini are the most versatile.

TOMATO PRODUCTS

Start with tomato paste (in a tube) as well as canned diced and canned whole tomatoes.

OILS

Extra-virgin olive oil and toasted sesame oil are the most flavorful and useful. Add a neutral-tasting vegetable oil if you like.

VINEGARS

Wine vinegar (red or white) is essential. Add others (sherry, balsamic, Chinese black) based on the cuisines you like.

WINE

White wine or vermouth is the most versatile. Add others (red, Shaoxing, dry sherry, sake, mirin) based on the cuisines you like.

SALT & PEPPER

It's worth keeping table, kosher, and flake salt on hand as well as black pepper—in a mill, please!

SPICES

Cayenne, coriander, and cumin are workhorses in this book, followed by smoked paprika, chili powder, dried oregano, and cinnamon.

ALLIUMS

Garlic and yellow onions are absolutely essential; shallots and scallions nearly so.

VEGETABLES & FRUITS

Carrots and celery are foundational in many recipes and refrigerate well. Try to keep lemons, limes, and oranges on hand, too. Raisins are surprisingly useful as well.

DAIRY

Start with milk, heavy cream, and plain Greek yogurt. See Smart Substitutions on page 9 for tips on fashioning other types of dairy from these ingredients.

EGGS & CHEESE

Always have large eggs, Parmesan, and a crumbly cheese (feta or goat) in the fridge.

CONDIMENTS & SAUCES

Start with anchovies, olives, Dijon mustard, fish sauce, hot sauce, soy sauce, tahini, and white miso. Add capers, kimchi, pepperoncini, gochujang, harissa, mayonnaise, hoisin sauce, oyster sauce, sriracha, and Thai curry paste as needed.

PANTRY BASICS

You should have all-purpose flour, cornstarch, granulated sugar, brown sugar, honey, and chicken or vegetable broth. Crispy food is so appealing, and panko is the best coating option.

10 THINGS TO ALWAYS KEEP IN THE FREEZER

CHICKEN

Keep boneless, skinless chicken breasts and thighs in original packaging when possible.

SAUSAGE

A few links of Italian sweet or hot sausage can form the basis of a pasta sauce or soup.

BACON

Coil up individual strips, freeze on a plate, and transfer to a zipper-lock bag.

SHRIMP

Individually quick-frozen shrimp (with no additional ingredients on the label) are high quality and ready to use. Defrost in a bowl of cold water.

BREAD

Slice bread, wrap it tightly in aluminum foil, and seal in a zipper-lock bag before freezing. Store flatbreads and tortillas in original packaging.

BUTTER

Freeze butter in its wrapper. Move individual sticks to the fridge as needed.

VEGETABLES

Frozen corn, edamame, peas, and spinach are worth stocking.

NUTS & SEEDS

Due to their high fat content, nuts and seeds go rancid quickly unless frozen. Toasted sesame seeds, walnuts, and pistachios are especially versatile.

CHIPOTLE CHILES IN ADOBO

Freeze spoonfuls of chiles and sauce on a parchment paper–lined baking sheet. Transfer frozen chiles to a zipper-lock bag to store.

GINGER

Peel and cut fresh ginger into 1-inch pieces and freeze in a zipper-lock bag. To use, chop or grate ginger directly from the freezer.

how to adapt recipes like a pro

You don't have the required ingredients, or maybe you like the recipe but not all the components. You're ready to freestyle. The substitutions at right will reliably work in most recipes. But what if you want to make larger changes? Here are some guidelines I think about when I'm retooling a recipe.

PROTEINS

Switch like cuts with each other—for example, ground meats and poultry are often interchangeable, as are boneless chops and boneless steaks and even tofu. Pay attention to cooking times and desired internal temperatures (they will vary), and be prepared to use more or less fat in the pan if necessary.

VEGETABLES

If you want to use another vegetable than the one called for, try to pick something similar. Peas and edamame, zucchini and eggplant, spinach and arugula, fennel and celery, as well as carrots and sweet potatoes generally can be swapped for one another. If a recipe calls for two or three veggies and you don't have one, just bulk up on the vegetables you do have.

PASTA, RICE & GRAINS

Lots of latitude here if you're boiling the noodles or grains because you can easily adjust the cooking time. Be more circumspect if you're cooking these ingredients pilaf style and won't be draining off excess liquid.

SPICES

Cumin and paprika aren't terribly potent and are often used by the teaspoon, or even tablespoon. In contrast, a quarter teaspoon of nutmeg or cloves goes a long, long way. Pay attention to intensity when changing spices, and don't replace a mild spice with a potent one.

FRUITS & NUTS

Go ahead and make changes as you like here. But do pay attention to salted vs. unsalted when it comes to nuts. And look for a similar texture when changing fruits, replacing apples with pears, oranges with grapefruits, and peaches with plums or mangoes.

CHEESES

If you divide the world of cheeses into three broad categories—hard, crumbly, and creamy—and then substitute within a category, you are likely to be successful. Hard cheeses include Parmesan, Pecorino Romano, Grana Padano, cotija, and Manchego. Crumbly cheeses include feta, goat, ricotta salata, and queso blanco. Creamy cheeses include cheddar, fontina, Gruyère, Havarti, and Monterey Jack.

FRESH HERBS

Delicate herbs (basil, parsley, cilantro, mint, tarragon, dill, chives) are best used fresh (with mint as the only exception). Sturdy herbs (sage, oregano, thyme, marjoram) are best fresh, but you can substitute dried at a 3:1 ratio. It's fine to trade one fresh herb for another within a category (delicate or sturdy).

If you cook a lot, buy a bunch of parsley and/or cilantro every week—these herbs are the most versatile. Rubber bands and twist ties will encourage rot, so take them off when you get home. Many markets mist so much that the herbs are actually soggy. Wrap herbs in a paper towel and slide the herbs and towel inside an open bag and stow in the crisper. I find these steps keep parsley and cilantro in decent shape for up to a week. Wash and dry only what you're using that day.

smart substitutions

Knowing when you can sub in an ingredient you have on hand makes cooking easier and more foolproof.

produce	substitution
1 medium onion	4 large shallots or 5 to 6 medium shallots
1 medium leek	1 large onion
1 clove garlic	¼ teaspoon granulated garlic
1 tablespoon fresh ginger	¼ to ⅓ teaspoon ground ginger, to taste
1 medium fennel bulb	3 celery ribs
3 teaspoons fresh herb	1 teaspoon dried
1 lemon	1½ to 2 limes
1 medium vine-ripened tomato	6 ounces cherry or grape tomatoes
2 red bell peppers, roasted	1 cup jarred roasted red peppers
Canned crushed tomatoes	canned whole or diced tomatoes with their juice (pulse in a food processor)
10 ounces fresh tomatoes	1 (14.5-ounce) can whole peeled tomatoes, drained (in cooked applications)

chiles and spice blends	substitution
1 tablespoon minced fresh jalapeños	2 tablespoons jarred jalapeños
1 chipotle in adobo	½ teaspoon chipotle chile powder or ½ teaspoon smoked paprika + ⅛ teaspoon cayenne pepper
Sambal oelek	chile-garlic sauce
¼ teaspoon red pepper flakes	⅛ teaspoon cayenne pepper
1 tablespoon ancho chile powder	1 tablespoon mild paprika + pinch cayenne pepper
1 tablespoon gochugaru	1 tablespoon ancho chile powder + pinch cayenne pepper or 1 tablespoon Aleppo pepper
1 tablespoon Sichuan chili powder	1 tablespoon gochugaru
Cajun seasoning	Old Bay or Creole seasoning

liquids	substitution
1 tablespoon lemon or lime juice	2 teaspoons white wine vinegar
2 tablespoons mirin	2 tablespoons sake or white wine + 1 teaspoon sugar; or 2 tablespoons sweet sherry
White wine	dry vermouth
½ cup red/white wine or vermouth	½ cup broth + 1 teaspoon wine vinegar or lemon juice (add the vinegar or lemon juice just before serving)
Chinese black vinegar	balsamic vinegar
Shaoxing wine	dry sherry
Pomegranate molasses	equivalent amount of half lemon juice, half molasses

dairy	substitution
1 cup whole milk	⅝ cup skim milk + ⅜ cup half-and-half; or ⅔ cup 1 percent low-fat milk + ⅓ cup half-and-half; or ¾ cup 2 percent low-fat milk + ¼ cup half-and-half
1 cup half-and-half	¾ cup whole milk + ¼ cup heavy cream; or ⅔ cup skim or low-fat milk + ⅓ cup heavy cream; or ⅞ cup skim milk + ⅛ cup heavy cream
Sour cream	full-fat Greek yogurt
1 cup plain yogurt	⅔ cup Greek yogurt + ⅓ cup milk or water

other	substitution
1 cup tahini	6 tablespoons peanut butter + 2 tablespoons toasted sesame oil (you'll use half the amount of tahini)
1 anchovy fillet (if anchovy is a background flavor)	½ teaspoon fish sauce
Pasta, specific shape	substitute other pastas by weight, not by volume
1 teaspoon table salt	1½ teaspoons Morton Kosher Salt or 2 teaspoons Diamond Crystal Kosher Salt

kitchen gear faq

This book assumes that you have basic pieces of equipment in your kitchen. If you're investing in new gear, check out americastestkitchen.com for the latest brand recommendations based on our rigorous, independent product testing. Even though I'm the "ingredient guy" on our TV shows, I get a lot of questions about gear. Here are the most common queries and what you need to know.

Do I really need both a food processor and blender?

Sort of. For pureeing liquids and solids, a blender really is best. Food processors can leak (you can mitigate this risk by not overfilling the workbowl), and they don't produce as smooth a puree. If you don't make a lot of pureed soups, you can get away with just a food processor, which is the far-more-versatile appliance. One more thought: If you're short on counter space, pair your food processor with an immersion blender. You can't make daiquiris, but you will be able to puree soup.

Do I need fancy knives?

When I come to dinner, many friends want to show me their fancy knife collection. I smile and don't say what I really think: What a waste! You need just three knives—a chef's knife, a paring knife, and a serrated bread knife. They don't need to be terribly expensive—expect to spend $100 for the trio. They must be sharp, so you're better off investing in a good sharpener (I use an electric model but there are good manual options) than more knives that will just sit in the drawer.

So many of your recipes call for a microwave!

More a complaint than a question, but I hear from readers of my newsletter that they don't own a microwave. Before I give you some workarounds, let me make a quick pitch for owning a cheap microwave—it's handy for prepping ingredients (removing liquid from eggplant, blooming spices in oil, toasting bread crumbs), and a microwave precook will significantly cut roasting or sautéing time for slow-cooking veggies like sweet potatoes. That said, you can certainly bloom spices and toast bread crumbs in a skillet—the timing will be different but the visual cues remain the same. In recipes that use a microwave to cut total cook time, increase the roasting or sautéing time for the item in question (usually a vegetable) by 10 to 15 minutes.

What's your favorite gadget?

My rasp grater. I use it for grating Parmesan and Pecorino as well as zesting citrus fruits. It's the only way that I prepare ginger, which is too fibrous when chopped with a knife. When I want garlic that is perfectly smooth (e.g., for a dressing or uncooked sauce), I use the grater rather than a knife.

What cookware is essential?

You need a 12-inch traditional skillet (something clad, please) and a 12-inch nonstick skillet. A Dutch oven (6 to 7 quarts is most useful) is very handy, as is a large saucepan (3 to 4 quarts). Don't forget rimmed baking sheets—I own six in various sizes but two will suffice. If you cook many Asian dishes, a wok is a must-have.

What am I missing?

Good cooking starts with accurate measuring. In addition to the obvious dry measuring cups, liquid measuring cups, and measuring spoons, I strongly recommend that you invest in a scale and an instant-read thermometer. No more guessing about how much those veggies weigh. And no more overcooked steaks, roasts, and chops.

the leftovers dilemma

Some cooks love leftovers (less cooking in the days to come), but others dread them because of worry about waste and repetition. The first question to ask yourself—do you like leftovers or not? Keep that answer in mind as you put the advice on this page into practice.

Upcycling Leftovers

Some leftover lovers just want to repeat the same dinner later in the week. Check out the Storage and Reheating Tips that follow. Others prefer to upcycle leftovers as components in a future meal. This approach requires a bit more planning.

- Distinct components are much easier to repurpose than a leftover dish. If you know you're going to have leftovers, reserve them before the final assembly: If you have roasted chicken breasts and veggies that are drizzled with a sauce, set aside some chicken, veggies, and sauce before final assembly of the dish. Likewise, leftover salad is usually terrible, but if you set aside the undressed components you will have many options.
- Sauces are easily reimagined, like a vinaigrette that dresses salad one night and then is drizzled over fish later in the week.
- Many leftover proteins are lovely in salads. Wait to shred chicken or slice steak until ready to use.
- Roasted veggies often can be used in salads, soups, and pasta sauces.
- Most oil-based pastas (especially those with veggies or bits of meat) work nicely in a frittata. Beat six to eight eggs in a bowl, add chilled pasta and grated cheese, and cook this mixture in an oiled nonstick pan as you would any frittata.

Storage and Reheating Tips

Many bad leftovers would have been perfectly fine if handled differently. Start by storing leftovers in airtight containers and remember that flavors will be dulled in the fridge. Taste all reheated dishes before serving. Add more salt and pepper, drizzle with olive oil, sprinkle with a fresh herb, or add a squeeze of lemon or drizzle of vinegar.

Here's how to revive specific leftovers so they shine again on the dinner table:

- Place proteins on a wire rack set inside a rimmed baking sheet, cover with aluminum foil, and reheat in a 350-degree oven. The wire rack allows for better air circulation and more even heating.
- Reheat soups and stews in a pot on the stovetop. Or use a microwave and stir several times to avoid hot spots. Add a little water if the soup or stew seems too thick.
- Reheat casseroles and skillet dishes in a baking dish covered with foil in a 350-degree oven.
- Place pizza, tarts, and quesadillas on a rimmed baking sheet, tent with foil, and reheat in a 350-degree oven. Or, reheat pieces on the stove in a loosely covered nonstick skillet over medium heat to crisp up the dough and melt the cheese.
- An uncovered dish in the microwave works best with rice and grains. Add a tablespoon of water to up to 4 cups of cooked rice or grains and heat until steaming, stirring once about halfway through.

finding the right recipe for tonight

These lists are designed to help you find just the right thing to cook for dinner tonight.

Easy Sheet-Pan Dinners

Complete meals with minimal clean up.

Skillet Suppers

These need a bit more attention than a sheet-pan supper, but the components of skillet suppers pick up flavor from each other, with delicious results.

Celebrate Spring

The start of a new season is a great time to shake up your cooking routine and make the best of local produce.

Here Comes Summer

Make the best of summer produce with these recipes.

Easy Sheet-Pan Dinners

When It's Just Too Hot to Cook

These recipes require little or no cooking and are designed to be served chilled or at room temperature.

Here Comes Summer

When It's Just Too Hot to Cook

Harvest Time Suppers

Say hello to autumn with apples and squash.

- Pan-Seared Pork Chops with Apples and Spinach, 101
- Roasted Cabbage with Kielbasa and Pierogi, 110
- Stuffed Delicata Squash, 194
- Cacio e Pepe Beans with Squash, Sage, and Walnuts, 228
- East African Coconut Curry with Tofu and Squash, 231
- Creamy Pumpkin Ramen, 271
- Spiced Chicken Soup with Squash and Navy Beans, 294

Comfort Food

Hearty dishes designed for a cold night.

- Seared Scallops with Polenta, Bacon, and Poblano Chiles, 172
- Spicy Polenta with White Beans and Kale, 213
- Chana Masala, 223
- Vegetarian Ramen with Shiitakes and Soft Eggs, 288
- Chicken and Leek Soup with Parmesan Dumplings, 292
- Posole Verde, 301
- Spicy Tomato Soup with Tortellini and Sausage, 308
- Quick Mediterranean Beef Stew, 320

Perfect for Leftovers

Recipes that are perfect when you're cooking for one or two people and want leftovers.

- Barbecue-Rubbed Chicken Thighs with Deviled Egg Potato Salad, 27
- Thai Curry Chicken with Sweet Potatoes and Green Beans, 36
- One-Pot Lamb Meatballs with Eggplant and Chickpeas, 122
- Creamy Butternut and Fennel Soup, 312
- Picadillo-Style Beef Chili, 323
- Creamy Chickpea and Sweet Potato Stew, 325

Harvest Time Suppers

Perfect for Leftovers

COOKING FOR TWO 101

This has been my world since our youngest left for college nine years ago. Here's what I do to halve a recipe.

- Sheet-pan suppers and salads can almost always be halved, without adjustment.
- Pasta sauces can usually be halved, just save extra pasta cooking water in case things seem dry.
- Sautés and stir-fries are a bit trickier to halve. Sometimes you need to cut cooking time—fewer veggies in the pan means faster cooking, and less liquid translates to faster reduction. Switching from a 12-inch pan to a 10-inch pan will compensate here, but I often just stick with the larger pan and watch the clock and/or lower the heat a bit.
- Skillet casseroles and frittatas are the trickiest. You definitely need to trade down the pan size (replace a 12-inch pan with a 10-inch) and adjust cook time.

Cooking for Two

These recipes are easily scaled to serve two (see Cooking for Two 101).

Almost-No-Shopping Dinners

If you have a well-stocked pantry (see page 6), you'll need to buy just one or two ingredients to make these recipes.

Cooking for Two

Start with a Rotisserie Chicken

How to make things really simple.

- Chicken and Leek Soup with Parmesan Dumplings, 292
- Chicken and Arugula Salad with Cherries and Feta, 329
- Chicken Salad with Cabbage and Fish Sauce, 330
- Orecchiette Salad with Roasted Vegetables, Chicken, and Jalapeño-Lime Dressing, 339
- Avocado Chicken Salad Sandwiches with Jicama and Banana Peppers, 366

My Favorite Recipes

My Favorite Recipes

Enough said.

- Sesame-Glazed Meatballs and Broccoli, 79
- One-Pot Lamb Meatballs with Eggplant and Chickpeas, 122
- Calabrian Chile White Beans with Almond Romesco, 227
- Chili Crisp Noodles, 245
- Spaghetti al Tonno, 260
- Hummus Bowls with Roasted Chicken and Cauliflower, 336
- White Beans and Chorizo with Quick Marinated Tomatoes and Onion, 344

Assemble-Your-Own Dinners for Families

These dinners can come to the table with sauces and garnishes in separate bowls, allowing kids plenty of options.

- Maple-Soy Salmon Bowls with Quinoa and Brussels Sprouts, 136
- Spicy Salmon Sushi Bowls, 139
- Loaded Sweet Potato Wedges with Tempeh, 193
- Hummus Bowls with Roasted Chicken and Cauliflower, 336
- Chicken and Plantain Lettuce Wraps with Mafé Sauce, 370
- Korean Sizzling Beef Lettuce Wraps, 381

- Cast-Iron Pork Fajitas, 382
- Honey-Sriracha Shrimp Lettuce Wraps, 389
- Blackened Salmon Tacos with Slaw, Avocado, and Grapefruit, 390

Readers' Favorite Recipes

The recipes featured in the Dinner Tonight newsletter that have driven lots of engagement on the ATK app and website.

- Murgh Makhani (Indian Butter Chicken), 52
- Couscous Risotto with Chicken and Spinach, 66
- Salmon with Old Bay Butter and Confetti Grits, 135
- One-Pan Cod and Green Rice, 157
- Seared Shrimp with Tomato, Lime, and Avocado, 176
- Penne with Pancetta and Asparagus, 263
- Carrot Ribbon, Chicken, and Coconut Curry Soup, 298
- Red Lentil Soup with Warm Spices, 316
- Pasta e Fagioli, 319
- Honey-Sriracha Shrimp Lettuce Wraps, 389

Readers' Favorite Recipes

never boring chicken

chapter 1

crispy za'atar chicken cutlets WITH sweet potato wedges

Serves 4 • Total Time: 35 minutes

- **½ cup plus 3 tablespoons extra-virgin olive oil, divided**
- **¼ cup chopped fresh dill, parsley, and/or tarragon**
- **1 shallot, minced**
- **2 tablespoons red wine vinegar**
- **¾ teaspoon plus ⅛ teaspoon table salt, divided**
- **1½ pounds sweet potatoes, unpeeled, cut lengthwise into 1-inch-wide wedges**
- **2 large eggs**
- **1 cup panko bread crumbs**
- **2 tablespoons za'atar**
- **2 (8-ounce) boneless, skinless chicken breasts, trimmed**

A SPOONFUL of za'atar elevates the humble breaded chicken cutlet with no extra effort. While you make the chicken, sweet potato wedges roast in the oven. A zippy, herb-forward vinaigrette balances the sweetness of the potatoes and makes the side just as special as the cutlets.

1 Adjust oven rack to middle position and heat oven to 450 degrees. Whisk 2 tablespoons oil, dill, shallot, vinegar, and ⅛ teaspoon salt together in bowl; set vinaigrette aside.

2 Toss potatoes with 1 tablespoon oil and ¼ teaspoon salt and arrange cut side down in even layer on rimmed baking sheet. Roast until potatoes are softened and bottoms are well browned, about 15 minutes.

3 Meanwhile, lightly beat eggs in shallow dish. Combine panko and za'atar in second shallow dish. Halve each breast horizontally and pound between 2 sheets of plastic wrap to uniform ½-inch thickness. Pat cutlets dry with paper towels and sprinkle with remaining ½ teaspoon salt. Working with 1 cutlet at a time, dip in egg, allow excess to drip off, then coat with panko mixture, pressing gently to adhere; transfer to large plate.

4 Line serving platter with double layer of paper towels. Heat remaining ½ cup oil in 12-inch skillet over medium-high heat until shimmering. Place 2 cutlets in skillet and cook until deep golden brown, about 2 minutes per side. Transfer cutlets to prepared platter and repeat with remaining 2 cutlets. Season with salt and pepper to taste. Discard paper towels and arrange potatoes on platter with chicken. Drizzle potatoes with vinaigrette and serve.

NOTES

The breasts will be easier to slice into cutlets if you chill them in the freezer for about 15 minutes. You can also skip halving the breasts and use four (4-ounce) chicken cutlets.

KITCHEN IMPROV

Make a quick tahini sauce to serve with the chicken by combining ¼ cup each tahini and water, 2 tablespoons lemon juice, and 2 garlic cloves, minced to paste; season with salt to taste. Pork or veal cutlets also work well. Try other herb or spice blends, such as herbes de Provence or ras el hanout, in place of the za'atar.

skillet chicken breasts WITH burst cherry tomato sauce

Serves 4 • Total Time: 40 minutes

- 4 (6- to 8-ounce) boneless, skinless chicken breasts, trimmed
- 1 tablespoon herbes de Provence
- 1¼ teaspoons table salt, divided
- ¼ cup extra-virgin olive oil, divided
- 4 garlic cloves, sliced thin
- 3 anchovy fillets
- 1 pound cherry tomatoes
- ½ cup dry white wine
- 1 tablespoon chopped fresh oregano, divided
- ¼ teaspoon red pepper flakes
- 2 tablespoons unsalted butter, cut into 2 pieces and chilled

WHITE WINE, butter, and anchovies give richness and savory depth to a jammy, fresh tomato sauce that's ready in 10 minutes. Pour that sauce over sautéed chicken breasts flavored with herbes de Provence, add a baguette, and dream of France.

1 Pat chicken dry with paper towels and sprinkle with herbes de Provence and 1 teaspoon salt. Heat 1 tablespoon oil in 12-inch nonstick skillet over medium-high heat until just smoking. Place chicken in skillet and cook, flipping occasionally, until chicken is well browned and registers 160 degrees, 10 to 12 minutes. Transfer chicken to serving platter, tent with aluminum foil, and let rest while preparing sauce.

2 Cook remaining 3 tablespoons oil, garlic, and anchovies in now-empty skillet over medium heat until garlic is just beginning to brown, about 1 minute, breaking up anchovies with wooden spoon. Add tomatoes, wine, 1½ teaspoons oregano, pepper flakes, and remaining ¼ teaspoon salt and bring to simmer. Cover and cook, stirring occasionally, until most of tomatoes have burst, about 5 minutes.

3 Uncover and continue to cook, breaking up tomatoes with back of wooden spoon, until juices are thickened and saucy, about 5 minutes. Off heat, stir in butter until evenly incorporated. Top chicken with sauce and sprinkle with remaining 1½ teaspoons oregano. Serve.

NOTES

To ensure even cooking, look for chicken breasts of even thickness; if necessary, pound the breasts to even thickness using a meat pounder.

KITCHEN IMPROV

You can substitute 1½ pounds boneless, skinless thighs for the breasts; cook the thighs to at least 175 degrees, increasing the cooking time range in step 1 to 12 to 15 minutes. The skillet will initially be crowded; however, the thighs will shrink as they cook. Crusty bread is great here, but rice, egg noodles, and polenta are also good options.

crispy ranch chicken AND broccoli

Serves 4 • Total Time: 45 minutes

- **1/2 cup mayonnaise, divided**
- **1/3 cup whole milk**
- **1 tablespoon chopped fresh dill**
- **5 teaspoons ranch seasoning mix, divided**
- **1/4 teaspoon cayenne pepper**
- **2/3 cup panko bread crumbs**
- **6 tablespoons unsalted butter, melted, divided**
- **1 pound broccoli florets, cut into 2-inch pieces**
- **1 1/2 teaspoons table salt, divided**
- **3/4 teaspoon pepper, divided**
- **4 (6- to 8-ounce) boneless, skinless chicken breasts, trimmed**

ZESTY RANCH seasoning mix is the hero of this sheet-pan dinner that will have everyone smiling. For maximum impact, use it three ways: on the chicken, in the crispy panko coating, and in a sauce to spoon over everything.

1 Adjust oven rack to middle position and heat oven to 400 degrees. Whisk 6 tablespoons mayonnaise, milk, dill, 1 tablespoon ranch seasoning, and cayenne together in bowl; refrigerate sauce until ready to serve.

2 Combine panko, 2 tablespoons melted butter, and 1 teaspoon ranch seasoning in second bowl and microwave until golden brown, about 2 minutes, stirring occasionally. Toss broccoli, 1/2 teaspoon salt, 1/4 teaspoon pepper, and remaining 4 tablespoons melted butter together on rimmed baking sheet. Roast for 10 minutes.

3 Meanwhile, pat chicken dry with paper towels and sprinkle with remaining 1 teaspoon ranch seasoning, remaining 1 teaspoon salt, and remaining 1/2 teaspoon pepper. Spread remaining 2 tablespoons mayonnaise over tops of chicken, then sprinkle with panko mixture. Push broccoli to 1 half of sheet and arrange chicken panko side up on empty half. Roast until chicken registers 160 degrees and broccoli is crisp-tender, about 15 minutes. Serve with sauce.

NOTES

To ensure even cooking, look for chicken breasts of even thickness; if necessary, pound breasts to even thickness using a meat pounder.

This recipe was developed using Hidden Valley Original Ranch Seasoning.

KITCHEN IMPROV

Make the ranch sauce extra tangy by using buttermilk, if you have it, in place of whole milk. (Low-fat milk is also fine in a pinch.) For bolder herb flavor, increase the amount of dill to up to 1/4 cup and/or include other herbs such as parsley, cilantro, basil, or tarragon.

SLATHERING BARBECUE spice rub on boneless chicken thighs brings outdoor flavors indoors, with some help from the broiler. Add a mustardy deviled potato salad for a dinner that tastes of summer, no grill required.

barbecue-rubbed chicken thighs WITH deviled egg potato salad

Serves 4 • Total Time: 35 minutes

- **1½ pounds red or Yukon gold potatoes, unpeeled, cut into ½-inch pieces**
- **1½ teaspoons table salt, divided, plus salt for cooking potatoes**
- **2 tablespoons distilled white vinegar**
- **2 pounds boneless, skinless chicken thighs, trimmed**
- **2 tablespoons barbecue spice rub**
- **1 tablespoon vegetable oil**
- **4 hard-cooked large eggs, separated, whites chopped**
- **⅓ cup mayonnaise**
- **1 tablespoon Dijon mustard**
- **1 celery rib, chopped fine**

1 Adjust oven rack 6 inches from broiler element and heat broiler. Bring 2 quarts water to boil in large saucepan over medium-high heat. Add potatoes and 2 tablespoons salt, return to boil, and cook until tender, 8 to 10 minutes. Drain potatoes, rinse under cold water, then drain well. Spread potatoes over rimmed baking sheet, drizzle with vinegar, and toss to combine; refrigerate until needed.

2 Meanwhile, set wire rack in aluminum foil–lined rimmed baking sheet. Pat chicken dry with paper towels, then toss with barbecue spice rub, oil, and 1 teaspoon salt and arrange in single layer on prepared rack. Broil until chicken is well browned and registers at least 175 degrees, 14 to 18 minutes, flipping chicken halfway through broiling. Let rest while preparing salad.

3 Whisk egg yolks, mayonnaise, mustard, and remaining ½ teaspoon salt together in large bowl. Add celery, egg whites, and potatoes and toss to coat. Season with salt and pepper to taste. Serve chicken with potato salad.

NOTES

Use a store-bought barbecue rub, or make your own: Combine 1 tablespoon packed brown sugar, 1 teaspoon paprika, 1 teaspoon chili powder, ½ teaspoon garlic powder, ½ teaspoon table salt, and a pinch of cayenne pepper. Have time to plan ahead? The vinegar-dressed potatoes can be refrigerated, covered, for up to 3 days.

KITCHEN IMPROV

Tap into your pantry and shake things up with the potato salad. Add more tang by swapping a portion of the mayonnaise for sour cream or yogurt, or add kick by using prepared horseradish in place of the mustard. Bulk up the salad by including pantry-friendly vegetables such as thawed frozen peas, chopped roasted red peppers, or thinly sliced radishes.

sticky gochujang chicken thighs WITH carrot-kimchi salad

Serves 4 • Total Time: 45 minutes

- ¼ cup gochujang
- 3½ tablespoons sugar, divided
- 3 tablespoons soy sauce, divided
- 2½ tablespoons toasted sesame oil, divided
- 8 (5- to 7-ounce) bone-in chicken thighs, trimmed
- ½ teaspoon table salt
- ½ teaspoon pepper
- 1 tablespoon vegetable oil
- 3 cups cilantro leaves and tender stems, cut into 3-inch lengths
- 2 cups cabbage kimchi, drained and cut into 1½-inch pieces
- 3 carrots, peeled and shredded
- 3 scallions, sliced thin on bias
- 2 teaspoons toasted sesame seeds

A FOUR-INGREDIENT gochujang sauce transforms roasted chicken thighs into a mouthwatering main. Pair with a vibrant salad of kimchi, crisp carrots, and fresh cilantro to strike an ideal balance between spicy and savory versus crunchy and bright.

1 Adjust oven rack to middle position and heat oven to 450 degrees. Whisk gochujang, 3 tablespoons sugar, 2 tablespoons soy sauce, and 2 tablespoons sesame oil together in small bowl; measure out and reserve 6 tablespoons sauce.

2 Pat chicken dry with paper towels and sprinkle with salt and pepper. Heat vegetable oil in 12-inch ovensafe skillet over medium-high heat until just smoking. Place chicken skin side down in skillet and cook until lightly browned on first side, 5 to 7 minutes. Off heat, flip chicken and brush with remaining gochujang sauce. Transfer skillet to oven and roast until chicken registers at least 175 degrees, about 15 minutes.

3 Remove skillet from oven. Being careful of hot skillet handle, brush chicken with reserved sauce and let rest while preparing salad.

4 Whisk remaining 1½ teaspoons sugar, remaining 1 tablespoon soy sauce, and remaining 1½ teaspoons sesame oil together in large bowl. Add cilantro, kimchi, and carrots and toss to combine. Arrange salad and chicken on serving platter and sprinkle with scallions and sesame seeds. Serve.

NOTES

Don't substitute store-bought gochujang sauce, which contains additional ingredients. The skillet will initially be crowded; however, the thighs will shrink as they cook. Use the large holes of a box grater to shred the carrots.

KITCHEN IMPROV

You can substitute four (12-ounce) bone-in split chicken breasts, halved crosswise, for the thighs; cook the breasts to 160 degrees, increasing the roasting time range in step 2 to 15 to 18 minutes.

SLICED RAW ASPARAGUS shines in a salad dressed with a lemony, toasted-walnut vinaigrette. Start the chicken thighs in a nonstick skillet to render the fat and crisp the skin; finish them in the oven to cook the meat through.

roasted chicken thighs WITH asparagus, arugula AND walnut salad

Serves 4 • Total Time: 40 minutes

- **8 (5- to 7-ounce) bone-in chicken thighs, trimmed**
- **1¾ teaspoons table salt, divided**
- **¾ teaspoon pepper, divided**
- **1 tablespoon grated lemon zest plus 3 tablespoons juice**
- **¼ cup extra-virgin olive oil, divided**
- **¾ cup walnuts or almonds, toasted and chopped, divided**
- **1 small shallot, chopped**
- **1 tablespoon water**
- **1 teaspoon honey**
- **1 pound thick asparagus, trimmed**
- **5 ounces (5 cups) baby arugula**

1 Adjust oven rack to middle position and heat oven to 450 degrees. Pat chicken dry with paper towels and sprinkle with 1 teaspoon salt and ½ teaspoon pepper. Sprinkle flesh sides of thighs with lemon zest.

2 Heat 1 tablespoon oil in 12-inch ovensafe skillet over medium-high heat until just smoking. Place chicken skin side down in skillet and cook until lightly browned on first side, 5 to 7 minutes. Flip chicken, transfer skillet to oven, and roast until chicken registers at least 175 degrees, about 15 minutes.

3 Meanwhile, process ½ cup walnuts, shallot, water, honey, lemon juice, remaining ¾ teaspoon salt, remaining ¼ teaspoon pepper, and remaining 3 tablespoons oil in food processor until mostly smooth, about 30 seconds, scraping down sides of bowl as needed.

4 Cut asparagus tips from spears into ¾-inch-long pieces. Thinly slice remaining asparagus spears on bias. Toss asparagus, arugula, and remaining walnuts with dressing in large bowl until well combined. Season with salt and pepper to taste. Serve chicken with salad.

NOTES

The skillet will initially be crowded; however, the chicken thighs will shrink as they cook. Make the salad while the chicken is in the oven. For easier slicing, select large asparagus spears, about ½ inch thick.

KITCHEN IMPROV

Other thinly sliced vegetables work here, too. Replace the asparagus with thinly sliced celery or shaved zucchini. Mixed baby greens or torn butter lettuce would be nice instead of the arugula. If you prefer to use chicken breasts, substitute four (12-ounce) bone-in split chicken breasts, halved crosswise, for the thighs and cook to 160 degrees, increasing the roasting time range in step 2 to 15 to 18 minutes.

honey-glazed chicken drumsticks WITH charred corn AND pineapple salad

Serves 4 to 6 • Total Time: 45 minutes

- **2½ pounds chicken drumsticks, trimmed**
- **1¾ teaspoons table salt, divided**
- **1 teaspoon pepper, divided**
- **¼ cup honey**
- **1½ tablespoons red wine vinegar**
- **2 garlic cloves, minced**
- **1 tablespoon vegetable oil**
- **5 ears corn, kernels cut from cobs**
- **1 red onion, halved and sliced ¼ inch thick**
- **1½ cups 1-inch pineapple pieces**
- **2 jalapeños, stemmed, seeded, and minced**
- **1 tablespoon Tajín Clásico seasoning**
- **½ cup fresh cilantro leaves**

1 Adjust oven rack to middle position and heat oven to 450 degrees. Line rimmed baking sheet with aluminum foil and spray with vegetable oil spray. Pat chicken dry with paper towels and sprinkle with 1¼ teaspoons salt and ½ teaspoon pepper. Arrange chicken on prepared sheet and roast for 15 minutes.

2 Meanwhile, whisk honey, vinegar, and garlic together in small bowl. Microwave until bubbling and fragrant, about 1 minute, stirring frequently to prevent mixture from bubbling over. Measure out and reserve 2 tablespoons honey mixture.

3 Brush chicken with remaining honey mixture and continue to roast until chicken registers at least 175 degrees, 10 to 15 minutes. Brush chicken with reserved honey mixture and let rest for 5 minutes.

4 While chicken is roasting, heat oil in 12-inch nonstick skillet over medium-high heat until shimmering. Add corn, onion, remaining ½ teaspoon salt, and remaining ½ teaspoon pepper and cook, without stirring, until corn is lightly charred, about 3 minutes. Stir mixture and cook until corn and onion are tender, about 2 minutes. Transfer corn mixture to large bowl, add pineapple, jalapeños, and Tajín, and toss to combine. Arrange salad and chicken on serving platter and sprinkle with cilantro. Serve.

NOTES

Look for drumsticks that are between 5 and 7 ounces each. To help reduce prep time, use already peeled pineapple. For a spicier salad, include all or a portion of the jalapeño seeds.

KITCHEN IMPROV

If fresh corn isn't in season, you can substitute 4 cups thawed frozen corn. If you can't find Tajín Clásico seasoning, use chili powder instead. If you like, substitute eight (5- to 7-ounce) bone-in chicken thighs for the drumsticks.

INEXPENSIVE BUT MEATY chicken drumsticks taste great when glazed and roasted. Brush them with two coats of a honey-vinegar glaze for sweet yet sophisticated tang. The salsa-like salad turns this into an easy summer dinner.

skillet-roasted chicken WITH garlicky spinach AND beans

Serves 4 to 6 • Total Time: 45 minutes

- **2½ pounds bone-in chicken pieces (split breasts cut in half, thighs, and/or drumsticks), trimmed**
- **1½ teaspoons table salt, divided**
- **1 tablespoon extra-virgin olive oil, plus extra for drizzling**
- **1 shallot, minced**
- **6 garlic cloves, sliced thin**
- **⅛ teaspoon pepper flakes**
- **1 (15-ounce) can cannellini beans, rinsed**
- **½ cup dry white wine**
- **1 pound (16 cups) baby spinach, divided**
- **1 teaspoon grated lemon zest**

THE COMBINATION of searing and high-heat roasting leaves plenty of caramelized drippings in the skillet to use as the base for a flavorful side dish of greens and beans.

1 Adjust oven rack to middle position and heat oven to 450 degrees. Pat chicken dry with paper towels and sprinkle with 1 teaspoon salt. Heat oil in 12-inch ovensafe skillet over medium-high heat until just smoking. Place chicken skin side down in skillet and cook until lightly browned, 5 to 7 minutes. Flip chicken, transfer skillet to oven, and roast until breasts register 160 degrees and drumsticks and thighs register at least 175 degrees, 10 to 15 minutes.

2 Remove skillet from oven. Being careful of hot skillet handle, transfer chicken to platter skin side up and let rest while preparing beans and spinach.

3 Add shallot, garlic, pepper flakes, and ¼ teaspoon salt to fat remaining in skillet and cook over medium heat until fragrant, about 1 minute. Stir in beans and wine, bring to simmer, and cook, stirring occasionally, until beans are just beginning to break down, about 5 minutes.

4 Mound half of spinach over beans and cook, covered, until spinach is mostly wilted, about 2 minutes. Using tongs, stir in remaining spinach and remaining ¼ teaspoon salt. Cook, covered, until spinach is fully wilted, about 2 minutes. Off heat, stir in lemon zest and season with salt and pepper to taste. Drizzle bean-spinach mixture with extra oil and serve with chicken.

NOTES

Any mix of bone-in chicken parts works well here. If using thighs or drumsticks, look for pieces that are between 5 and 7 ounces. You will need a 12-inch ovensafe skillet with a tight-fitting lid. The skillet will initially be crowded in step 1; however, the chicken will shrink as it cooks.

KITCHEN IMPROV

Other styles of white beans will work; consider great northern or butter beans. Baby kale or chopped escarole can also be substituted for the spinach.

thai curry chicken WITH sweet potatoes AND green beans

Serves 4 to 6 • Total Time: 45 minutes

- **1 (14-ounce) can coconut milk, divided**
- **3 tablespoons Thai yellow or red curry paste, divided**
- **2½ pounds bone-in chicken thighs and/or drumsticks**
- **¾ teaspoon table salt**
- **1 tablespoon vegetable oil**
- **1 pound sweet potatoes, unpeeled, halved lengthwise and sliced ¼ inch thick**
- **8 ounces green beans, trimmed**
- **1 tablespoon fish sauce**
- **1 tablespoon sugar**
- **1 cup Thai basil, mint, and/or cilantro leaves**
- **3 scallions, sliced thin on bias**
- **Lime wedges**

1 Adjust oven rack to middle position and heat oven to 400 degrees. Whisk 1½ teaspoons coconut milk and 1½ teaspoons curry paste together in small bowl. Pat chicken dry with paper towels and sprinkle with salt. Heat oil in 12-inch ovensafe skillet or sauté pan over medium-high heat until just smoking. Place chicken skin side down in skillet and cook until lightly browned on first side, 5 to 7 minutes. Transfer chicken to plate skin side up and brush with curry mixture.

2 Meanwhile, microwave potatoes and green beans in large covered bowl until tender, 8 to 10 minutes, tossing vegetables after 5 minutes of microwaving; drain off excess liquid.

3 Pour off all but 1 tablespoon fat from skillet. Add remaining 2½ tablespoons curry paste to fat left in skillet and cook over medium heat, stirring constantly, until fragrant, about 1 minute. Whisk in remaining coconut milk, fish sauce, and sugar, scraping up any browned bits. Stir in vegetables and bring to simmer.

4 Nestle chicken skin side up into skillet (skin should remain above liquid). Transfer skillet to oven and roast until chicken registers at least 175 degrees, 20 to 25 minutes. Sprinkle chicken and vegetables with basil and scallions. Serve with lime wedges.

NOTES

Give the can of coconut milk a good shake before opening; this will make it easier to measure out a portion of it in step 1. Look for thighs and drumsticks that are between 5 and 7 ounces. The skillet will initially be crowded in step 1; however, the chicken will shrink as it cooks. For the crispiest chicken, be sure to arrange the browned pieces in the pan so the skin stays above the liquid in step 4.

KITCHEN IMPROV

You can substitute four (12-ounce) bone-in split chicken breasts, halved crosswise, for the thighs; cook the breasts to 160 degrees, reducing the roasting time range in step 4 to 15 to 20 minutes. Choose a variety of sweet potatoes, including purple or white, to add vibrancy to this dish.

CANNED COCONUT MILK and a few tablespoons of Thai curry paste are your shortcut to burnished, succulent chicken and vegetables in a rich, aromatic scuce. The veggies parcook in the microwave while you tend to browning the chicken; then everything goes into the skillet to finish in the oven.

coriander-cumin chicken WITH potatoes AND carrots

Serves 4 • Total Time: 45 minutes

- 1½ pounds small red or Yukon Gold potatoes, unpeeled, halved
- 12 ounces carrots, peeled and sliced ½ inch thick on bias
- 1 teaspoon table salt, plus salt for cooking vegetables
- ½ cup mayonnaise
- 2 tablespoons minced canned chipotle chile in adobo sauce
- 1 teaspoon grated lime zest plus 1 teaspoon juice
- 4 garlic cloves (3 peeled and smashed, 1 minced to paste)
- 8 (5- to 7-ounce) bone-in chicken thighs, trimmed
- 1 tablespoon vegetable oil
- 2 tablespoons coriander seeds
- 2 teaspoons cumin seeds
- 3 scallions, sliced thin

1 Adjust oven rack to middle position and heat oven to 450 degrees. Place potatoes and carrots in large saucepan and add water to cover by 1 inch. Bring to boil over medium-high heat. Add 1 teaspoon salt, reduce heat to medium, and simmer, stirring once or twice, until vegetables are tender, about 10 minutes; drain and set aside.

2 Meanwhile, whisk mayonnaise, chipotle, lime zest and juice, and minced garlic together in bowl; refrigerate until ready to serve. Pat chicken dry with paper towels and sprinkle with salt. Heat oil in 12-inch ovensafe skillet over medium-high heat until just smoking. Place chicken skin side down in skillet and cook until well browned on first side, 7 to 9 minutes. Transfer chicken to plate skin side up.

3 Pour off all but 1 tablespoon fat from skillet. Stir coriander seeds, cumin seeds, and smashed garlic into fat left in skillet, then add vegetables and toss to coat with spices. Arrange chicken skin side up on top of vegetables. Transfer skillet to oven and roast until chicken registers at least 175 degrees, 15 to 20 minutes.

4 Remove skillet from oven. Being careful of hot skillet handle, transfer chicken to serving platter and let rest while finishing vegetables. Stir potatoes and carrots, then return skillet to oven and roast until vegetables are fully softened, about 5 minutes. Stir scallions into vegetables. Serve chicken with vegetables and chipotle mayonnaise.

ROASTED CHICKEN with root vegetables, crunchy pops of whole spices, and a finishing dollcp of chipotle mayonnaise—all in 45 minutes: Now this is weeknight cooking with weekend flair.

NOTES

Use small potatoes measuring 1 to 2 inches in diameter. A rasp grater makes quick work of turning the garlic into a paste. To make the best use of time, start boiling the vegetables in step 1 before preparing the remaining ingredients. The skillet will initially be crowded in step 2 however, the chicken will shrink as it cooks.

KITCHEN IMPROV

You can substitute four (12-ounce) bone-in split chicken breasts, halved crosswise, for the thighs; cook the breasts to 160 degrees.

sheet-pan jerk chicken WITH sweet potatoes AND crispy collard greens

Serves 4 • Total Time: 45 minutes

- **1½ pounds sweet potatoes, unpeeled, sliced into ½-inch-thick rounds**
- **3 tablespoons plus 2 teaspoons vegetable oil, divided**
- **¼ teaspoon plus ⅛ teaspoon table salt, divided**
- **1 pound collard greens, stemmed and cut into 2-inch pieces**
- **3 tablespoons jerk seasoning**
- **4 (10-ounce) chicken leg quarters, trimmed**
- **Lime wedges**

1 Adjust oven rack to upper-middle position and heat oven to 475 degrees. Toss sweet potatoes with 1 tablespoon oil and ⅛ teaspoon salt in large bowl, then arrange cut side down in single layer on rimmed baking sheet. Toss collards with 2 teaspoons oil and ⅛ teaspoon salt in now-empty bowl, then arrange in even layer over potatoes.

2 Whisk jerk seasoning, remaining 2 tablespoons oil, and remaining ⅛ teaspoon salt together in again-empty bowl. Pat chicken dry with paper towels, then toss with spice mixture until well coated. Place 1 piece chicken skin side up in each corner of sheet on top of vegetables. Roast until chicken registers at least 175 degrees and sweet potatoes are softened, 25 to 35 minutes.

3 Transfer chicken to serving platter and let rest while finishing vegetables. Return sheet to oven and roast until collards are crisp, about 5 minutes. Gently toss vegetables with any accumulated chicken juices. Serve chicken and vegetables with lime wedges.

NOTES

Store-bought jerk seasoning is convenient, but you can also make your own by combining 1 tablespoon packed brown sugar, 1½ teaspoons ground allspice, 1½ teaspoons pepper, 1 teaspoon garlic powder, ¾ teaspoon dried thyme, ¾ teaspoon dry mustard, and ½ teaspoon cayenne.

KITCHEN IMPROV

Kale can be substituted for the collards. Consider using another seasoning blend such as Cajun, Creole, or barbecue. You can use eight (5- to 7-ounce) bone-in chicken thighs instead of leg quarters; arrange two thighs in each corner of the pan and roast for 20 to 25 minutes in step 2.

ASSERTIVELY SPICED chicken and some thoughtful organization on a sheet pan bring the flavors of Jamaican barbecue to the weeknight dinner table. Chicken leg quarters roast over sweet potatoes and collards, producing a mix of creamy and crispy vegetables.

glazed chicken breasts WITH currant-pistachio couscous

Serves 4 • Total Time: 40 minutes

- **2 tablespoons apricot preserves**
- **1 tablespoon harissa**
- **5 tablespoons extra-virgin olive oil, divided**
- **¼ cup dried currants or raisins**
- **1 teaspoon grated lemon zest plus 2 tablespoons juice**
- **1 garlic clove, minced**
- **1½ teaspoons table salt, divided**
- **4 (6- to 8-ounce) boneless, skinless chicken breasts, trimmed**
- **1½ cups water**
- **1¼ cups couscous**
- **½ cup shelled pistachios, toasted and chopped**
- **¼ cup fresh mint leaves, torn**

APRICOT PRESERVES and harissa pull double duty, glazing the chicken breasts and flavoring the couscous. In the same two-for-one spirit, the couscous cooks in the same skillet that's first used to sauté the chicken.

1 Combine preserves, harissa, and 1 tablespoon oil in bowl. Transfer 1 tablespoon harissa mixture to second bowl and stir in currants, lemon zest and juice, garlic, ½ teaspoon salt, and 3 tablespoons oil; set aside.

2 Pat chicken dry with paper towels and sprinkle with remaining 1 teaspoon salt. Heat remaining 1 tablespoon oil in 12-inch non-stick skillet over medium-high heat until just smoking. Place chicken in skillet and cook, flipping occasionally, until chicken is well browned and registers 160 degrees, 10 to 12 minutes. Transfer chicken to serving platter and brush with remaining harissa-apricot mixture. Tent with aluminum foil and let rest while preparing couscous.

3 Bring water to boil in now-empty skillet over high heat. Off heat, stir in couscous, cover, and let sit for 5 minutes. Add pistachios, mint, and harissa-currant mixture and fluff with fork to combine. Serve chicken with couscous.

NOTES

To ensure even cooking, look for chicken breasts of even thickness; if necessary, pound the breasts to even thickness using a meat pounder. Harissa can be found in both mild and spicy versions; use whichever you prefer.

KITCHEN IMPROV

You can substitute 1½ pounds boneless, skinless chicken thighs for breasts; cook them for 12 to 15 minutes in step 2, until at least 175 degrees. The skillet will be crowded at first, but the thighs will shrink as they cook. Try apple or peach preserves in place of apricot preserves. Substitute sliced almonds for pistachios.

lemon-oregano chicken WITH farro salad

Serves 4 • Total Time: 30 minutes

- 1½ cups whole farro
- 1 teaspoon table salt, plus salt for cooking farro
- 6 tablespoons extra-virgin olive oil, divided
- 1 tablespoon minced fresh oregano
- 1½ teaspoons grated lemon zest plus 2 tablespoons juice
- ¾ teaspoon pepper
- 4 (6- to 8-ounce) boneless, skinless chicken breasts, trimmed
- ¼ cup thinly sliced pepperoncini, plus 1 tablespoon brine
- ½ English cucumber, cut into ½-inch pieces (3 cups)
- 1 tomato, cored and cut into ½-inch pieces
- 2 ounces feta cheese, crumbled (½ cup)

1 Bring 2 quarts water to boil in large saucepan. Add farro and 1 tablespoon salt, return to boil, and cook until farro is tender with slight chew, 15 to 30 minutes. Drain farro, rinse under cold water, then drain well; set aside.

2 Meanwhile, combine 1 tablespoon oil, oregano, lemon zest, pepper, and salt in small bowl; measure out and reserve 1 tablespoon oregano mixture. Rub chicken breasts evenly with remaining oregano mixture. Heat 1 tablespoon oil in 12-inch nonstick skillet over medium-high heat until just smoking. Place chicken in skillet and cook, flipping occasionally, until chicken is well browned and registers 160 degrees, 10 to 12 minutes. Transfer chicken to cutting board, tent with aluminum foil, and let rest while preparing salad.

3 Whisk pepperoncini brine, lemon juice, remaining ¼ cup oil, and reserved oregano mixture together in large bowl. Measure out and reserve 2 tablespoons dressing. Add cucumber, tomato, feta, farro, and pepperoncini to remaining dressing in large bowl and toss to combine. Slice chicken ½ inch thick and serve with farro salad, drizzling chicken with reserved dressing.

NOTES

To ensure even cooking, look for chicken breasts of even thickness; if necessary, pound the breasts to even thickness using a meat pounder. If using pearl, quick-cooking, or presteamed farro (check the ingredient list on the package to determine this) instead of whole farro, be prepared to reduce the cooking time in step 1.

KITCHEN IMPROV

Other whole grains can be used in place of the farro; keep in mind that cooking times may change. Switch up the veggies with bell peppers, radishes, edamame, asparagus, or grated carrots. Try just about any crumbled cheese, such as queso fresco, goat, or blue. Or level up the salad with chopped olives, roasted red peppers, a sprinkle of fresh herbs, or chopped toasted nuts before serving.

AN ENDLESSLY riffable meal of protein plus grain-and-veggie salad should be in every cook's weeknight arsenal. The recipe here (a blueprint, really) offers a good mix of flavors and textures whether you switch up the protein, veggies, or dressing.

YOUR OVEN is a faster route to this favorite NYC street food than any delivery app. Baking the turmeric-scented rice in a covered dish is foolproof and convenient since the chicken is already roasting in the oven. While that's happening, whip up a creamy garlic sauce and shawarma-spiced oil.

halal-cart chicken AND rice

Serves 4 • Total Time: 40 minutes

- **1¾ cups boiling water**
- **1½ cups long-grain white rice, rinsed**
- **3 tablespoons extra-virgin olive oil, divided**
- **1¼ teaspoons table salt, divided**
- **½ teaspoon ground turmeric**
- **1½ pounds boneless, skinless chicken thighs, trimmed**
- **1¼ teaspoons shawarma spice blend, divided**
- **1 teaspoon minced garlic, divided**
- **½ teaspoon dried oregano**
- **½ teaspoon grated lemon zest plus 2 tablespoons juice**
- **1 cup mayonnaise**
- **2 tablespoons water**
- **4 cups shredded iceberg or romaine lettuce**
- **6 ounces cherry tomatoes, halved**

1 Adjust oven rack to upper-middle and lower-middle positions and heat oven to 450 degrees. Combine boiling water, rice, 1 tablespoon oil, ½ teaspoon salt, and turmeric in 8-inch square baking dish. Cover dish tightly with aluminum foil and bake on lower rack until rice is tender and water has been fully absorbed, about 15 minutes.

2 Meanwhile, pat chicken dry with paper towels, then toss with 1 tablespoon oil and ½ teaspoon salt on rimmed baking sheet. Arrange chicken in even layer and roast on upper rack until just beginning to brown and registers at least 175 degrees, 12 to 15 minutes.

3 While chicken and rice cook, combine remaining 1 tablespoon oil, ½ teaspoon shawarma spice blend, ½ teaspoon garlic, oregano, lemon zest, and remaining ¼ teaspoon salt in large bowl; set spiced oil aside. Whisk mayonnaise, water, lemon juice, remaining ¾ teaspoon shawarma spice blend, and remaining ½ teaspoon minced garlic together in small bowl; set sauce aside.

4 Remove dish from oven and let rice sit for 5 minutes. Cut chicken into ½-inch pieces and toss with spiced oil. Fluff rice with fork and serve with chicken, lettuce, and tomatoes, passing white sauce separately.

NOTES

Serve with warmed pita and hot sauce. You can substitute baharat or hawaij for the shawarma spice blend; or make your own by combining ¼ teaspoon ground coriander, ¼ teaspoon ground cumin, ¼ teaspoon ground cardamom, ¼ teaspoon paprika, ⅛ teaspoon ground turmeric, and ⅛ teaspoon pepper.

KITCHEN IMPROV

This recipe also works well with lamb. Toss four (8- to 12-ounce) lamb shoulder chops (blade or round bone), about ¾ inch thick, with oil and salt. Arrange the lamb on a baking sheet as directed and roast until the meat registers 130 to 135 degrees (for medium), about 15 minutes. Carve the meat from the bone before cutting it into pieces and tossing it with the spiced oil.

chicken sausages AND apples WITH smoky cheese grits

Serves 4 • Total Time: 35 minutes

- **3 cups chicken broth**
- **1 cup whole milk**
- **4 tablespoons unsalted butter, divided**
- **½ teaspoon table salt, divided**
- **1 cup quick-cooking grits**
- **4 ounces smoked gouda cheese, shredded (1 cup)**
- **1½ pounds chicken sausage**
- **2 red apples, cored and cut into ¾-inch pieces**
- **2 shallots, chopped**
- **2 teaspoons sugar**
- **1 teaspoon lemon juice**

SMOKED GOUDA and apples elevate a comforting dinner of sausage and grits without adding extra time.

1 Bring broth, milk, 3 tablespoons butter, and ¼ teaspoon salt to simmer in large saucepan over medium-high heat. Slowly whisk in grits. Reduce heat to medium-low and cook, stirring often, until grits are thick and creamy, 5 to 7 minutes. Off heat, whisk in gouda. Cover and set aside.

2 Meanwhile, bring sausages and ½ cup water to simmer in 12-inch skillet over medium heat. Cover and cook until sausages register at least 135 degrees, 5 to 7 minutes. (If skillet contents begin to sizzle, add ¼ cup water.) Uncover and, using paring knife, pierce each sausage in 8 to 10 spots to release fat and juices. Continue to cook, uncovered, moving sausages as necessary, until dark fond forms on bottom of skillet and sausages register 160 degrees, 2 to 4 minutes. Transfer sausages to plate, tent with aluminum foil, and let rest while preparing apples.

3 Melt remaining 1 tablespoon butter in now-empty skillet over medium-high heat. Add apples, shallots, sugar, and remaining ¼ teaspoon salt and cook, stirring frequently, until tender and lightly browned, about 5 minutes. Stir in lemon juice. Serve sausages with grits and apples.

NOTES

Quick-cooking grits help expedite this dinner. You can certainly use old-fashioned, but you'll need to increase the simmering time by 25 minutes and may need to add more water during simmering.

KITCHEN IMPROV

Swap the chicken sausage for turkey or pork sausage. Use another semisoft cheese such as smoked cheddar or extra-sharp cheddar. Want your grits extra-cheesy? Go ahead and double the gouda. While you're at it, stir in some minced fresh chives.

coconut-braised chicken WITH plantains AND peppers

Serves 4 • Total Time: 45 minutes

- 3 tablespoons vegetable oil
- 2 large ripe plantains, peeled, quartered lengthwise, and cut into 2- to 3-inch lengths
- 4 (6- to 8-ounce) boneless, skinless chicken breasts, trimmed
- 1½ teaspoons table salt, divided
- 1 onion, chopped
- 2 red or green bell peppers, stemmed, seeded, and cut into ¼-inch-wide strips
- 3 garlic cloves, minced
- 1 teaspoon sazón
- 1 (14-ounce) can coconut milk
- 2 tablespoons chopped fresh cilantro
- 1 jalapeño chile, stemmed and sliced thin
- Lime wedges

GOLDEN PLANTAINS meet juicy chicken in a rich, coconut milk–laced skillet meal inspired by the stews of coastal Central and South America. This dish demands plenty of rice to soak up the sauce.

1 Heat oil in 12-inch nonstick skillet over medium heat until shimmering. Add plantains and cook, turning as needed, until golden brown, 5 to 7 minutes; transfer to bowl.

2 Pat chicken dry with paper towels and sprinkle with 1 teaspoon salt. Add chicken to fat left in skillet and cook over medium-high heat until browned on first side, about 3 minutes. Transfer chicken to plate browned side up.

3 Add onion, bell peppers, and remaining ½ teaspoon salt to fat left in skillet and cook over medium-high heat until softened, 5 to 7 minutes. Stir in garlic and sazón and cook until fragrant, about 30 seconds. Stir in coconut milk, scraping up any browned bits. Nestle plantains and chicken, browned side up, into skillet and add any accumulated juices. Bring to simmer, then reduce heat to medium-low, cover, and simmer until chicken registers 140 degrees, 6 to 12 minutes.

4 Uncover, increase heat to medium-high, and cook until chicken registers 160 degrees, 3 to 6 minutes. Sprinkle with cilantro and jalapeño and serve with lime wedges.

NOTES

Look for plantains that are almost completely black and yield to firm pressure, like a ripe avocado. To ensure even cooking, look for chicken breasts of even thickness; if necessary, pound the breasts to even thickness using a meat pounder. Look for sazón with culantro and achiote (also called annatto); avoid those without salt.

KITCHEN IMPROV

You can substitute 1½ pounds boneless, skinless thighs for the breasts; cook the thighs to at least 175 degrees, increasing the cooking time range in step 4 to 5 to 7 minutes.

murgh makhani (INDIAN BUTTER CHICKEN)

Serves 4 to 6 • Total Time: 35 minutes

- **2 pounds boneless, skinless chicken thighs, trimmed**
- **½ cup plain Greek yogurt**
- **2 teaspoons table salt, divided**
- **4 tablespoons unsalted butter, cut into 4 pieces and chilled, divided**
- **1 onion, chopped fine**
- **4 garlic cloves, minced**
- **4 teaspoons grated fresh ginger**
- **1 serrano chile, stemmed, seeded, and minced**
- **1 tablespoon garam masala**
- **1 teaspoon ground coriander**
- **½ teaspoon ground cumin**
- **½ teaspoon pepper**
- **1½ cups water**
- **½ cup tomato paste**
- **1 tablespoon sugar**
- **1 cup heavy cream**
- **2 tablespoons chopped fresh cilantro**

1 Adjust oven rack 6 inches from broiler element and heat broiler. Set wire rack in aluminum foil–lined rimmed baking sheet. Pat chicken dry with paper towels, then toss with yogurt and 1 teaspoon salt in bowl until well coated. Arrange chicken evenly on prepared rack and broil until evenly charred and registers at least 175 degrees, 16 to 20 minutes, flipping chicken halfway through broiling.

2 Meanwhile, melt 2 tablespoons butter in large saucepan over medium heat. Add onion, garlic, ginger, and serrano and cook, stirring frequently, until mixture is softened and onion begins to brown, 8 to 10 minutes. Add garam masala, coriander, cumin, and pepper and cook, stirring frequently, until fragrant, about 3 minutes. Add water and tomato paste and whisk until no lumps of tomato paste remain. Add sugar and remaining 1 teaspoon salt and bring to boil. Off heat, stir in cream. Using immersion blender or blender, process until smooth, 30 to 60 seconds. Return sauce to simmer over medium heat and whisk in remaining 2 tablespoons butter.

3 Cut chicken into ¾-inch pieces and stir into sauce. Stir in cilantro and season with salt to taste. Serve.

NOTES

Butter chicken is usually mild; if you prefer a spicier dish, add the minced ribs and seeds from the chile.

KITCHEN IMPROV

The butter sauce is so good there's no reason to limit it to chicken. Make Tofu Makhani by substituting two (14-ounce) blocks firm tofu, cut into ¾-inch planks, for the chicken. Chickpea Makhani is also easy: Skip step 1 and add two (15-ounce) cans chickpeas, drained, with the water. After bringing the chickpeas and sauce to a boil, reduce to a gentle simmer and cook for 10 minutes before stirring in the cream. You can also bulk up your makhani by stirring in thawed frozen peas, cut green beans, or sliced okra with the cut chicken; gently simmer to heat through before adding the cilantro.

THE MARRIAGE of broiled chicken and creamy spiced tomato sauce is an all-time favorite. The pantry-friendly blend of aromatics and spices (including convenient garam masala) creates flavor in a flash. Serve with Simple Rice Pilaf (page 54) and/or naan.

easy rice AND grain side dishes

simple rice pilaf

Serves 4 • Total Time: 35 minutes

ABSOLUTELY PLAIN rice has its place at the table. But why not invite something a little more interesting?

- **3 tablespoons unsalted butter**
- **1½ cups long-grain white rice, rinsed**
- **2 garlic cloves, minced**
- **1 teaspoon minced fresh thyme**
- **2¼ cups chicken or vegetable broth or water**
- **¾ teaspoon table salt**

1. Melt butter in large saucepan over medium-high heat. Add rice and cook, stirring frequently, until edges begin to turn translucent, about 2 minutes. Stir in garlic and thyme and cook until fragrant, about 30 seconds.
2. Stir in broth and salt and bring to boil. Cover, reduce heat to low, and cook until liquid is absorbed and rice is tender, about 20 minutes. Off heat, let rice rest, covered, for 10 minutes. Fluff rice with fork. Serve.

NOTES

Any long-grain white rice will work here, including jasmine, basmati, or Texmati.

KITCHEN IMPROV

Boost the aromatics by adding 1 cup finely chopped onion or shallot to the saucepan before the rice and sautéing until just beginning to soften, about 3 minutes. Swap the thyme for ½ teaspoon dried spice such as coriander, cumin, turmeric, or paprika.

---

mexican red rice

Serves 4 • Total Time: 45 minutes

THIS STAPLE side's beauty lies in its simplicity and a careful balance of fresh flavors.

- **1 tomato, cored and quartered**
- **1 jalapeño chile, stemmed, halved, and seeded**
- **1½ teaspoons table salt**
- **¼ teaspoon pepper**
- **1 garlic clove, chopped**
- **1–1¾ cups chicken or vegetable broth or water**
- **3 tablespoons extra-virgin olive oil**
- **1½ cups long-grain white rice, rinsed**
- **1 tablespoon tomato paste**
- **¼ cup chopped fresh cilantro**

1. Process tomato, jalapeño, salt, pepper, and garlic in food processor until smooth, about 30 seconds, scraping down sides of bowl as needed. Transfer mixture to 4-cup liquid measuring cup. Stir to deflate foam, if necessary, then add enough broth to equal 2½ cups.
2. Heat oil in large saucepan over medium-high heat until shimmering. Add rice and cook, stirring frequently, until edges begin to turn translucent, about 2 minutes. Add tomato paste and cook, stirring constantly, until mixture is uniformly colored, about 1 minute. Stir in tomato mixture and bring to boil. Cover, reduce heat to low, and cook until liquid is absorbed and rice is tender, about 20 minutes. Off heat, let rice rest, covered, for 10 minutes. Add cilantro and fluff with fork to combine. Serve.

NOTES

Any long-grain white rice will work here, including jasmine, basmati, or Texmati.

KITCHEN IMPROV

You can easily turn this into a rice and bean side dish by adding one (15-ounce) can black or pinto beans, rinsed, to the saucepan following the tomato mixture; do not stir the beans into the rice.

creamy parmesan polenta

Serves 4 • Total Time: 45 minutes

4½ cups water
1 cup coarse-ground polenta
1 teaspoon table salt
Pinch baking soda
1 ounce Parmesan cheese, grated (½ cup)
1 tablespoon unsalted butter

1 Bring water to boil in medium saucepan over high heat. Whisk in polenta, salt, and baking soda. Bring mixture to boil, stirring frequently. Reduce heat to lowest possible setting, cover, and cook for 5 minutes. Whisk until smooth, cover, and continue to cook until grains are tender but slightly al dente, about 25 minutes longer. (Polenta should be loose and barely hold its shape when drizzled from whisk; it will continue to thicken as it cools.)

2 Remove from heat, whisk in Parmesan and butter, and season with salt and pepper to taste. Serve.

THE PINCH of baking soda cuts the cooking time in half, and covering the pan means there's no need for constant stirring.

NOTES

Look for Bob's Red Mill yellow corn polenta. Coarse-ground grits also work well. Avoid quick-cooking or instant polenta or cornmeal.

KITCHEN IMPROV

You can use just about any hard cheese, such as Pecorino Romano, aged Manchego, or aged Gouda, in place of the Parmesan. Level up your polenta by sprinkling it with fresh herbs, toasted sliced almonds or pine nuts, and/or chopped sun-dried tomatoes.

cooking hearty grains

THERE ARE several ways to cook hearty grains, but boiling them is arguably the easiest. Simply bring 4 quarts water to boil in large pot and add 1 teaspoon table salt. Stir in 1 cup grains and cook until tender, following the timing below; drain well.

grain	cook time
Pearl barley	20 to 40 minutes
Farro	15 to 30 minutes
Freekeh	30 to 45 minutes
Long-grain brown rice	25 to 30 minutes
Oat berries	30 to 40 minutes
Wild rice	35 to 40 minutes

NOTES

One cup dry grains will yield 2½ cups cooked grains; feel free to double the amount of grains if you want leftovers. Refrigerate cooled cooked grains for up to 3 days.

KITCHEN IMPROV

Cooked grains are easy to level up. Start by stirring in chopped fresh herbs, toasted nuts, and/or dried fruit. Next, drizzle with a flavorful oil such as extra-virgin olive oil or toasted sesame oil. Finally, add some tang with fresh citrus juice or vinegar.

san bei ji (THREE-CUP CHICKEN)

Serves 4 • Total Time: 45 minutes

- 1½ pounds boneless, skinless chicken thighs, trimmed and cut into 2-inch pieces
- ⅓ cup soy sauce
- ⅓ cup Shaoxing wine
- 1 tablespoon packed brown sugar
- 3 tablespoons vegetable oil
- 1 (2-inch) piece ginger, peeled, halved lengthwise, and sliced into thin half-moons
- 12 garlic cloves, peeled and halved lengthwise
- ½–¾ teaspoon red pepper flakes
- 6 scallions, white and green parts separated and sliced thin on bias
- 1 tablespoon water
- 1 teaspoon cornstarch
- 1 cup fresh Thai basil leaves, large leaves halved lengthwise
- 1 tablespoon toasted sesame oil

1. Toss chicken with soy sauce, Shaoxing wine, and sugar in bowl until well coated; set aside.
2. Add vegetable oil, ginger, garlic, and pepper flakes to 14-inch flat-bottomed wok or 12-inch nonstick skillet and heat over medium-low heat. Cook, tossing slowly but constantly, until garlic is golden brown and beginning to soften, 8 to 10 minutes.
3. Add chicken and marinade to skillet, increase heat to medium-high, and bring to simmer. Reduce heat to medium-low and simmer for 10 minutes, tossing occasionally. Stir in scallion whites and continue to cook until chicken registers about 200 degrees, 8 to 10 minutes longer.
4. Whisk water and cornstarch together in small bowl, then stir into sauce. Simmer until sauce is slightly thickened, about 1 minute. Off heat, stir in basil, sesame oil, and scallion greens and serve.

THIS TAKE on the Taiwanese classic retools the original one-cup-each formula for the soy sauce, sesame oil, and rice wine, and uses quick-cooking boneless, skinless chicken thigh pieces. Serve with rice.

NOTES

For a dish with more heat, use the larger amount of red pepper flakes. Since the chicken will require your attention on the stovetop, consider a simple oven-roasted vegetable (see page 142).

KITCHEN IMPROV

If Shaoxing wine or Thai basil are unavailable, substitute dry sherry and Italian basil respectively. Instead of rice, serve this over another grain or over noodles.

cashew chicken

Serves 4 • Total Time: 30 minutes

- **5 tablespoons soy sauce, divided**
- **1 tablespoon Shaoxing wine**
- **1 teaspoon toasted sesame oil**
- **1 teaspoon cornstarch**
- **1½ pounds boneless, skinless chicken breasts, trimmed and cut into ¾-inch pieces**
- **⅓ cup hoisin sauce**
- **⅓ cup water**
- **1 tablespoon Chinese black vinegar**
- **3 tablespoons vegetable oil**
- **1 cup raw cashews**
- **2 celery ribs, sliced ¼ inch thick on bias**
- **6 scallions, white parts sliced thin, green parts cut into 1-inch pieces**
- **2 garlic cloves, minced**
- **1 teaspoon grated fresh ginger**
- **½ teaspoon red pepper flakes**

1 Whisk 2 tablespoons soy sauce, Shaoxing wine, sesame oil, and cornstarch together in large bowl. Add chicken and toss to coat. Whisk hoisin, water, vinegar, and remaining 3 tablespoons soy sauce together in separate bowl and set aside.

2 Heat vegetable oil in 14-inch flat-bottomed wok or 12-inch nonstick skillet over medium heat until shimmering. Add cashews and cook, tossing slowly but constantly, until golden brown, 4 to 6 minutes, reducing heat if cashews begin to darken too quickly. Using slotted spoon, transfer cashews to small bowl.

3 Heat oil left in pan over medium-high heat until just smoking. Add chicken and increase heat to high. Cook, tossing slowly but constantly, until no longer pink, 2 to 6 minutes. Add celery, scallion whites, garlic, ginger, and pepper flakes and cook, tossing constantly, until celery is just beginning to soften, about 2 minutes.

4 Add hoisin mixture, bring to boil, and cook until chicken is cooked through and sauce is thickened, 1 to 3 minutes. Off heat, stir in scallion greens and cashews. Serve.

NOTES

This recipe moves quickly; be sure to have all the ingredients prepared and close by so that you're equipped for fast cooking. Since the chicken will require your attention on the stovetop, pair with a simple oven-roasted vegetable (see page 142).

KITCHEN IMPROV

If Shaoxing wine or Chinese black vinegar are unavailable, substitute dry sherry and balsamic vinegar respectively. Peanuts can be used in place of the cashews. Double or triple the amount of celery if you're looking for more vegetables; increase the cooking time in step 3 by 1 to 2 minutes. Cashew Chicken also makes an excellent filling for lettuce wraps.

THIS STIR-FRY doesn't skimp on flavor. Chinese pantry staples produce an umami-rich sauce with balanced sweetness, but the cashews are the star: Deeply toasted in the same oil used for the stir-fry, their flavor permeates the dish. Serve with rice.

SIX THAI CHILES make the heat component plenty loud, but the salty, sweet, and umami-packed ingredients are blasting just as forcefully. The balance of flavors is pitch-perfect. Serve with rice.

gai pad krapow (SPICY THAI BASIL CHICKEN)

Serves 4 • Total Time: 25 minutes

- **2 cups tightly packed fresh Thai basil leaves, divided**
- **3 garlic cloves, peeled**
- **6 green or red Thai chiles, stemmed**
- **2 tablespoons fish sauce, divided, plus extra for serving**
- **1 tablespoon oyster sauce**
- **1 tablespoon sugar, plus extra for serving**
- **1 teaspoon distilled white vinegar, plus extra for serving**
- **1 pound 93 percent lean ground chicken**
- **3 shallots, sliced thin (about 3/4 cup)**
- **2 tablespoons vegetable oil**
- **Red pepper flakes**

1 Pulse 1 cup basil, garlic, and chiles in food processor until finely chopped, 6 to 10 pulses, scraping down sides of bowl as needed. Transfer 1 tablespoon basil mixture to small bowl and stir in 1 tablespoon fish sauce, oyster sauce, sugar, and vinegar; set aside. Transfer remaining basil mixture to 14-inch flat-bottomed wok or 12-inch nonstick skillet.

2 Pulse chicken and remaining 1 tablespoon fish sauce in now-empty processor until just combined, about 4 pulses.

3 Add shallots and oil to wok with basil mixture and cook over medium-low heat, stirring constantly, until garlic and shallots are golden brown, 5 to 8 minutes (mixture should start to sizzle after about 1½ minutes; if it doesn't, adjust heat accordingly).

4 Add chicken mixture, increase heat to medium, and cook, breaking up chicken with wooden spoon, until only traces of pink remain, 2 to 4 minutes. Add reserved basil–fish sauce mixture and continue to cook, stirring constantly, until chicken is no longer pink, about 1 minute longer. Stir in remaining 1 cup basil and cook, stirring constantly, until basil is wilted, 30 to 60 seconds. Serve immediately, passing pepper flakes, extra fish sauce, extra sugar, and extra vinegar separately.

NOTES

For a milder version, remove the ribs and seeds from the chiles. Passing red pepper flakes, sugar, fish sauce, and vinegar at the table allows everyone to adjust flavors to suit their tastes. Be sure to use ground chicken, not ground chicken breast (also labeled 99 percent fat-free).

KITCHEN IMPROV

You can use Italian basil in place of the Thai basil. If fresh Thai chiles are unavailable, substitute 2 serranos or 1 medium jalapeño. You can substitute ground turkey, lean ground beef, ground pork, or crumbled extra-firm tofu for the chicken, if desired. Instead of rice, serve with another grain or with noodles. This recipe also makes an excellent filling for lettuce wraps.

chicken piccata meatballs

Serves 4 • Total Time: 45 minutes

- **2 lemons**
- **1/3 cup extra-virgin olive oil**
- **2 ounces Parmesan cheese, grated (1 cup)**
- **1/2 cup panko bread crumbs**
- **1 large egg, lightly beaten**
- **3/4 teaspoon pepper**
- **1/2 teaspoon table salt**
- **1 pound 93 percent lean ground chicken**
- **1 shallot, minced**
- **2 teaspoons all-purpose flour**
- **1 cup chicken broth, plus extra as needed**
- **2 tablespoons capers, rinsed**
- **3 tablespoons unsalted butter, cut into 1/2-inch cubes**
- **1 tablespoon chopped fresh parsley**

SEASONED WITH lemon zest, black pepper, and Parmesan and simmered in a velvety lemon-butter sauce with briny capers, these meatballs deliver the brightness of piccata from the inside out. The tangy, rich sauce begs to be soaked up with egg noodles, pasta, bread, or even mashed potatoes.

1 Halve 1 lemon lengthwise. Trim ends from 1 half, halve lengthwise again, then cut crosswise into very thin slices; set aside. Zest and juice remaining 1½ lemons to yield 1½ teaspoons zest and 3 tablespoons juice.

2 Add oil to 12-inch nonstick skillet. Combine Parmesan, panko, egg, pepper, salt, and lemon zest in large bowl. Add chicken and mix with your hands until thoroughly combined. Using moistened hands, pinch off and roll mixture into 24 meatballs (about 1 tablespoon each); arrange in even layer in skillet. Place skillet over medium-high heat and cook until meatballs are well browned on one side, about 4 minutes. Gently turn meatballs and continue to cook, turning as needed, until well browned on all sides, 4 to 6 minutes; transfer to plate.

3 Add shallot to fat left in skillet and cook over medium heat until softened, about 30 seconds. Stir in flour and cook for 1 minute. Slowly whisk in broth, then stir in capers, lemon slices, and lemon juice and bring to simmer. Return meatballs and any accumulated juices to skillet and simmer until meatballs register 160 degrees, 3 to 5 minutes, turning meatballs halfway through simmering.

4 Transfer meatballs to serving platter. Off heat, whisk butter into sauce in skillet, 1 piece at a time, until incorporated. Season with salt and pepper to taste and adjust consistency of sauce with extra broth as needed. Spoon sauce over meatballs and sprinkle with parsley. Serve.

NOTES

Be sure to use ground chicken, not ground chicken breast (also labeled 99 percent fat-free). If you're able to plan ahead, shape and refrigerate the meatballs up to 2 days in advance.

KITCHEN IMPROV

You can substitute ground turkey or ground pork for the chicken. Other fresh herbs such as tarragon, basil, or chives can be used in place of the parsley.

OXO

skillet orzo WITH chicken meatballs, green olives AND feta

Serves 4 • Total Time: 45 minutes

- 1 shallot, chopped coarse
- ¼ cup panko bread crumbs
- ¾ teaspoon pepper, divided
- ½ teaspoon table salt, divided
- 1 pound 93 percent lean ground chicken
- ¼ cup milk
- 2 tablespoons unsalted butter, melted and cooled
- 1 tablespoon Worcestershire sauce
- ¼ cup extra-virgin olive oil, divided
- 4 cups chicken broth
- 2 cups orzo
- ½ teaspoon grated lemon zest plus 2 tablespoons juice, divided
- ⅓ cup pitted green olives, chopped fine
- ⅓ cup minced fresh parsley
- 4 ounces feta, crumbled (1 cup)

MELTED BUTTER ensures these chicken meatballs aren't dry, while Worcestershire amps up the meaty element. Cooking orzo in the meatball drippings makes it extra-tasty. A no-cook olive, lemon, and parsley sauce makes everything shine.

1 Process shallot, panko, ¼ teaspoon pepper, and ¼ teaspoon salt in food processor until shallot is finely ground, about 20 seconds, scraping down sides of bowl as needed. Add chicken, milk, melted butter, and Worcestershire and pulse until just combined, 8 to 12 pulses.

2 Add 1 tablespoon oil to 12-inch nonstick skillet. Pinch off and roll chicken mixture into 12 meatballs (about 3 tablespoons each), and transfer to skillet. Place skillet over medium-high heat and cook until meatballs are browned on first side, about 3 minutes. Gently turn meatballs and continue to cook, turning as needed until browned on all sides, 4 to 6 minutes. Transfer to plate.

3 Add broth, orzo, 1 tablespoon lemon juice, remaining ½ teaspoon pepper, and remaining ¼ teaspoon salt to fat left in skillet. Bring to boil over high heat, then reduce heat to gentle simmer, cover, and cook for 6 minutes. Nestle meatballs into orzo mixture and add any accumulated juices. Cover and cook for 3 minutes. Uncover and continue to cook until orzo begins to sizzle, 3 to 5 minutes. Remove from heat and let rest for 5 minutes.

4 Meanwhile, combine olives, parsley, lemon zest and remaining 1 tablespoon juice, and remaining 3 tablespoons oil in bowl. Spoon olive sauce over meatballs and orzo and sprinkle with feta. Serve.

NOTES

Handle the meatballs delicately when turning them. Your best bet is to wait until the first sides are well browned so that they will easily release from the pan. You can shape and refrigerate the meatballs up to 2 days in advance.

KITCHEN IMPROV

You can substitute ground turkey or ground pork for the ground chicken. Two tablespoons rinsed capers can be used in place of olives.

couscous risotto WITH chicken AND spinach

Serves 4 • Total Time: 45 minutes

- 2 pounds boneless, skinless chicken breasts, trimmed and cut into 1-inch pieces
- 1½ teaspoons table salt, divided
- ½ teaspoon pepper
- 3 tablespoons unsalted butter, divided
- 2 leeks, white and light green parts only, halved lengthwise, sliced thin, and washed thoroughly
- 1½ cups pearl couscous
- 3 cups chicken broth
- 2 ounces (2 cups) baby spinach, chopped coarse
- 1½ ounces Parmesan cheese, grated (¾ cup), plus extra for serving
- ½ cup thawed frozen peas
- ⅓ cup heavy cream
- Red pepper flakes

1 Sprinkle chicken with 1 teaspoon salt and pepper. Melt 1 tablespoon butter in Dutch oven over medium-high heat. Add chicken and cook until no longer pink, about 5 minutes; transfer to bowl.

2 Melt remaining 2 tablespoons butter in now-empty pot over medium heat. Add leeks and couscous and cook until leeks have softened and couscous is lightly toasted, 4 to 6 minutes. Stir in broth and remaining ½ teaspoon salt and bring to simmer. Reduce heat to medium-low, cover, and cook, stirring occasionally, for 6 minutes. Stir in chicken and any accumulated juices and cover. Cook, stirring occasionally, until chicken is cooked through, about 6 minutes.

3 Off heat, stir in spinach, Parmesan, peas, and cream and let sit until heated through, about 5 minutes. Serve, passing pepper flakes and extra Parmesan separately.

NOTES

Pearl couscous is often labeled Israeli couscous in the supermarket. Don't substitute regular couscous, as it requires a different cooking method and will not work in this recipe.

KITCHEN IMPROV

You can substitute 2 cups of thinly sliced onion or shallot for the leeks. Baby kale can be used in place of the spinach, and frozen corn, lima beans, or cut green beans can be used in place of the peas. Other hard cheeses, such as Pecorino Romano, aged Manchego, or aged gouda, are a good substitute for the Parmesan.

PEARL COUSCOUS produces an almost effortless risotto with a unique texture and lovely nutty flavor. The addition of chicken and vegetables, along with Parmesan, peas, and heavy cream, creates a satisfying one-pot supper.

cheesy green chile, chicken, AND bean skillet

Serves 4 • Total Time: 35 minutes

- 2 tablespoons vegetable oil
- 1 poblano chile, stemmed, seeded, and chopped fine
- 1 white onion, chopped fine, divided
- 1/4 teaspoon table salt
- 2 garlic cloves, minced
- 2 teaspoons ground cumin
- 1 teaspoon dried oregano
- 1 pound 93 percent lean ground chicken
- 1 (15-ounce) can black beans, rinsed
- 1 cup jarred salsa verde
- 1/2 cup chopped fresh cilantro, plus 1/2 cup fresh cilantro leaves
- 2 tablespoons water
- 8 ounces Monterey Jack cheese, shredded (2 cups)
- 1 jalapeño chile, stemmed and sliced thin
- 8–12 (6-inch) corn or flour tortillas, warmed
- Lime wedges

1 Adjust oven rack 6 inches from broiler element and heat broiler. Heat oil in 12-inch broiler-safe skillet over medium heat until shimmering. Add poblano, three-quarters onion, and salt and cook until softened, about 5 minutes. Stir in garlic, cumin, and oregano and cook until fragrant, about 30 seconds.

2 Add chicken and cook, breaking up meat with wooden spoon, until no longer pink, 3 to 5 minutes. Stir in black beans, salsa verde, chopped cilantro, and water and bring to simmer. Season with salt and pepper to taste.

3 Spread chicken and bean mixture into even layer and sprinkle with Monterey Jack. Transfer skillet to oven and broil until cheese is melted and spotty brown, about 3 minutes. Sprinkle with jalapeño, cilantro leaves, and remaining onion. Serve with tortillas and lime wedges.

NOTES

Be sure to use ground chicken and not ground chicken breast (also labeled 99 percent fat-free).

KITCHEN IMPROV

If you like, substitute ground turkey or ground pork for the chicken. Colby or block mozzarella cheese can be used in place of the Monterey Jack. Jalapeño, cilantro, and onion are a good start in terms of toppings, but you can certainly go further with sour cream, sliced avocado, chopped tomatoes, and/or sliced radishes.

THIS SCOOPABLE skillet meal gives you all the melty cheese and tart-grassy flavors of green chicken enchiladas, but without all the filling, rolling, and extended baking needed for the traditional dish. Pair with tortillas or the vehicle of your choice: tostadas, chips, or rice.

beyond steaks and chops

chapter 2

seared skirt steak WITH hominy AND tomatoes

Serves 4 • Total Time: 35 minutes

- **1½ pounds outside skirt steak, trimmed**
- **2¼ teaspoons table salt, divided**
- **1½ teaspoons dried oregano**
- **½ teaspoon pepper**
- **½ teaspoon ground cumin**
- **2 tablespoons vegetable oil, divided**
- **1 white onion, halved and sliced ¼ inch thick**
- **1½ pounds plum tomatoes, cored and cut into 1-inch pieces**
- **2 serrano chiles, stemmed, seeded, and minced**
- **2 garlic cloves, minced**
- **1 (15-ounce) can hominy, rinsed**
- **2 ounces queso fresco, crumbled (½ cup)**
- **¼ cup chopped fresh cilantro**

SKIRT STEAK, a flavorful, thin cut, is often marinated and grilled. But rubbed with spices and seared on the stovetop, it makes for a satisfyingly quick dinner. Pair it with a side of chewy hominy, chiles, and stewy tomatoes that evokes Western-style cookouts.

1 Slice steak with grain into 3-inch-wide pieces. Combine 1¼ teaspoons salt, oregano, pepper, and cumin in bowl. Pat steaks dry with paper towels and sprinkle with spice mixture. Heat 1 tablespoon oil in 12-inch nonstick skillet over medium-high heat until just smoking. Add steaks and cook until well browned on both sides and meat registers 120 to 125 degrees (for medium-rare) or 130 to 135 degrees (for medium), about 2 minutes per side. Transfer steaks to cutting board, tent with aluminum foil, and let rest while preparing tomato-hominy mixture.

2 Heat remaining 1 tablespoon oil in now-empty skillet over medium heat until shimmering. Add onion and cook until softened and lightly browned, 5 to 7 minutes. Stir in tomatoes, serranos, garlic, and remaining 1 teaspoon salt and cook until tomatoes are softened, 5 to 7 minutes. Stir in hominy and cook until heated through, about 1 minute. Season with salt and pepper to taste. Sprinkle with queso fresco and cilantro.

3 Slice steaks thin against grain and serve with tomato-hominy mixture.

NOTES

Skirt steaks come from two different muscles, sometimes (not always) labeled as "inside" skirt steak and "outside" skirt steak. Look for the more tender outside cut, which is 3 to 4 inches wide and ½ to 1 inch thick. If you can only find the inside cut (typically 5 to 7 inches wide and ¼ to ½ inch thick), halve the steaks lengthwise before slicing them in step 1.

KITCHEN IMPROV

If you like, serve with warmed tortillas, crema, and lime wedges. Flank steak works in place of skirt steak.

moroccan steak tips WITH spiced couscous AND chickpeas

Serves 4 • Total Time: 35 minutes

- **4 teaspoons ras el hanout**
- **2 teaspoons table salt**
- **1½ pounds sirloin steak tips, trimmed and cut into 2-inch pieces**
- **1 tablespoon vegetable oil**
- **1¼ cups water**
- **1 (15-ounce) can chickpeas, rinsed**
- **¾ cup couscous**
- **½ cup golden raisins**
- **2 ounces (2 cups) baby spinach**
- **Lemon wedges for serving**

WARM SPICES and dried fruit—common in Moroccan cuisine—add character to this quick steak dinner. Flavor gets layered in (and dirty dishes are minimized) by using the same skillet to cook all the components.

1 Combine ras el hanout and salt in bowl. Pat steak tips dry with paper towels and sprinkle with 1 tablespoon spice mixture. Heat oil in 12-inch skillet over medium-high heat until just smoking. Add steak tips and cook until browned on all sides and meat registers 120 to 125 degrees (for medium-rare) or 130 to 135 degrees (for medium), 7 to 10 minutes. Transfer steak tips to plate, tent with aluminum foil, and let rest while preparing couscous.

2 Combine water, chickpeas, couscous, raisins, and remaining spice mixture in now-empty skillet and bring to boil over medium-high heat. Off heat, cover and let sit until couscous is tender, about 5 minutes. Fold in spinach, one handful at a time. Serve couscous with steak tips and lemon wedges.

NOTES

Sirloin steak tips can also be labeled "flap meat" or "bavette steak" and may be sold as whole steaks, strips, or pieces. Try to buy whole steaks or strips and cut them into pieces yourself. If steak tips are unavailable, look for tri-tip or flank steak. If you prefer, you can make your own ras el hanout blend by combining 1 teaspoon each of cardamom, coriander, cumin, and pepper.

KITCHEN IMPROV

Use another bean such as cannellini, pinto, or butter beans. Swap in chopped dried fruits like apricots or figs for the raisins. You can use baby kale in place of spinach.

steak tips WITH creamy summer squash orzo

Serves 4 • Total Time: 45 minutes

- **2 tablespoons unsalted butter**
- **2 summer squash (8 ounces each), quartered lengthwise and sliced thin**
- **1 onion, chopped**
- **3 garlic cloves, sliced thin**
- **1½ teaspoons table salt, divided**
- **1 teaspoon pepper, divided**
- **1½ cups orzo**
- **3 cups chicken broth**
- **1½ pounds sirloin steak tips, trimmed and cut into 2-inch pieces**
- **1 tablespoon vegetable oil**
- **1 (5.2-ounce) package Boursin Garlic & Fine Herbs cheese, room temperature**
- **3 ounces (3 cups) baby spinach, chopped coarse**

1 Melt butter in large saucepan over medium-high heat. Stir in squash, onion, garlic, ¾ teaspoon salt, and ¼ teaspoon pepper. Cover and cook, stirring occasionally, until vegetables are softened and saucepan is mostly dry, 10 to 12 minutes. Stir in orzo and cook for 1 minute. Stir in broth and bring to boil. Reduce heat to medium-low and simmer, stirring often, until orzo is tender and broth has been absorbed, about 15 minutes.

2 Meanwhile, pat steak tips dry with paper towels and sprinkle with remaining ¾ teaspoon salt and remaining ¾ teaspoon pepper. Heat oil in 12-inch skillet over medium-high heat until just smoking. Add steak tips and cook until browned on all sides and meat registers 120 to 125 degrees (for medium-rare) or 130 to 135 degrees (for medium), 7 to 10 minutes. Transfer steak tips to plate, tent with aluminum foil, and let rest while finishing orzo.

3 Off heat, stir Boursin and spinach into orzo until cheese is incorporated and spinach is wilted. Season with salt and pepper to taste. Serve steak tips with orzo.

SUMMER SQUASH adds velvety texture to a creamy risotto-style orzo that's served alongside simply cooked steak tips. Boursin cheese, stirred into the orzo just before serving, is a great shortcut to boosting flavor and richness.

NOTES

Sirloin steak tips can also be labeled "flap meat" or "bavette steak" and may be sold as whole steaks, strips, or pieces. For best results, try to buy whole steaks or strips and cut them into pieces yourself. If steak tips are unavailable, look for tri-tip or flank steak.

KITCHEN IMPROV

Zucchini works well in place of summer squash. You can swap baby kale for the spinach. You can make your own seasoned cheese, if desired, by using an equal weight of crumbled goat cheese and including 2 tablespoons of your favorite minced fresh herbs and finely grated citrus zest.

40002

sesame-glazed meatballs AND broccoli

Serves 4 • Total Time: 45 minutes

- **1 cup panko bread crumbs**
- **2 large eggs, lightly beaten**
- **4 scallions, white parts minced, green parts sliced thin on bias**
- **2 tablespoons chili-garlic sauce**
- **2 tablespoons toasted sesame oil, divided**
- **1½ teaspoons table salt, divided**
- **1½ pounds 90 percent lean ground beef**
- **1 pound broccoli florets, cut into 2-inch pieces**
- **2 tablespoons vegetable oil**
- **¼ cup hoisin sauce, plus extra for serving**
- **1½ tablespoons sesame seeds, toasted**

FLAVOR-PACKED meatballs take center stage in this easy sheet-pan dinner, a homey spin on the classic Chinese stir-fry of beef and broccoli. Serve with rice.

1 Adjust oven rack 8 inches from broiler element and heat oven to 450 degrees. Line rimmed baking sheet with aluminum foil and spray with vegetable oil spray. Combine panko, eggs, scallion whites, chili-garlic sauce, 1 tablespoon sesame oil, and 1¼ teaspoons salt in large bowl. Add ground beef and mix with your hands until thoroughly combined. Pinch off and roll mixture into 16 meatballs (about ¼ cup each) and arrange on half of prepared sheet.

2 Toss broccoli, vegetable oil, remaining 1 tablespoon sesame oil, and remaining ¼ teaspoon salt together in clean bowl. Arrange broccoli on other half of sheet. Roast until meatballs register 160 degrees and broccoli is crisp-tender, 15 to 20 minutes.

3 Remove sheet from oven and heat broiler. Combine hoisin and sesame seeds in bowl. Brush hoisin mixture over meatballs. Broil until glaze is bubbling and tops of broccoli are browned, about 3 minutes, rotating sheet halfway through broiling. Sprinkle with scallion greens and serve with extra hoisin.

NOTES

The meatballs can be shaped and refrigerated up to 2 days in advance.

KITCHEN IMPROV

You can use 93 percent lean ground chicken or turkey instead of ground beef. Swap in other condiments for hoisin to create new flavors of meatballs, such as gochujang, pomegranate molasses, or even peach preserves.

easy stovetop vegetable side dishes

pan-roasted broccoli

Serves 4 • Total Time: 20 minutes

PAN ROASTING brings this easy-to-overlook vegetable to new heights.

- **3 tablespoons water**
- **1/4 teaspoon table salt**
- **1/8 teaspoon pepper**
- **2 tablespoons extra-virgin olive oil**
- **1 1/4 pounds broccoli, florets cut into 1 1/2-inch pieces, stalks peeled and cut on bias into 1/4-inch-thick slices**

1 Stir water, salt, and pepper together in small bowl until salt dissolves; set aside. Heat oil in 12-inch nonstick skillet over medium-high heat until just smoking. Add broccoli stalks in even layer and cook, without stirring, until browned on bottoms, about 2 minutes. Add florets to skillet and toss to combine. Cook, without stirring, until bottoms of florets just begin to brown, 1 to 2 minutes.

2 Add water mixture and cover skillet. Cook until broccoli is bright green but still crisp, about 2 minutes. Uncover and continue to cook until water has evaporated, broccoli stalks are tender, and florets are crisp-tender, about 2 minutes longer. Serve.

NOTES

You will need a 12-inch nonstick skillet with a tight-fitting lid.

KITCHEN IMPROV

Roasted broccoli is a blank canvas for adding flavors. Start with a drizzle of citrus juice, vinegar, and/or flavorful oil. Add crunch with a sprinkle of dukkah, shichimi togarashi, or whatever toasted nuts and seeds you have on hand.

---

sautéed baby bok choy

Serves 4 • Total Time: 15 minutes

TENDER-CRISP TEXTURE and mild flavor are big assets in this quick side.

- **4 teaspoons vegetable oil, divided**
- **2 garlic cloves, minced**
- **8 small heads baby bok choy (1 1/2 to 2 ounces each), halved, washed thoroughly, and spun dry**
- **2 tablespoons water**
- **1/4 teaspoon table salt**

1 Combine 1 teaspoon oil and garlic in small bowl; set aside.

2 Heat remaining 1 tablespoon oil in 12-inch nonstick skillet over medium heat until shimmering. Add bok choy and water and immediately cover. Cook, covered, shaking skillet occasionally, for 2 minutes. Uncover, toss bok choy, then push bok choy to sides of skillet. Add garlic mixture to center of skillet and cook, stirring constantly, until fragrant, about 20 seconds. Stir garlic mixture into bok choy, sprinkle with salt, and continue to cook, stirring constantly, until all water has evaporated, stems are crisp-tender, and leaves are wilted, about 2 minutes. Serve.

NOTES

If using heads weighing more than 2 ounces each, quarter them rather than halve them. Spinning the bok choy dry in a salad spinner prevents adding too much water to the pan.

KITCHEN IMPROV

You can flavor the bok choy by swapping half of the water with soy sauce, fish sauce, or oyster sauce. Add up to 1 tablespoon grated fresh ginger or minced lemongrass with the garlic. Drizzle the bok choy with Chinese black vinegar, sesame oil, or chili crisp before serving.

fastest, easiest mashed potatoes

Serves 4 • Total Time: 25 minutes

- 2 pounds Yukon Gold or russet potatoes, peeled and sliced 1/4 inch thick
- 8–10 tablespoons half-and-half
- 4 tablespoons unsalted butter, cut into 1/4-inch slices
- 1 teaspoon table salt

1. Bring 1 quart water to boil in medium saucepan over high heat. Add potatoes, making sure they are fully submerged in water. (If not, add just enough water to cover.) Return water to boil, then adjust heat to maintain very gentle simmer. Cover and cook until paring knife meets no resistance when slipped into center of potatoes, about 12 minutes.
2. Drain potatoes and return to saucepan. Use potato masher, ricer, or food mill to process potatoes to desired consistency. Stir in 1/2 cup half-and-half, butter, and salt until combined. Adjust consistency with remaining half-and-half as desired. Season with salt and pepper to taste, and serve.

A MODERATELY sized pot and sliced (not cubed) potatoes produce faster, more evenly cooked results that come out perfectly fluffy.

NOTES

Yukon Gold potatoes will deliver buttery flavor and color; for earthier flavor, use russets. For a chunkier texture, use a potato masher; for a smoother mash, use a ricer or food mill.

KITCHEN IMPROV

You can really use any type of dairy: Heavy cream makes a rich mash, while whole milk will be leaner. If you're a fan of tangy mashed potatoes, reach for yogurt or sour cream and adjust the consistency with water or broth as needed. Level up your potatoes by stirring in roasted garlic, fresh herbs, prepared horseradish, scallions, and/or shredded cheese.

---

boiled carrots with lemon and chives

Serves 4 • Total Time: 25 minutes

- 1 pound carrots, peeled
- 2 teaspoons table salt
- 1 tablespoon unsalted butter, cut into 4 pieces
- 1 tablespoon chopped fresh chives
- 1 teaspoon lemon juice, plus extra for serving
- 1/8 teaspoon pepper

1. Cut carrots into 1½- to 2-inch lengths. Leave thin pieces whole, halve medium pieces lengthwise, and quarter thick pieces lengthwise.
2. Bring 2 cups water to boil in medium saucepan over high heat. Add carrots and salt, cover, and cook until tender throughout, about 6 minutes.
3. Drain carrots and return them to saucepan. Add butter, chives, lemon juice, and pepper and stir until butter is melted. Season with salt and pepper to taste. Serve.

GET REACQUAINTED with a neglected but worthwhile cooking method.

NOTES

For even cooking, it's important that the carrot pieces are of similar size.

KITCHEN IMPROV

The lemon-and-chive flavor combo works with a variety of dishes, but you can also try lime and cilantro, ginger and scallion, or orange and tarragon. Sprinkle the carrots with something crunchy like toasted nuts or seeds.

new york strip steaks WITH crispy potatoes AND parsley sauce

Serves 4 • Total Time: 45 minutes

- **1 cup chopped fresh parsley**
- **½ cup plus 3 tablespoons extra-virgin olive oil, divided**
- **¼ cup finely chopped red onion**
- **¼ cup red wine vinegar**
- **2 tablespoons water**
- **4 garlic cloves, minced**
- **1½ teaspoons table salt, divided**
- **¼ teaspoon red pepper flakes**
- **1½ pounds red or Yukon Gold potatoes, unpeeled, cut into 1-inch wedges**
- **2 (12- to 16-ounce) boneless strip steaks, 1½ inches thick, trimmed**
- **¾ teaspoon pepper**

THE COLD-START method used here will become your favorite way to sear steak. There's no splatter or smoke, and the steaks cook evenly and develop an incredible crust. Jump-starting the potatoes in the microwave means they brown after just 10 minutes in the skillet.

1 Combine parsley, ½ cup oil, onion, vinegar, water, garlic, ¼ teaspoon salt, and pepper flakes in bowl; set aside for serving.

2 Toss potatoes with 1 tablespoon oil and ¼ teaspoon salt in bowl. Cover and microwave, stirring occasionally, until potatoes begin to soften, 5 to 7 minutes; drain well.

3 Meanwhile, pat steaks dry with paper towels and sprinkle with remaining 1 teaspoon salt and pepper. Place steaks 1 inch apart in cold 12-inch nonstick skillet. Place skillet over high heat and cook steaks for 2 minutes. Flip steaks and cook on second side for 2 minutes. (Neither side of steaks will be browned at this point.)

4 Flip steaks, reduce heat to medium, and continue to cook, flipping steaks every 2 minutes, until browned and meat registers 120 to 125 degrees (for medium-rare) or 130 to 135 degrees (for medium), 4 to 10 minutes. (Steaks should be sizzling gently; if not, increase heat slightly. Reduce heat if skillet starts to smoke.) Transfer steaks to cutting board, tent with aluminum foil, and let rest while finishing potatoes.

5 Add remaining 2 tablespoons oil to now-empty skillet and heat over medium heat until shimmering. Add potatoes and cook, turning occasionally, until well browned, about 10 minutes. Slice steaks thin and serve with potatoes, passing parsley sauce separately.

NOTES

Avoid potatoes smaller than 3 inches in diameter.

KITCHEN IMPROV

This recipe also works with boneless rib-eye steaks of a similar thickness. The parsley sauce is well suited for flavor swaps: Start by using other herbs for all or a portion of the parsley. You can incorporate intensely flavored ingredients, such as chopped olives, sun-dried tomatoes, capers, or anchovies, into the sauce.

Laguiole

hoisin-glazed rib-eye steaks WITH baby bok choy

Serves 4 • Total Time: 35 minutes

- **1 tablespoon toasted sesame oil**
- **2 garlic cloves, minced**
- **1½ teaspoons table salt, divided**
- **1¼ teaspoons pepper, divided**
- **1 teaspoon ground coriander**
- **1 teaspoon smoked paprika**
- **2 (12- to 16-ounce) boneless rib-eye steaks, 1½ inches thick, trimmed**
- **3 tablespoons hoisin sauce**
- **8 small heads baby bok choy (1½ to 2 ounces each), halved, washed thoroughly, and spun dry**
- **1 red Fresno chile, stemmed and sliced thin**

SAVORY HOISIN sauce makes a surprisingly complex one-ingredient glaze. Adding a spice rub before cooking and brushing on hoisin after yields flavorful steaks with a glaze that stays put. Use the skillet to sear baby bok choy (covered, so that they also steam and cook through) for an easy side.

1 Combine sesame oil, garlic, ½ teaspoon salt, and ¼ teaspoon pepper in bowl; set aside. Combine coriander, paprika, remaining 1 teaspoon salt, and remaining 1 teaspoon pepper in separate bowl. Pat steaks dry with paper towels and sprinkle with spice mixture.

2 Place steaks 1 inch apart in cold 12-inch nonstick skillet. Place skillet over high heat and cook steaks for 2 minutes. Flip steaks and cook on second side for 2 minutes. (Neither side of steaks will be browned at this point.)

3 Flip steaks, reduce heat to medium, and continue to cook, flipping steaks every 2 minutes, until browned and meat registers 120 to 125 degrees (for medium-rare) or 130 to 135 degrees (for medium), 4 to 10 minutes. (Steaks should be sizzling gently; if not, increase heat slightly. Reduce heat if skillet starts to smoke.) Transfer steaks to cutting board, brush with hoisin, and tent with aluminum foil. Let rest while preparing bok choy.

4 Return skillet to medium-high heat and heat fat left in skillet until just smoking. Add bok choy, cut side down, and Fresno chile and cook, covered and without stirring, until bok choy is charred on bottom and can be easily pierced with tip of paring knife, about 4 minutes. Off heat, stir in sesame oil mixture and toss to coat. Slice steaks thin and serve with bok choy.

NOTES

If a Fresno chile isn't available, substitute a jalapeño chile. Be sure to wash the bok choy after it's halved so that the insides are exposed and any dirt can be easily washed away. You will need a 12-inch nonstick skillet with a tight-fitting lid.

KITCHEN IMPROV

Try this with boneless strip steaks of a similar thickness.

bourbon-glazed rib-eye steaks WITH collard greens salad

Serves 4 • Total Time: 35 minutes

- 1/4 cup cider vinegar, divided
- 3 tablespoons vegetable oil
- 1 teaspoon plus 2 tablespoons Worcestershire sauce, divided
- 2 tablespoons maple syrup, divided
- 1½ teaspoons table salt, divided
- 1¼ teaspoons pepper, divided
- 1 pound collard greens, stemmed and sliced thin crosswise
- 2 (12- to 16-ounce) boneless rib-eye steaks, 1½ inches thick, trimmed
- 1/4 cup bourbon
- 1/2 cup pecans, toasted and chopped
- 1/4 cup dried cherries

MASSAGING DRESSING into collards tenderizes them and imbues them with the same tangy-sweet flavors that go into a bourbon glaze for steak.

1 Whisk 3 tablespoons vinegar, oil, 1 teaspoon Worcestershire, 1 tablespoon maple syrup, 1/2 teaspoon salt, and 1/4 teaspoon pepper together in large bowl. Add collard greens and toss to combine, gently massaging to tenderize.

2 Pat steaks dry with paper towels and sprinkle with remaining 1 teaspoon salt and remaining 1 teaspoon pepper. Place steaks 1 inch apart in cold 12-inch nonstick skillet. Set skillet over high heat and cook steaks for 2 minutes. Flip steaks and cook on second side for 2 minutes. (Neither side of steaks will be browned at this point.)

3 Flip steaks, reduce heat to medium, and continue to cook, flipping steaks every 2 minutes, until browned and meat registers 120 to 125 degrees (for medium-rare) or 130 to 135 degrees (for medium), 4 to 10 minutes. (Steaks should be sizzling gently; if not, increase heat slightly. Reduce heat if skillet starts to smoke.) Transfer to wire rack set in rimmed baking sheet. Wipe skillet clean with paper towels.

4 Cook bourbon and remaining 1 tablespoon vinegar, 2 tablespoons Worcestershire, and 1 tablespoon maple syrup in now-empty skillet over medium-high heat, stirring often, until thickened, about 2 minutes. Off heat, return steaks to skillet and turn to coat, then return to wire rack and let rest for 5 minutes. Slice steaks and top salad with pecans and cherries. Serve, drizzling steaks with extra glaze.

NOTES

Look for bunches of collards with smaller leaves, which are more tender. White wine vinegar can be used in place of the cider vinegar; Lacinato kale is a suitable alternative to collards. If you prefer to avoid alcohol, you can use chicken broth in place of the bourbon.

KITCHEN IMPROV

Try this with boneless strip steaks of a similar thickness. Any type of nut or dried fruit (cut into 1/2-inch pieces if necessary) can be used in place of the pecans or cherries.

A BRILLIANT GREEN, creamy, and herb-forward avocado sauce unites smoky ancho-rubbed flank steak and black bean–studded rice, but it would improve practically anything. Stirring a portion of cilantro and jalapeño into the rice intensifies its flavor and color.

ancho-rubbed flank steak AND cilantro rice WITH avocado sauce

Serves 4 • Total Time: 40 minutes

- **1 cup long-grain white rice**
- **1 (15-ounce) can black or pinto beans, rinsed**
- **1 tablespoon ancho chile powder**
- **1½ teaspoons table salt, divided**
- **¾ teaspoon pepper, divided**
- **1 (1½-pound) flank steak, trimmed and cut into 4 equal steaks**
- **2 tablespoons vegetable oil**
- **2 cups fresh cilantro leaves and tender stems, chopped coarse**
- **¼ cup jarred sliced jalapeño chiles**
- **1 teaspoon grated lime zest plus 2 tablespoons juice, plus lime wedges for serving**
- **1 avocado, halved, pitted, and chopped coarse**

1 Bring 2 quarts water to boil in large saucepan over high heat. Add rice and cook, stirring occasionally, until just tender, about 12 minutes. Drain rice and return to saucepan. Gently stir in beans and cover to keep warm.

2 Meanwhile, combine chile powder, 1 teaspoon salt, and ½ teaspoon pepper in bowl. Pat steaks dry with paper towels and rub with spice mixture. Heat oil in 12-inch nonstick skillet over medium-high heat until just smoking. Lay steaks in skillet and cook until well browned on first side, 3 to 5 minutes, reducing heat if spices begin to burn. Flip steaks, reduce heat to medium, and continue to cook until meat registers 120 to 125 degrees (for medium-rare) or 130 to 135 degrees (for medium), 4 to 10 minutes. Transfer steaks to cutting board, tent with aluminum foil, and let rest while preparing sauce.

3 Pulse cilantro, jalapeños, lime zest and juice, remaining ½ teaspoon salt, and remaining ¼ teaspoon pepper in food processor until finely chopped, about 10 pulses, scraping down sides of bowl as needed. Transfer 2 tablespoons cilantro mixture to rice and stir to combine. Add avocado and ½ cup water to processor and process until smooth, about 30 seconds. Season with salt and pepper to taste. Slice steaks thin and serve with rice and beans and lime wedges, passing sauce separately.

NOTES

Any long-grain white rice will work, including jasmine or Texmati.

KITCHEN IMPROV

Skirt steak works too; reduce the cooking time to 2 to 3 minutes per side. The spice mixture used here is simple, but you can also use 1 tablespoon of your favorite steak seasoning in place of the chile powder, salt, and pepper in step 2. The avocado sauce also makes a great dressing for salads. Turn this dinner into taco night with the addition of warmed tortillas.

stir-fried cumin beef

Serves 4 • Total Time: 45 minutes

- **1 tablespoon water**
- **1/4 teaspoon baking soda**
- **1 pound flank steak, trimmed**
- **4 garlic cloves, minced**
- **1 tablespoon grated fresh ginger**
- **1 tablespoon cumin seeds, ground coarse**
- **2 teaspoons Sichuan chili powder**
- **1 1/4 teaspoons Sichuan peppercorns, ground**
- **1/2 teaspoon table salt, divided**
- **1 tablespoon Shaoxing wine or dry sherry**
- **1 tablespoon soy sauce**
- **2 teaspoons molasses**
- **1/2 teaspoon cornstarch**
- **1/4 cup vegetable oil, divided**
- **1/2 small onion, sliced thin**
- **2 tablespoons coarsely chopped fresh cilantro**

1 Combine water and baking soda in medium bowl. Cut steak with grain into 2- to 2 1/2-inch-wide strips, then slice each strip against grain 1/4 inch thick. Add beef to baking soda mixture and toss to coat. Let sit at room temperature for 5 minutes.

2 Meanwhile, combine garlic and ginger in small bowl. Combine cumin, chili powder, peppercorns, and 1/4 teaspoon salt in second small bowl. Add Shaoxing wine, soy sauce, molasses, cornstarch, and remaining 1/4 teaspoon salt to beef mixture. Toss until well combined.

3 Heat 1 tablespoon oil in 14-inch flat-bottomed wok or 12-inch nonstick skillet over medium-high heat until just smoking. Add half of beef mixture and increase heat to high. Using tongs, toss beef slowly but constantly until exuded juices have evaporated and meat begins to sizzle, 2 to 6 minutes. Transfer to clean bowl. Repeat with 1 tablespoon oil and remaining beef mixture.

4 Heat remaining 2 tablespoons oil in now-empty wok over medium heat until shimmering. Add garlic mixture (oil will splatter) and cook, stirring constantly, until fragrant, 15 to 30 seconds. Add onion and cook, tossing slowly but constantly with tongs, until onion begins to soften, 1 to 2 minutes. Return beef to wok and toss to combine. Sprinkle cumin mixture over beef and toss until onion takes on pale orange color. Transfer to serving platter, sprinkle with cilantro, and serve immediately.

SICHUAN CHILI powder, Sichuan peppercorns, and cumin add plenty of fragrance and mild heat to this Hunanese-inspired stir-fry. Coating the beef with a little baking soda before cooking promotes juicy meat.

NOTES

The steak will be easier to slice thin if you put it in the freezer for 15 minutes. We prefer the flavor and texture of freshly ground cumin seeds here; however, you can substitute 1 tablespoon store-bought ground cumin. If you can't find Sichuan chili powder, gochugaru (Korean red pepper flakes) is a good substitute. This recipe moves quickly, so make sure to have all the ingredients prepped and close by before you start cooking.

KITCHEN IMPROV

Lamb also works well here. Remove bones and trim excess fat from 2 (14- to 16-ounce) lamb shoulder chops before slicing as directed in step 1.

rice bowls WITH harissa beef, chickpeas AND olives

Serves 4 • Total Time: 40 minutes

- **2 tablespoons extra-virgin olive oil**
- **1 onion, chopped**
- **1 teaspoon table salt, divided**
- **3 garlic cloves, chopped**
- **1 pound 85 percent lean ground beef**
- **3 tablespoons harissa, plus extra for serving**
- **1 tablespoon tomato paste**
- **2 (15-ounce) cans chickpeas, undrained**
- **2 carrots, peeled and cut into ½-inch pieces (1 cup)**
- **½ cup pitted brine-cured green olives, chopped coarse**
- **½ teaspoon pepper**
- **4 cups cooked white rice**
- **¼ cup chopped fresh cilantro**

SPICY, AROMATIC harissa chile paste, used throughout North Africa and parts of the Middle East, lends potent flavor to this chili-like ground-beef-and-bean dinner.

1 Heat oil in 12-inch nonstick skillet over medium-high heat until shimmering. Add onion and ½ teaspoon salt and cook until softened, 3 to 5 minutes. Stir in garlic and cook until fragrant, about 30 seconds. Add beef, breaking up meat with wooden spoon, and cook until lightly browned, 5 to 7 minutes. Stir in harissa and tomato paste and cook until pastes darken slightly, about 2 minutes.

2 Stir in chickpeas and their liquid, carrots, olives, pepper, and remaining ½ teaspoon salt and bring to simmer. Reduce heat to medium-low and simmer, stirring occasionally, until carrots are tender and liquid is thickened and glossy, 10 to 12 minutes. Season with salt and pepper to taste. Serve over rice, sprinkling individual portions with cilantro and passing extra harissa separately.

NOTES

Harissa is available in both mild and spicy versions; use whichever you prefer. A rice cooker makes quick work of preparing steamed rice. You'll want to start with about 1½ cups long-grain white rice to yield 4 cups cooked rice. You can also use our recipe for Simple Rice Pilaf (page 54).

KITCHEN IMPROV

You can substitute ground lamb, ground pork, or 93 percent lean ground turkey or chicken for the beef. Try other root vegetables like celery root, parsnips, or turnips in place of the carrots. Add a cooling element by topping with a dollop of sour cream or yogurt.

rice and lentils WITH spiced beef AND crispy onions

Serves 4 • Total Time: 30 minutes

- 1/4 cup extra-virgin olive oil
- 1 large red onion, halved and sliced thin (about 1 1/2 cups)
- 1 1/4 teaspoons table salt, divided
- 1 pound 85 percent lean ground beef
- 3 garlic cloves, minced
- 1 teaspoon ground cumin
- 1 teaspoon ground coriander
- 1/2 teaspoon ground allspice
- 1/2 teaspoon pepper
- 3 cups cooked rice
- 1 (15-ounce) can lentils, rinsed
- 1/4 cup chopped fresh dill
- 1/2 cup plain whole-milk yogurt

1 Heat oil in 12-inch nonstick skillet over medium heat until shimmering. Add onion and 1/4 teaspoon salt and cook until well browned and beginning to crisp around edges, 8 to 10 minutes. Using slotted spoon, transfer onions to plate.

2 Add beef to fat left in skillet and cook, breaking up meat with wooden spoon, until no longer pink, 4 to 6 minutes. Add remaining 1 teaspoon salt, garlic, cumin, coriander, allspice, and pepper and cook until fragrant and beef is just beginning to brown, about 2 minutes. Add rice and lentils, increase heat to medium-high, and cook, stirring often, until heated through, about 2 minutes. Scatter onions over top and sprinkle with dill. Serve with yogurt.

CANNED LENTILS may be more unexpected than other canned beans, but they're ideal for this weeknight riff on mujaddara, the classic Lebanese spiced pilaf. It may seem like you're frying too much sliced onion—but you're not!

NOTES

A rice cooker makes quick work of preparing steamed rice. You'll want to start with about 1 cup long-grain white rice to yield 3 cups cooked rice. You can also use our recipe for Simple Rice Pilaf (page 54).

KITCHEN IMPROV

You can substitute ground lamb, ground pork, or 93 percent lean ground turkey or chicken for the beef. You can't go wrong with an abundance of fresh herbs here; add chopped fresh parsley and/or mint if you have them.

pork medallions WITH sautéed asparagus AND peas

Serves 4 • Total Time: 30 minutes

- 2 (12- to 16-ounce) pork tenderloins, trimmed and cut crosswise into 1½-inch-thick medallions
- 1½ teaspoons table salt, divided
- 1 teaspoon pepper, divided
- 4 tablespoons unsalted butter, divided
- 2 ounces pancetta, cut into ¼-inch pieces
- 1 leek, white and light green parts only, halved lengthwise, sliced thin, and washed thoroughly
- ¼ teaspoon red pepper flakes
- 1 pound asparagus, trimmed and cut into 2-inch lengths
- 1 cup frozen peas, thawed
- 1 tablespoon chopped fresh mint, basil, or tarragon
- 1 teaspoon grated lemon zest, plus lemon wedges for serving

1 Pat pork dry with paper towels and sprinkle with 1 teaspoon salt and ½ teaspoon pepper. Melt 2 tablespoons butter in 12-inch skillet over medium-high heat. Add pork cut side down and cook until well browned and meat registers 135 to 140 degrees, 4 to 6 minutes per side. Transfer to plate, tent with aluminum foil, and let rest while preparing vegetables.

2 Cook pancetta in now-empty skillet over medium-high heat until fat begins to render, about 1 minute. Add leek, pepper flakes, remaining ½ teaspoon salt, and remaining ½ teaspoon pepper and cook until softened, about 2 minutes. Stir in asparagus and peas and cook until asparagus is crisp-tender, about 5 minutes. Off heat, stir in mint, lemon zest, and remaining 2 tablespoons butter. Serve pork with vegetables and lemon wedges.

SKILLET-BROWNED medallions are a fast and attractive way of presenting pork tenderloin, rather than roasting it in the oven. Serve them with a trio of bright green vegetables (plus herbs and lemon zest) enriched with just enough butter and pancetta.

NOTES

If pancetta is unavailable, you can substitute bacon.

KITCHEN IMPROV

Try zucchini or summer squash instead of asparagus: After trimming the ends, halve the squash lengthwise and then slice crosswise ½ inch thick. Other frozen vegetables like cut green beans, lima beans, or corn can be used in place of the peas.

lemon AND herb pork chops WITH cauliflower puree

Serves 4 • Total Time: 45 minutes

- 1 large head cauliflower (3 pounds)
- ½ cup plus 2 tablespoons chicken broth, divided
- 8 tablespoons unsalted butter, divided
- 1¾ teaspoons table salt, divided
- 1 tablespoon grated lemon zest, divided, plus 1 tablespoon juice
- 1 tablespoon chopped fresh thyme, divided
- 1 teaspoon pepper
- 4 (6- to 8-ounce) boneless pork chops, ¾ to 1 inch thick, trimmed
- 2 garlic cloves, minced

1 Trim outer leaves of cauliflower and cut stem flush with bottom of head. Place cauliflower stem side up. Using kitchen shears, cut stems vertically around core to remove large florets. Cut florets through stems into 1-inch pieces; thinly slice core. Bring cauliflower, ½ cup broth, 3 tablespoons butter, and ¾ teaspoon salt to boil in large saucepan over high heat. Reduce heat to medium-low, cover, and simmer, stirring occasionally, until cauliflower is tender, about 20 minutes. Using immersion blender, process until smooth, about 2 minutes. Cover to keep warm.

2 Meanwhile, combine 2 teaspoons lemon zest, 1½ teaspoons thyme, pepper, and remaining 1 teaspoon salt in bowl. Pat pork chops dry with paper towels and rub pork with zest mixture. Melt 1 tablespoon butter in 12-inch skillet over medium-high heat. Cook pork until well browned and meat registers 140 to 145 degrees, about 6 minutes per side. Transfer to serving platter, tent with aluminum foil, and let rest while preparing sauce.

3 Cook garlic, 1 tablespoon butter, and remaining 1½ teaspoons thyme in now-empty skillet over medium heat until fragrant, about 30 seconds. Stir in remaining 2 tablespoons broth. Off heat, whisk in lemon juice, remaining 3 tablespoons butter, and remaining 1 teaspoon lemon zest until fully combined. Stir in any accumulated pork juices. Serve pork chops with cauliflower puree and sauce.

NOTES

You can use a countertop blender instead of an immersion blender to process the cauliflower.

KITCHEN IMPROV

Level up your cauliflower puree by adding roasted garlic or grated cheese before processing or by stirring in fresh herbs before serving. Other hearty herbs such as rosemary and sage can be used in place of the thyme.

VELVETY CAULIFLOWER puree is a wonderful accompaniment to lemony skillet-cooked pork chops. Simmering the cauliflower in broth and butter until completely tender makes for an ultrasmooth puree. A quick pan sauce of butter, lemon, and garlic ties the two together.

VICTORINOX
5.2000.12

pan-seared pork chops WITH apples AND spinach

Serves 4 • Total Time: 45 minutes

- **2 teaspoons ground coriander**
- **1¼ teaspoons table salt, divided**
- **½ teaspoon pepper**
- **4 (6- to 8-ounce) boneless pork chops, ¾ to 1 inch thick, trimmed**
- **3 tablespoons vegetable oil, divided**
- **2 apples, cored and cut into 1-inch wedges**
- **1 red onion, chopped**
- **12 ounces (12 cups) baby spinach**
- **1 tablespoon minced fresh tarragon**

SWEET-SAVORY PORK and apples is a favorite pairing, and this simple take doesn't disappoint. Getting the skillet very hot allows for a deep brown exterior and juicy interior on the chops, and adding an onion-spinach sauté ups the sophistication level.

1 Combine coriander, 1 teaspoon salt, and pepper in bowl. Pat pork chops dry with paper towels and sprinkle with spice mixture. Heat 12-inch cast-iron skillet over medium heat for 3 minutes. Add 1 tablespoon oil and heat until just smoking. Cook pork until well browned and meat registers 140 to 145 degrees, about 6 minutes per side. Transfer to serving platter, tent with aluminum foil, and let rest. Wipe skillet clean with paper towels.

2 Heat 1 tablespoon oil in now-empty skillet over medium-low heat until shimmering. Add apples cut side down and cook until caramelized and tender, about 2 minutes per side. Transfer to platter with pork.

3 Heat remaining 1 tablespoon oil in again-empty skillet over medium heat until shimmering. Add onion and remaining ¼ teaspoon salt and cook until softened, about 3 minutes. Add spinach and cook until wilted, about 2 minutes. Season with salt and pepper to taste. Sprinkle apples with tarragon. Serve pork chops with apples and spinach.

NOTES

Any variety of sweet apples, such as Gala, Fuji, or Braeburn, will work. If you don't have a cast-iron skillet, heat 1 tablespoon oil in 12-inch skillet over medium heat until just smoking; proceed with step 1 as directed.

KITCHEN IMPROV

Swap in baby kale or chopped escarole for the spinach. Parsley, dill, or basil are also great herbs to use for sprinkling on the apples before serving.

pork chops WITH creamy corn AND lima beans

Serves 4 • Total Time: 40 minutes

- **1½ teaspoons table salt, divided**
- **1½ teaspoons pepper, divided**
- **1 teaspoon smoked paprika**
- **¼ teaspoon cayenne pepper**
- **4 (8- to 10-ounce) bone-in pork rib chops, ¾ to 1 inch thick, trimmed**
- **4 slices bacon, chopped**
- **4 ears corn, kernels cut from cobs**
- **1½ cups frozen baby lima beans**
- **4 scallions, white and green parts separated and sliced thin**
- **½ cup heavy cream**
- **2 teaspoons lemon juice**

SUCCOTASH STARS in this stunning one-pan pork chop dinner. Cooking spice-rubbed pork chops in bacon fat is always a good idea. As the chops rest, prepare the quick succotash in the empty pan and then finish with bits of crispy bacon and rich cream.

1 Combine 1 teaspoon salt, 1 teaspoon pepper, paprika, and cayenne in bowl. Pat pork chops dry with paper towels and sprinkle with spice mixture. Cook bacon in 12-inch nonstick skillet over medium heat until rendered and crisp, 5 to 7 minutes. Using slotted spoon, transfer bacon to plate; set aside.

2 Add pork chops to fat left in skillet and cook over medium-high heat until well browned and meat registers 140 to 145 degrees, about 6 minutes per side. Transfer to plate, tent with aluminum foil, and let rest.

3 Add corn, lima beans, scallion whites, remaining ½ teaspoon salt, and remaining ½ teaspoon pepper to fat left in skillet and cook until vegetables are softened, 3 to 5 minutes. Add cream and cook until slightly thickened, about 2 minutes. Off heat, stir in lemon juice, scallion greens, and bacon. Season with salt and pepper to taste. Serve pork chops with vegetable mixture.

NOTES

If fresh corn isn't in season, substitute 3 cups thawed frozen corn.

KITCHEN IMPROV

Feel free to substitute other frozen vegetables for the lima beans; cut green beans and peas are both good choices. You can also add a diced bell pepper to the pan along with the other veggies. If you have a few extra minutes and want even more sweet corn flavor, after removing the kernels from the cobs, scrape the cobs with the back of a knife and add the creamy pulp to the skillet with the kernels.

ITALIAN BREAD SALAD turns roast pork tenderloin into a satisfying one-dish supper. The toasted bread and roasted veggies emerge from the oven supercharged with flavor. Toss them with a briny caper dressing and add cucumbers, tomatoes, and basil for freshness.

NOTES

Buy tenderloins that are of equal size and weight so that they cook at the same rate. Ripe, in-season tomatoes are best here, but supermarket vine-ripened tomatoes (or cherry or grape tomatoes) will work; avoid plum tomatoes, which are less juicy.

KITCHEN IMPROV

Beyond a baguette, any rustic bread with a thick crust will do. Olives are a great option if you're not a fan of capers, or you can swap in shaved Parmesan. You can easily bulk up the salad with a can of white beans or a few handfuls of baby arugula or spinach.

one-pan pork tenderloin AND panzanella salad

Serves 4 to 6 • Total Time: 45 minutes

- **3 tablespoons balsamic vinegar, divided**
- **2 tablespoons whole-grain mustard, divided**
- **1 tablespoon packed brown sugar**
- **1 teaspoon cornstarch**
- **2 (12- to 16-ounce) pork tenderloins, trimmed**
- **1½ teaspoons plus ⅛ teaspoon table salt, divided**
- **1⅛ teaspoons pepper, divided**
- **1 (12-inch) baguette, cut into 1-inch pieces (5 cups)**
- **1 red onion, cut into 1-inch pieces**
- **1 red bell pepper, stemmed, seeded, and cut into ½-inch-wide strips**
- **1 yellow summer squash, quartered lengthwise and cut into 1-inch pieces**
- **½ cup extra-virgin olive oil, divided**
- **1 tablespoon capers, rinsed, plus 1 tablespoon brine**
- **1 garlic clove, minced**
- **½ English cucumber, quartered lengthwise and sliced ½ inch thick**
- **2 tomatoes, cored and cut into 1-inch pieces, or 6 ounces cherry or grape tomatoes, halved**
- **½ cup chopped fresh basil**

1. Adjust oven rack to middle position and heat oven to 450 degrees. Whisk 1 tablespoon vinegar, 1 tablespoon mustard, sugar, and cornstarch in bowl until no lumps of cornstarch remain. Pat tenderloins dry with paper towels and sprinkle with 1 teaspoon salt and ½ teaspoon pepper. Place tenderloins in center of rimmed baking sheet (it's OK if they are touching) and brush tops and sides with all of vinegar mixture.

2. Toss baguette, onion, bell pepper, squash, ¼ cup oil, ½ teaspoon salt, and ½ teaspoon pepper in large bowl until baguette and vegetables are well coated with oil. Distribute vegetable mixture around tenderloins on sheet. Roast until pork registers 135 degrees, about 20 minutes, stirring vegetable mixture halfway through roasting.

3. Meanwhile, whisk capers and brine, garlic, remaining 2 tablespoons vinegar, remaining 1 tablespoon mustard, remaining ⅛ teaspoon salt, remaining ⅛ teaspoon pepper, and remaining ¼ cup oil together in now-empty bowl.

4. Transfer tenderloins to cutting board, tent with aluminum foil, and let rest for 5 minutes. Meanwhile, add cucumber, tomatoes, basil, and vegetable mixture to bowl with caper dressing and toss to combine. Slice tenderloins ½ inch thick and serve with panzanella salad.

pork tenderloin WITH white beans AND romesco

Serves 4 • Total Time: 45 minutes

- 2 (15-ounce) cans great northern beans, divided
- 2 (12- to 16-ounce) pork tenderloins, trimmed
- 1½ teaspoons table salt, divided
- ¼ teaspoon pepper
- 5 tablespoons extra-virgin olive oil, divided
- 3 garlic cloves, sliced thin, divided
- ½ teaspoon smoked paprika
- ¼ teaspoon cayenne pepper
- ⅔ cup jarred roasted red peppers, patted dry
- ¼ cup slivered or sliced almonds, toasted
- ⅓ cup coarsely chopped fresh parsley, divided
- 1 tablespoon sherry or red wine vinegar
- 3 ounces (3 cups) baby spinach

1. Adjust oven rack to middle position and heat oven to 400 degrees. Drain and rinse 1 can beans; set aside with remaining 1 can beans and their canning liquid. Pat tenderloins dry with paper towels and sprinkle with 1 teaspoon salt and pepper. Heat 1 tablespoon oil in 12-inch skillet over medium-high heat until just smoking. Add tenderloins and cook until well browned on all sides, about 5 minutes; transfer to plate.

2. Add 1 tablespoon oil, 2 garlic cloves, paprika, cayenne, and ¼ teaspoon salt to now-empty skillet and cook over medium heat until fragrant, about 30 seconds. Stir in beans and reserved canning liquid, scraping up any browned bits. Bring to simmer and cook, stirring frequently, until heated through, about 2 minutes. Nestle tenderloins into beans and add any accumulated juices. Transfer skillet to oven and roast until pork registers 135 degrees, 10 to 15 minutes.

3. Meanwhile, process red peppers, almonds, ¼ cup parsley, vinegar, remaining 3 tablespoons oil, remaining garlic clove, and remaining ¼ teaspoon salt in food processor until smooth, about 1 minute, scraping down sides of bowl as needed. Season with salt and pepper to taste. Transfer romesco to bowl.

4. Remove skillet from oven. Being careful of hot skillet handle, transfer tenderloins to cutting board, tent with aluminum foil, and let rest while finishing beans. Stir ¼ cup romesco into beans, then stir in spinach, one handful at a time, until wilted. Season with salt and pepper to taste. Slice tenderloins ½ inch thick and arrange on top of bean mixture. Sprinkle with remaining 2 tablespoons parsley and serve, passing remaining romesco separately.

CLASSIC PORK and beans gets an update with the addition of fresh spinach and a tangy-sweet, nutty romesco sauce. This comforting dinner needs only one skillet, a little stovetop time, and a short trip to the oven.

NOTES

Buy tenderloins that are of equal size and weight so that they cook at the same rate. The romesco sauce can be refrigerated for up to 3 days; bring it to room temperature before using.

KITCHEN IMPROV

Other types of white beans will work here, such as cannellini or butter beans. Baby kale or chopped escarole can be substituted for the spinach.

jammy skillet sausages WITH blackberries AND fennel

Serves 4 • Total Time: 35 minutes

- **1 tablespoon extra-virgin olive oil**
- **1½ pounds hot or sweet Italian sausage**
- **1 fennel bulb, 2 tablespoons fronds chopped coarse; stalks discarded; bulb halved and cut into 1½-inch wedges**
- **½ cup chicken broth**
- **1 shallot, minced**
- **½ cup balsamic vinegar**
- **2 tablespoons honey**
- **½ teaspoon table salt**
- **¼ teaspoon pepper**
- **10 ounces (2 cups) blackberries**

DARK, MOODY good looks belie the bright summer flavor of this sweet-savory one-pan meal. Balsamic vinegar and honey amp up the jamminess of blackberries, while fennel lends aromatic contrast.

1. Heat oil in 12-inch skillet over medium heat until shimmering. Add sausages and brown on all sides, about 5 minutes. Nestle fennel cut side down among sausages. Add broth, cover, and cook until sausages register 160 degrees and fennel is tender and can be easily pierced with fork, 8 to 10 minutes.

2. Using slotted spoon, transfer sausages and fennel to plate. Add shallot, vinegar, honey, salt, and pepper to cooking liquid left in skillet. Bring to simmer and cook until slightly thickened, about 2 minutes. Add blackberries and cook, mashing some berries with back of fork, until sauce is thickened and silicone spatula dragged through it leaves wide trail before filling back in, about 3 minutes. Season with salt and pepper to taste. Nestle sausages and fennel into sauce and sprinkle with fennel fronds. Serve.

NOTES

Do not remove the fennel bulb core; it will help keep the wedges intact. If your fennel doesn't have the fronds attached, a sprinkle of fresh dill or parsley would make a nice garnish. Thawed frozen blackberries can be used instead of fresh.

KITCHEN IMPROV

You can substitute raw chicken or turkey sausages for the pork sausages. Serve with crusty bread or polenta.

roasted cabbage WITH kielbasa AND pierogi

Serves 4 • Total Time: 45 minutes

- 1/4 **cup extra-virgin olive oil, divided**
- 2 **tablespoons whole-grain mustard, divided**
- 1/2 **teaspoon plus 1/8 teaspoon table salt, divided**
- 1/4 **teaspoon plus pinch pepper, divided**
- 1 **small head green cabbage (1 1/2 pounds), cut through core into 1 1/4-inch-wedges**
- 14 **ounces kielbasa sausage, sliced 3/4 inch thick on bias**
- 1 **pound frozen pierogi**
- 1/3 **cup plus 1 tablespoon water, divided**
- 2 **tablespoons unsalted butter**
- 1/4 **cup torn fresh dill**

CLASSIC COMFORT is the name of the game here. Cabbage wedges and kielbasa slices roast in the oven while plush pierogi steam in a skillet. A mustardy butter sauce and a flurry of dill elevate everything. Keeping the core on the cabbage wedges holds them together.

1 Adjust oven rack to middle position and heat oven to 450 degrees. Spray rimmed baking sheet with vegetable oil spray. Whisk 2 tablespoons oil, 1 tablespoon mustard, 1/2 teaspoon salt, and 1/4 teaspoon pepper together in bowl. Brush cabbage wedges with oil mixture, then arrange cut side down on prepared sheet. Roast cabbage until beginning to brown around edges, about 12 minutes.

2 Remove sheet from oven and arrange kielbasa cut side down on sheet around cabbage. Return sheet to oven and roast until cabbage is tender and kielbasa is browned, about 10 minutes. Transfer cabbage and kielbasa to serving platter; cover to keep warm.

3 Meanwhile, heat remaining 2 tablespoons oil in 12-inch nonstick skillet over medium heat until shimmering. Add still-frozen pierogi (they will overlap) and cook until light golden brown, about 3 minutes per side. Carefully add 1/3 cup water, cover, and cook until pierogi are tender and water has been mostly absorbed, about 3 minutes. Uncover skillet and continue to cook until remaining water has evaporated, about 1 minute. Transfer pierogi to platter with cabbage and kielbasa.

4 Melt butter in now-empty skillet over medium heat. Whisk in remaining 1 tablespoon water, remaining 1 tablespoon mustard, remaining 1/8 teaspoon salt, and remaining pinch pepper. Drizzle cabbage, kielbasa, and pierogi with sauce and sprinkle with dill. Serve.

NOTES

This recipe was developed using cheddar pierogi, but other fillings work too. Just make sure to use frozen pierogi and precooked smoked kielbasa. You will need a 12-inch nonstick skillet with a tight-fitting lid.

KITCHEN IMPROV

Try swapping out the kielbasa for andouille or smoked chorizo sausage. Dollops of sour cream or plain Greek yogurt will enrich this meal in a very good way.

kimchi bokkeumbap (KIMCHI FRIED RICE)

Serves 4 • Total Time: 35 minutes

- **1 (8-inch square) sheet gim**
- **2 tablespoons vegetable oil, divided**
- **2 (¼-inch-thick) slices deli ham, cut into ¼-inch pieces (about 4 ounces)**
- **1 large onion, chopped**
- **6 scallions, white and green parts separated and sliced**
- **1¼ cups cabbage kimchi, drained with ¼ cup juice reserved, cut into ¼-inch strips**
- **¼ cup water**
- **4 teaspoons soy sauce**
- **4 teaspoons gochujang**
- **½ teaspoon pepper**
- **3 cups cooked short-grain white rice, room temperature**
- **4 teaspoons toasted sesame oil**
- **1 tablespoon sesame seeds, toasted**

1 Grip gim with tongs and hold 2 inches above low flame on gas burner. Toast gim, turning every 3 to 5 seconds, until gim is aromatic and shrinks slightly, about 20 seconds. (If you don't have a gas stove, toast gim on rimmed baking sheet in 275-degree oven until gim is aromatic and shrinks slightly, 20 to 25 minutes, flipping gim halfway through toasting.) Using kitchen shears, cut gim into four 2-inch-wide strips. Stack strips and cut crosswise into thin strips.

2 Heat 1 tablespoon vegetable oil in 14-inch flat-bottomed wok or 12-inch nonstick skillet over medium-high heat until shimmering. Add ham, onion, and scallion whites and cook, stirring frequently, until onion is softened and ham is beginning to brown at edges, 6 to 8 minutes. Stir in kimchi and reserved juice, water, soy sauce, gochujang, and pepper. Cook, stirring occasionally, until kimchi turns soft and translucent, 4 to 6 minutes.

3 Add rice, reduce heat to medium-low, and cook, tossing slowly but constantly until mixture is evenly coated, about 3 minutes. Stir in sesame oil and remaining 1 tablespoon vegetable oil. Increase heat to medium-high and cook, stirring occasionally, until mixture begins to stick to wok, about 4 minutes. Divide bokkeumbap among individual bowls and sprinkle with sesame seeds, scallion greens, and gim. Serve.

LEFTOVER RICE is transformed into a punchy, radiant dinner with the barest of efforts in this unfussy Korean comfort-food staple. This recipe leans on deli ham to keep things simple.

NOTES

This recipe works best with day-old rice; alternatively, cook your rice 2 hours ahead, spread it on a rimmed baking sheet, and let it cool completely before chilling it for 30 minutes. You'll need at least a 16-ounce jar of kimchi; if it doesn't yield ¼ cup of juice, make up the difference with water. This recipe moves quickly; be sure to have all the ingredients prepared and close by so that you're equipped for fast cooking.

KITCHEN IMPROV

Plain pretoasted seaweed snacks can be substituted for the gim; omit the toasting in step 1. If you like, top each portion with a fried egg.

miso pork AND eggplant stir-fry

Serves 4 • Total Time: 40 minutes

- 1/4 cup white miso
- 3 tablespoons mirin
- 2 tablespoons toasted sesame oil
- 2 tablespoons seasoned rice vinegar
- 2 teaspoons honey
- 2 teaspoons red pepper flakes
- 1 pound ground pork
- 1 tablespoon water
- 3/4 teaspoon table salt, divided
- 1/2 teaspoon baking soda
- 1 tablespoon vegetable oil
- 3 garlic cloves, minced
- 1 1/2 pounds Japanese or Chinese eggplant, halved lengthwise and sliced 1 inch thick
- 6 scallions, white and green parts separated and sliced 1/2 inch thick on bias
- 1 tablespoon sesame seeds

JUICY PORK (tenderized with baking soda) and creamy eggplant unite in this flavorful stir-fry, melded together by an umami-forward miso sauce with honey and red pepper flakes. Serve over rice or noodles.

1 Whisk miso, mirin, sesame oil, vinegar, honey, and pepper flakes in large bowl until well combined. Measure out and reserve 1/4 cup sauce for serving. Toss pork with water, 1/2 teaspoon salt, and baking soda in separate bowl until thoroughly combined.

2 Heat vegetable oil in 14-inch flat-bottomed wok or 12-inch nonstick skillet over medium-high heat until shimmering. Add pork and cook, breaking up meat into small pieces, until no longer pink, 5 to 7 minutes. Stir in garlic and cook until fragrant, about 30 seconds. Using slotted spoon, transfer pork to bowl with remaining sauce.

3 Add eggplant, scallion whites, and remaining 1/4 teaspoon salt to now-empty wok and toss to combine. Cover and cook over medium heat, stirring occasionally, until eggplant is very soft, about 10 minutes. Off heat, add pork and sauce and gently toss to combine. Sprinkle with scallion greens and sesame seeds. Serve, passing reserved sauce separately.

NOTES

You can substitute 3 tablespoons of white wine or sake mixed with 1 tablespoon of sugar for the mirin. You will need a 14-inch flat-bottomed wok or 12-inch nonstick skillet with a tight-fitting lid. This recipe moves quickly; be sure to have all the ingredients prepared and close by so that you're equipped for fast cooking.

KITCHEN IMPROV

Yellow, red, or brown miso paste can be used instead of white. You can substitute ground lamb, ground beef, or 93 percent lean ground turkey or chicken for the pork. Small and narrow Italian eggplant can also be used here, but avoid globe eggplant, which are too large and will turn mushy.

white pizza WITH peach AND prosciutto

Serves 4 to 6 • Total Time: 40 minutes

- **3 tablespoons extra-virgin olive oil, divided**
- **4 ounces (1/2 cup) small-curd cottage cheese**
- **1/4 cup chopped fresh basil**
- **1/4 teaspoon table salt**
- **1/4 teaspoon pepper**
- **1 pound pizza dough, room temperature**
- **8 ounces fontina cheese, shredded (2 cups)**
- **1/2 red onion, sliced thin**
- **2 ounces (2 cups) baby arugula**
- **1 peach, halved, pitted, and sliced thin**
- **4 thin slices prosciutto, torn into 1-inch pieces**

SALTY PROSCIUTTO ribbons, sweet peach slices, peppery arugula, and a cheese duo make this pizza a summertime go-to. And thanks to the convenience of store-bought dough, it gets to the table in under 45 minutes.

1 Adjust oven rack to lowest position and heat oven to 500 degrees. Brush rimmed baking sheet with 1 tablespoon oil. Combine cottage cheese, basil, salt, pepper, and 1 tablespoon oil in bowl.

2 Press and roll dough into 15 by 11-inch rectangle, about 1/4 inch thick, on lightly floured counter. Transfer dough to prepared sheet and brush edges with 2 teaspoons oil. Spread cottage cheese mixture over dough, then sprinkle evenly with fontina and onion. Bake until cheese is spotty brown and crust is deep golden, 12 to 16 minutes, rotating sheet halfway through baking.

3 Transfer pizza to wire rack and let cool for 5 minutes. Toss arugula and peach with remaining 1 teaspoon oil and season with salt and pepper to taste. Top pizza with arugula mixture and prosciutto. Slice and serve.

NOTES

Use a ripe but firm peach here so that it holds its shape when sliced. Let the dough sit at room temperature while preparing the ingredients and heating the oven, or it will be difficult to stretch. If the dough springs back while shaping, let it rest for a few minutes before rolling it again.

KITCHEN IMPROV

Consider other stone fruits, such as nectarines or apricots. Feel free to substitute any good melting cheese for the fontina, such as Gruyère, Havarti, or whole-milk block mozzarella.

smoky peppers AND eggs WITH chorizo AND garlic toast

Serves 4 • Total Time: 45 minutes

- **4 ounces Spanish-style chorizo sausage, cut into ¼-inch pieces**
- **5 tablespoons extra-virgin olive oil, divided, plus extra for drizzling**
- **1 onion, halved and sliced thin**
- **2 tablespoons tomato paste**
- **1½ teaspoons table salt**
- **½ teaspoon smoked paprika**
- **¼ teaspoon pepper**
- **2 red or yellow bell peppers, stemmed, seeded, and cut into ½-inch strips**
- **1½ pounds tomatoes, cored, seeded, and cut into 1-inch pieces**
- **1 tablespoon sherry vinegar**
- **4 large eggs**
- **4 (1-inch-thick) slices rustic white bread**
- **1 garlic clove, peeled**
- **2 tablespoons chopped fresh parsley**

1. Adjust oven rack 6 inches from broiler element and heat broiler. Cook chorizo and ¼ cup oil in 12-inch skillet over medium heat, stirring occasionally, until rendered and crisp, about 3 minutes. Using slotted spoon, transfer chorizo to paper towel–lined plate; set aside.

2. Add onion, tomato paste, salt, paprika, and pepper to fat left in skillet and cook until onion is beginning to soften, about 3 minutes. Add bell peppers and tomatoes and cook until bell peppers begin to soften, about 3 minutes. Stir in vinegar, cover, and cook, stirring occasionally, until tomatoes have broken down into sauce-like consistency, 10 to 12 minutes. Remove skillet from heat.

3. Using back of spoon, make 4 shallow indentations (about 1 inch wide) in surface of vegetable mixture. Crack 1 egg into each indentation (which will hold yolk in place but not fully contain egg). Bring to simmer over medium-low heat. Cover and cook until yolks film over, 3 to 6 minutes, adjusting heat to maintain gentle simmer. Continue to cook, covered, until whites are softly but uniformly set (if skillet is shaken lightly, each egg should jiggle as single unit), 1 to 3 minutes longer.

4. Meanwhile, arrange bread on rimmed baking sheet and broil, flipping as needed, until well toasted, about 4 minutes. Rub 1 side of each toast with garlic, then drizzle with remaining 1 tablespoon oil. Sprinkle chorizo and parsley over bell peppers and eggs and drizzle with extra oil. Serve with garlic toasts.

VEGGIE-PACKED and enriched with crispy chorizo, this sauté of peppers, onions, and tomatoes is a riff on Spanish pisto. Eggs cooked right on top and broiler-toasted rustic bread alongside make it a meal.

NOTES

Since eggs cook so quickly, crack each egg into an individual small bowl so that you can get them into the pan at about the same time.

Use Spanish-style chorizo, which is cured and smoked; Mexican chorizo, which is raw and crumbly, will produce different results.

KITCHEN IMPROV

You can use a 28-ounce can of whole peeled tomatoes, drained with 1/4 cup juice reserved. Add the tomatoes and reserved juice to the skillet with the peppers, lightly crushing each tomato with the back of a spoon. Green or orange bell peppers also work. Make the meal heartier by using 8 eggs; create 8 divots (7 around the perimeter and 1 in the center) in step 3. Spice things up by adding a pinch of cayenne pepper along with the smoked paprika.

ONE DOUBLE-DUTY blend of cilantro, garlic, serrano, and lime juice works as both a marinade for quick-cooking lamb rib chops and a dressing for the snappy salad. For a little extra kick, leave the seeds in the serrano chile.

cilantro-lime lamb chops WITH cucumber-pea salad

Serves 4 • Total Time: 45 minutes

- **3 cups fresh cilantro leaves and tender stems**
- **1/3 cup extra-virgin olive oil, plus extra for drizzling**
- **1 serrano chile, stemmed and seeded**
- **3 tablespoons lime juice, divided**
- **1 tablespoon water**
- **1 tablespoon honey**
- **2 large garlic cloves**
- **1 1/4 teaspoons table salt, divided**
- **1 teaspoon ground cumin**
- **8 (5- to 6-ounce) lamb rib chops, 1 1/4 to 1 1/2 inches thick, trimmed**
- **5 Persian cucumbers, sliced thin**
- **2 cups frozen peas, thawed**
- **1 cup plain Greek yogurt**
- **2 tablespoons dukkah**

1 Process cilantro, oil, serrano, 1 tablespoon lime juice, water, honey, garlic, 1 teaspoon salt, and cumin in blender until smooth, about 1 minute, scraping down sides of blender jar as needed. Measure out and reserve 1/3 cup marinade.

2 Add remaining marinade and lamb chops to 1-gallon zipper-lock bag. Seal bag, turn to distribute marinade, and refrigerate for 15 minutes, flipping halfway through marinating.

3 Heat 12-inch cast-iron skillet over medium heat for 3 minutes. Remove lamb chops from bag, allowing excess marinade to drip off, and season with remaining 1/4 teaspoon salt. Arrange lamb in even layer in hot skillet and cook until well browned and meat registers 120 to 125 degrees (for medium-rare) or 130 to 135 degrees (for medium), 2 to 4 minutes per side. Transfer to plate and let rest while preparing salad.

4 Toss cucumbers, peas, reserved marinade, and remaining 2 tablespoons lime juice together in bowl. Spread yogurt evenly among four plates. Arrange salad and lamb chops on top of yogurt. Sprinkle with dukkah and drizzle with extra oil. Serve.

NOTES

Look for domestic lamb, which is typically grass-fed and finished on grain and has a less gamy flavor and better fat marbling than imported lamb. Lamb loin chops, which are slightly thicker than rib chops, can also be used; cook them for an additional 1 to 2 minutes per side. If you don't have a cast-iron skillet, heat 1 tablespoon oil in a 12-inch skillet over medium-high heat until just smoking; proceed with step 3 as directed. Have time to plan ahead? The lamb chops can be marinated for up to 2 hours.

KITCHEN IMPROV

In a pinch, you can use a combination of 1 tablespoon finely chopped peanuts and 1 tablespoon toasted sesame seeds for the dukkah. Mini Persian cucumber looks nice in this salad, but you can sub one large English cucumber, quartered lengthwise and sliced thin. If you prefer, grill the marinated lamb chops.

one-pot lamb meatballs WITH eggplant AND chickpeas

Serves 4 • Total Time: 45 minutes

- **½ cup panko bread crumbs**
- **1 large egg, lightly beaten**
- **2 tablespoons ras el hanout, divided**
- **4 teaspoons grated lemon zest, divided (2 lemons)**
- **6 garlic cloves, minced, divided**
- **1¼ teaspoons table salt, divided**
- **1 pound ground lamb**
- **2 tablespoons extra-virgin olive oil**
- **1 pound eggplant, cut into ½-inch pieces**
- **1 onion, chopped fine**
- **1 (28-ounce) can crushed tomatoes**
- **1 (15-ounce) can chickpeas, rinsed**
- **¾ cup golden raisins**
- **½ cup water**
- **½ cup pitted green olives, halved**
- **¼ cup harissa**
- **1 cup coarsely chopped fresh cilantro, parsley, and/or mint, divided**

1 Combine panko, egg, 1 tablespoon ras el hanout, 2 teaspoons lemon zest, one-third of garlic, and 1 teaspoon salt in large bowl. Add lamb and mix with your hands until thoroughly combined. Pinch off and roll mixture into 16 meatballs (about 3 tablespoons each).

2 Heat oil in Dutch oven over medium-high heat until just smoking. Add meatballs and cook until well browned on all sides, about 5 minutes; transfer to plate.

3 Add eggplant, onion, remaining garlic, remaining 1 tablespoon ras el hanout, and remaining ¼ teaspoon salt to fat left in pot and cook, stirring frequently, until vegetables are beginning to soften, 8 to 10 minutes. Stir in tomatoes, chickpeas, raisins, water, olives, harissa, and remaining 2 teaspoons lemon zest. Nestle meatballs into sauce and add any accumulated juices. Reduce heat to medium-low, cover, and cook until eggplant is very tender and meatballs register 160 degrees, about 10 minutes.

4 Off heat, stir in ½ cup cilantro. Sprinkle remaining ½ cup cilantro over top and serve.

ZESTY MEATBALLS anchor this Dutch-oven dinner inspired by the flavors of Moroccan tagines. The eggplant and chickpeas soak up loads of bold flavors from tomatoes, ras el hanout, harissa, lemon zest, garlic, onions, green olives, and raisins.

NOTES

Harissa is available in both mild and spicy versions; use whichever you prefer.

KITCHEN IMPROV

If you prefer, you can make your own ras el hanout by combining 1½ teaspoons each of cardamom, coriander, cumin, and pepper. You can substitute ground beef for the lamb, if desired. Other dried fruits can be used in place of the raisins (consider chopped apricots, figs, or dates). Serve this dish with flatbread, couscous, or rice.

spiced lamb patties WITH roasted cauliflower

Serves 4 • Total Time: 45 minutes

- **1 head cauliflower (2 pounds), cored and cut into 1½-inch florets**
- **1 red onion, cut through root end into 8 equal wedges, divided**
- **½ cup extra-virgin olive oil, divided**
- **2 teaspoons ground cumin, divided**
- **1¾ teaspoons table salt, divided**
- **¾ cup fresh mint, cilantro, or parsley leaves, divided**
- **¼ cup pine nuts, toasted**
- **¾ teaspoon ground cinnamon**
- **½ teaspoon pepper**
- **1 pound ground lamb**

LAMB PATTIES flavored with cinnamon and mint pair beautifully with roasted cauliflower and red onion. A food processor makes speedy work of both the patties and the accompanying mint sauce. You might find yourself making the cauliflower to serve with other simply cooked proteins.

1 Adjust oven rack to lower-middle position and heat oven to 450 degrees. Toss cauliflower, 6 onion wedges, 2 tablespoons oil, 1 teaspoon cumin, and ¾ teaspoon salt together on rimmed baking sheet. Roast until vegetables are tender and lightly browned, about 25 minutes, stirring halfway through roasting.

2 Meanwhile, pulse ½ cup mint, pine nuts, 5 tablespoons oil, and ¼ teaspoon salt in food processor until finely chopped, about 6 pulses, scraping down sides of bowl as needed; transfer sauce to bowl.

3 Add cinnamon, pepper, remaining 2 onion wedges, remaining 1 teaspoon cumin, remaining ¾ teaspoon salt, and remaining ¼ cup mint to now-empty processor and pulse until finely chopped, about 10 pulses. Add lamb and pulse until mixture is well combined, about 6 pulses. Using your lightly moistened hands, divide lamb mixture into 12 equal portions, then gently shape each portion into ½-inch-thick patties, about 2 inches in diameter.

4 Heat remaining 1 tablespoon oil in 12-inch nonstick skillet over medium-high heat until just smoking. Cook patties until browned and just cooked through, about 3 minutes per side. Serve patties with vegetables and mint sauce.

NOTES

The sauce and patties can be assembled and refrigerated up to 1 day in advance; bring the sauce to room temperature before serving.

KITCHEN IMPROV

You can substitute ground beef, ground pork, or 93 percent lean ground turkey or chicken for the lamb. To make this heartier, serve it with couscous or rice pilaf.

foolproof fish

chapter 3

salmon cakes WITH sugar snap pea salad

Serves 4 • Total Time: 35 minutes

- **1/4 cup plus 2 tablespoons mayonnaise, divided**
- **1/4 cup chopped fresh parsley, divided**
- **2 scallions, sliced thin, divided**
- **3 tablespoons lemon juice, divided**
- **4 teaspoons Dijon mustard, divided**
- **1 1/4 teaspoons table salt, divided**
- **1/2 teaspoon pepper, divided**
- **1 pound sugar snap peas, strings removed, cut in half diagonally**
- **1/2 English cucumber, quartered lengthwise and sliced 1/2 inch thick**
- **6 radishes, trimmed, halved, and sliced thin (1 cup)**
- **3 tablespoons plus 3/4 cup panko bread crumbs, divided**
- **1 (1 1/4-pound) skinless salmon fillet, cut into 1-inch pieces**
- **1/2 cup vegetable oil**
- **2 ounces (2 cups) baby arugula**

1. Whisk 1/4 cup mayonnaise, 2 tablespoons parsley, half of scallions, 2 tablespoons lemon juice, 1 tablespoon mustard, 1/2 teaspoon salt, and 1/4 teaspoon pepper together in large bowl. Add snap peas, cucumber, and radishes and toss to coat. Cover salad and refrigerate until needed.

2. Combine 3 tablespoons panko, remaining 2 tablespoons mayonnaise, remaining 2 tablespoons parsley, remaining scallions, remaining 1 tablespoon lemon juice, remaining 1 teaspoon mustard, remaining 3/4 teaspoon salt, and remaining 1/4 teaspoon pepper in bowl. Working in 3 batches, pulse salmon in food processor until coarsely chopped into 1/4-inch pieces, about 2 pulses, transferring each batch to bowl with panko mixture. Gently mix until uniformly combined.

3. Place remaining 3/4 cup panko in pie plate. Using 1/3-cup measure, scoop level amount of salmon mixture and transfer to baking sheet; repeat to make 8 cakes. Carefully coat each cake in bread crumbs, gently patting into disk measuring 2 3/4 inches in diameter and 1 inch high. Return coated cakes to baking sheet.

4. Heat oil in 12-inch nonstick skillet over medium-high heat until shimmering. Place salmon cakes in skillet and cook without moving until golden brown, about 2 minutes. Carefully flip cakes and cook until second sides are golden brown, 2 to 3 minutes. Transfer cakes to paper towel–lined plate to drain for 1 minute. Add arugula to salad, toss to combine, and season with salt and pepper to taste. Serve salmon cakes with salad.

FRESH FISH FILLETS are worth making into fish cakes for three good reasons: a crispy exterior, moist interior, and super-simple cooking technique. Salmon brings rich flavor to the cakes, and a just-as-simple springtime salad completes the meal.

NOTES

If you're buying a skin-on salmon fillet, purchase 1⅓ pounds of fish and ask your fishmonger to skin it for you. This will yield 1¼ pounds of salmon after skinning. When processing the salmon, it's OK to have some pieces that are larger than ¼ inch. It's important to avoid overprocessing the fish. The salad can be refrigerated for up to 1 hour before serving.

KITCHEN IMPROV

Consider swapping in other fresh herbs for the parsley and/or adding up to 2 tablespoons of briny ingredients to the salmon mixture, such as minced capers, olives, or pickles. Turn the salmon cakes into sliders by serving them on eight (2½-inch) slider buns or soft dinner rolls and topping them with tartar sauce.

A SWEET but slightly acidic tomato-mango salad dressed with honey-lime vinaigrette makes a perfect complement to rich coriander-dusted salmon. Cherry or grape tomatoes are go-to choices for year-round sweetness.

spiced crispy-skinned salmon WITH tomato-mango salad

Serves 4 • Total Time: 30 minutes

- 1/4 cup extra-virgin olive oil
- 1 tablespoon grated lime zest plus 2 tablespoons juice
- 1 tablespoon honey
- 1 teaspoon table salt, divided
- 1 teaspoon pepper, divided
- 1 pound cherry or grape tomatoes, halved (2 cups)
- 2 mangos, peeled, pitted, and cut into 1/2-inch pieces
- 1 large shallot, sliced thin
- 1/2 cup minced fresh cilantro, basil, and/or mint, divided
- 4 teaspoons ground coriander
- 4 (6- to 8-ounce) skin-on center-cut salmon fillets, 1 to 1 1/2 inches thick
- 1/4 cup roasted pepitas

1 Whisk oil, lime zest and juice, honey, 1/2 teaspoon salt, and 1/2 teaspoon pepper together in large bowl until honey has dissolved. Add tomatoes, mangos, shallot, and 1/4 cup cilantro and toss to combine; set salad aside.

2 Combine coriander, remaining 1/2 teaspoon salt, and remaining 1/2 teaspoon pepper in small bowl. Pat salmon dry with paper towels and sprinkle with spice mixture. Place salmon skin side down in cold 12-inch nonstick skillet and place over medium-high heat. Cook fillets, without moving them, until skins are golden brown and bottom 1/4 inch of fillets turns opaque, 6 to 8 minutes.

3 Using 2 spatulas, flip fillets skin side up and continue to cook without moving them until centers are still translucent when checked with tip of paring knife and salmon registers 125 degrees (for medium-rare), 6 to 8 minutes. Serve with salad, sprinkling with pepitas and remaining 1/4 cup cilantro.

NOTES

Properly ripened mangos make all the difference. The mangos are ready to use when their skins have turned yellow, they're a bit wrinkly and spotty, and they yield to gentle pressure. With that said, you can use frozen mango if you're unable to find fresh (or if you need an excuse to use it for more than your morning smoothie). Just be sure to thaw and drain it before using; you'll need about 3 cups. If using wild salmon (or arctic char), reduce cooking times to 4 to 6 minutes per side and cook until the fish registers 120 degrees.

KITCHEN IMPROV

Turn this salmon dinner into taco night by flaking the cooked salmon and including some warmed tortillas.

pan-seared salmon WITH braised beans AND greens

Serves 4 • Total Time: 35 minutes

- 1/4 cup extra-virgin olive oil, divided
- 4 garlic cloves, sliced thin
- 1 1/2 teaspoons chopped fresh thyme, divided
- 1 1/4 teaspoons table salt, divided
- 1/4 teaspoon red pepper flakes
- 2 (15-ounce) cans pinto beans, undrained
- 12 ounces Swiss chard, stemmed and cut into 1-inch pieces
- 1 teaspoon grated lemon zest plus 2 teaspoons juice
- 1/2 cup panko bread crumbs
- 4 (6- to 8-ounce) skin-on salmon fillets, 1 to 1 1/2 inches thick

CRISPY, LEMONY panko adds a finishing touch of tang and crunch to this simple supper. Cooking pinto beans in their starchy canning liquid gives them a rich, creamy consistency, making them taste like they cooked for longer than they did.

1 Heat 3 tablespoons oil in large saucepan over medium-high heat until shimmering. Add garlic, 1 teaspoon thyme, 1/4 teaspoon salt, and pepper flakes and cook until fragrant, about 1 minute. Add beans and their canning liquid and bring to simmer. Reduce heat to medium-low and simmer, stirring occasionally, until liquid is thickened and creamy, about 15 minutes. Stir in chard and cook until tender, about 5 minutes. Stir in lemon juice and season with salt and pepper to taste.

2 Meanwhile, heat remaining 1 tablespoon oil in 12-inch nonstick skillet over medium heat until shimmering. Add panko, lemon zest, 1/4 teaspoon salt, and remaining 1/2 teaspoon thyme and cook, stirring frequently, until golden brown, about 2 minutes; transfer to bowl and set aside. Wipe skillet clean with paper towels.

3 Pat salmon dry with paper towels and sprinkle with remaining 3/4 teaspoon salt. Place salmon skin side down in now-empty skillet and place over medium-high heat. Cook fillets, without moving them, until skins are golden brown and bottom 1/4 inch of fillets turns opaque, 6 to 8 minutes.

4 Using 2 spatulas, flip fillets skin side up and continue to cook without moving them until centers are still translucent when checked with tip of paring knife and salmon registers 125 degrees (for medium-rare), 6 to 8 minutes. Serve salmon over bean mixture, sprinkling panko mixture over top.

NOTES

If using wild salmon (or arctic char), reduce the cooking time to 4 to 6 minutes per side and cook until the fish registers 120 degrees.

KITCHEN IMPROV

Consider other beans such as cannellini or butter beans. Butter crackers or potato chips make for a unique twist on the panko crumbs. Plan on using about 2 ounces of crackers or chips, crushed into rough 1/8-inch pieces, in place of the panko.

salmon WITH old bay butter AND confetti grits

Serves 4 • Total Time: 30 minutes

- **4 tablespoons unsalted butter, softened, divided**
- **2 ears corn, kernels cut from cobs**
- **1 red bell pepper, stemmed, seeded, and chopped fine**
- **1 shallot, chopped fine**
- **1¾ teaspoons table salt, divided**
- **¾ teaspoon pepper, divided**
- **2 cups whole milk**
- **2 cups water**
- **1 cup quick grits**
- **1 teaspoon grated lemon zest plus 1 tablespoon juice, and lemon wedges for serving**
- **2 teaspoons Old Bay Seasoning**
- **4 (6- to 8-ounce) skin-on salmon fillets, 1 to 1½ inches thick**

1 Melt 2 tablespoons butter in large saucepan over medium-high heat. Add corn, bell pepper, shallot, 1¼ teaspoons salt, and ¼ teaspoon pepper and cook, stirring occasionally, until softened, 5 to 8 minutes. Add milk and water and bring to boil. Slowly whisk in grits. Reduce heat to medium-low and cook, stirring often, until grits are thick and creamy, 5 to 7 minutes. Off heat, stir in lemon juice and season with salt and pepper to taste; cover grits to keep warm.

2 Meanwhile, combine lemon zest, Old Bay, and remaining 2 tablespoons butter in small bowl; set aside. Pat salmon dry with paper towels and sprinkle with remaining ½ teaspoon salt and ½ teaspoon pepper. Place salmon skin side down in cold 12-inch nonstick skillet and place over medium-high heat. Cook fillets, without moving them, until skins are golden brown and bottom ¼ inch of fillets turn opaque, 6 to 8 minutes.

3 Using 2 spatulas, flip fillets skin side up and continue to cook without moving them until centers are still translucent when checked with tip of paring knife and salmon registers 125 degrees (for medium-rare), 6 to 8 minutes. Serve salmon atop grits with lemon wedges, dolloping individual portions with Old Bay–butter mixture.

SPICE BLENDS hold a lot of power. Savory and slightly spicy, slightly sweet, Old Bay packs multiple flavors to suffuse a lemony butter you dollop over salmon fillets. As the butter melts, it flavors both the fish and vegetable-studded grits below.

NOTES

If using wild salmon (or arctic char), reduce the cooking time to 4 to 6 minutes per side and cook until the fish registers 120 degrees.

KITCHEN IMPROV

You can substitute 1½ cups thawed frozen corn for the fresh. You can swap Creole or Cajun spice blends for the Old Bay seasoning (or simply use paprika).

maple-soy salmon bowls WITH quinoa AND brussels sprouts

Serves 4 • Total Time: 35 minutes

- **1½ cups white quinoa**
- **2¼ teaspoons table salt, divided**
- **1 pound small brussels sprouts, trimmed and halved**
- **¼ cup vegetable oil, divided**
- **1 (2-pound) skinless salmon fillet, 1 to 1½ inches thick, cut into 1½-inch pieces**
- **½ cup maple syrup**
- **1½ tablespoons soy sauce**
- **1 garlic clove, minced to a paste**
- **½ teaspoon grated fresh ginger**
- **¼ teaspoon red pepper flakes**
- **2 tablespoons lemon juice**
- **2 scallions, sliced thin on bias**
- **2 tablespoons toasted sesame seeds**

1. Bring 2 quarts water to boil in large saucepan over medium-high heat. Add quinoa and 1½ teaspoons salt, return to boil, and cook until quinoa is tender, 10 to 12 minutes. Drain quinoa, return to now-empty saucepan, and cover to keep warm.

2. Meanwhile, arrange brussels sprouts cut side down in single layer in 12-inch nonstick skillet. Drizzle with 3 tablespoons oil and sprinkle with ¼ teaspoon salt. Cover skillet, place over medium-high heat, and cook until sprouts are bright green and cut sides have started to brown, about 4 minutes. Uncover and continue to cook until cut sides are evenly browned, 1 to 2 minutes longer. Transfer sprouts to bowl and set aside.

3. Pat salmon dry with paper towels and sprinkle with remaining ½ teaspoon salt. Heat remaining 1 tablespoon oil in now-empty skillet over medium heat until shimmering. Add salmon skinned side up and cook until well browned on first side, 2 to 4 minutes. Using 2 spatulas, flip pieces and continue to cook until salmon registers 125 degrees, 2 to 4 minutes, removing pieces from skillet as they finish cooking. Transfer salmon to plate, tent with aluminum foil, and set aside. Pour off and discard fat; wipe skillet clean with paper towels.

4. Add maple syrup, soy sauce, garlic, ginger, and pepper flakes to again-empty skillet and bring to boil over medium-high heat. Cook until mixture has thickened and rubber spatula dragged through it leaves wide trail before filling back in, about 3 minutes. Add brussels sprouts and lemon juice and gently toss to coat. Divide quinoa among serving bowls, top with salmon and brussels sprouts, and drizzle any remaining glaze over top. Sprinkle with scallions and sesame seeds and serve.

QUICK-COOKING QUINOA provides a fluffy base for chunks of skillet-roasted salmon and maple-glazed brussels sprouts. Cooking the quinoa with the pasta method—in lots of boiling salted water—eliminates the need to pre-rinse the grains.

NOTES

If buying a skin-on salmon fillet, purchase 2¼ pounds of fish. This will yield 2 pounds of fish after skinning. If using wild salmon (or arctic char), reduce cooking times to about 2 minutes per side and cook until the fish registers 120 degrees. Look for brussels sprouts that are similar in size (and no more than 1½ inches in diameter) with small, tight heads.

KITCHEN IMPROV

Have fun with more toppings! Try adding shredded red cabbage, thinly sliced cucumber, pickled ginger, cilantro leaves, thinly sliced radishes, or toasted nuts.

spicy salmon sushi bowls

Serves 4 • Total Time: 45 minutes

- **1½ cups sushi rice**
- **½ teaspoon table salt, plus salt for cooking rice**
- **5 tablespoons seasoned rice vinegar, divided**
- **½ cup mayonnaise**
- **2–3 tablespoons sriracha**
- **4 (6- to 8-ounce) skin-on center-cut salmon fillets, 1 to 1½ inches thick**
- **1 avocado, halved, pitted, and sliced thin**
- **1 cup frozen edamame, thawed**
- **⅓ cup pickled ginger, drained**
- **½ cup crumbled roasted seaweed snacks**
- **1 tablespoon toasted sesame seeds**

ENDLESSLY CUSTOMIZABLE sushi bowls mean that everyone in the family gets exactly what they want. This recipe starts with sushi rice, pan-seared salmon, and a couple of essential toppings. From there, let your culinary imagination take over.

1. Bring 2 quarts water to boil in large saucepan. Add rice and 1½ teaspoons salt and cook until tender, 12 to 15 minutes. Drain rice and transfer to large bowl. Drizzle with ¼ cup vinegar and let cool while preparing other ingredients, occasionally tossing with wooden spoon.

2. Combine mayonnaise, sriracha, and remaining 1 tablespoon vinegar in bowl; set aside for serving. Pat salmon dry with paper towels and sprinkle with salt. Place salmon skin side down in cold 12-inch nonstick skillet and place over medium-high heat. Cook fillets without moving them until skins are golden brown and bottom ¼ inch of fillets turns opaque, 6 to 8 minutes.

3. Using two spatulas, flip fillets skin side up and continue to cook without moving them until centers are still translucent when checked with tip of paring knife and salmon registers 125 degrees (for medium-rare), 6 to 8 minutes. Transfer fillets to cutting board, let cool slightly, then flake into bite-size pieces; discard skin.

4. Divide rice among individual serving bowls. Arrange salmon, avocado, edamame, ginger, seaweed, and sesame seeds in individual bowls or on platter and serve, passing sriracha mayonnaise separately.

NOTES

Roasted seaweed snacks are sold in packages of various sizes; you will need about ¼ ounce. If you prefer a spicier mayonnaise, use the full 3 tablespoons of sriracha. If using wild salmon, cook it to 120 degrees.

KITCHEN IMPROV

The beauty of this recipe is allowing each person to customize their own bowl, so have fun setting out toppings. Consider adding thinly sliced cucumbers or radishes; carrot ribbons; mesclun; crispy shallots; or cubes of ripe mango or papaya.

spiced red snapper WITH creamy tahini sauce AND butter-toasted almonds

Serves 4 • Total Time: 35 minutes

- 1/4 cup tahini
- 2 tablespoons extra-virgin olive oil
- 2 tablespoons water, plus extra as needed
- 1/2 teaspoon grated lemon zest plus 2 tablespoons juice
- 1/4 teaspoon minced garlic
- 1 1/4 teaspoons table salt, divided
- 2 tablespoons minced fresh parsley
- 1/2 teaspoon ground coriander
- 1/2 teaspoon ground cumin
- 1/2 teaspoon black pepper
- 1/4 teaspoon cayenne pepper
- 4 (6- to 8-ounce) skin-on red snapper fillets, 3/4 to 1 inch thick
- 2 tablespoons unsalted butter
- 1/3 cup slivered almonds
- 1/3 cup pomegranate seeds

CREAMY TAHINI, sweet-tart pomegranate seeds, and golden toasted almonds adorn succulent fish in this stunning dish that brings together the warm spices and rich flavors of Levantine cuisine. A pantry-friendly spice blend and quick pan sear create restaurant-quality fish at home.

1. Whisk tahini, oil, water, lemon zest and juice, garlic, and 1/4 teaspoon salt together in bowl until smooth. (Sauce should be consistency of heavy cream; adjust consistency with extra water as needed.) Stir in parsley and set aside.

2. Combine remaining 1 teaspoon salt, coriander, cumin, pepper, and cayenne in small bowl. Pat snapper dry with paper towels. Using sharp knife, make 3 or 4 shallow slashes, 1/2 inch apart, in skin side of each fillet, being careful not to cut into flesh. Sprinkle flesh side of snapper with spice mixture.

3. Melt butter in 12-inch nonstick skillet over medium heat. Add almonds and cook, stirring frequently, until golden brown and fragrant, about 4 minutes. Using slotted spoon, transfer almonds to bowl and season with salt to taste.

4. Add snapper, flesh side down, to fat left in skillet and cook over medium heat until golden brown, about 4 minutes. Using 2 spatulas, gently flip snapper and continue to cook until fillets flake apart when gently prodded with tip of paring knife and fish registers 130 to 135 degrees, 3 to 5 minutes. Transfer fillets to serving platter. Spoon tahini sauce over top and sprinkle with toasted almonds and pomegranate seeds. Serve.

NOTES

Keep the skin on during cooking to prevent the fillets from drying out; you can remove it afterward if you choose not to serve it.

KITCHEN IMPROV

You can substitute striped bass or halibut for the snapper. Pine nuts, chopped pistachios, or chopped walnuts work well in place of almonds. Sprinkle with fresh parsley or tarragon for extra freshness if you want. Serve with Simple Rice Pilaf (page 54) or a simple oven-roasted vegetable (page 142).

simple vegetables from the oven

roasted asparagus

Serves 4 • Total Time: 30 minutes

- **2 pounds thick asparagus**
- **2 tablespoons plus 2 teaspoons extra-virgin olive oil, divided**
- **½ teaspoon table salt**
- **¼ teaspoon pepper**

1 Adjust oven rack to lowest position, place rimmed baking sheet on rack, and heat oven to 500 degrees. Trim bottom inch of asparagus spears and discard. Peel bottom halves of spears until white flesh is exposed. Place asparagus in large baking pan and toss with 2 tablespoons oil, salt, and pepper.

2 Transfer asparagus to preheated sheet and spread into even layer. Roast, without moving asparagus, until undersides of spears are browned, tops are vibrant green, and tip of paring knife inserted at base of largest spear meets little resistance, 8 to 10 minutes. Drizzle with remaining 2 teaspoons oil and serve.

A BLAZING-HOT oven is only part of the formula for deeply browned, crisp-tender spears. Peeling away the tough skin, preheating the baking sheet, and roasting the spears without moving them completes the equation.

NOTES

Look for thick asparagus spears that are between ½ and ¾ inch in diameter.

KITCHEN IMPROV

Sprinkle with toasted panko or grated Parmesan, or make a quick gremolata of minced garlic, fresh parsley, and grated lemon zest.

---

roasted butternut squash

Serves 4 • Total Time: 40 minutes

- **1 butternut squash (2 pounds), peeled, halved lengthwise, seeded, and sliced crosswise ½ inch thick**
- **4 teaspoons vegetable oil**
- **½ teaspoon table salt**
- **¼ teaspoon pepper**

Adjust oven rack to lowest position and heat oven to 450 degrees. Toss squash with oil, salt, and pepper and spread in even layer on aluminum foil–lined rimmed baking sheet. Roast until well browned and tender, 20 to 30 minutes, flipping slices once halfway through cooking. Season with salt and pepper to taste. Serve warm or at room temperature.

SUPREME TENDERNESS and great caramelization come from roasting butternut squash slices on high heat on the lowest rack of the oven.

NOTES

For the best texture, make sure to remove the fibrous flesh just below the squash's skin.

KITCHEN IMPROV

Add up to 1 teaspoon of a spice blend such as curry powder, baharat, or herbes de Provence with the oil. Sprinkle the roasted squash with chopped toasted nuts or seeds, za'atar, crumbled cheese (goat or feta), pomegranate seeds, chopped fresh herbs (cilantro, parsley, or mint), and/or pickled red onion.

broiled smashed zucchini

Serves 4 • Total Time: 25 minutes

- **2 pounds zucchini**
- **2 tablespoons extra-virgin olive oil, plus extra for drizzling**
- **4 teaspoons lemon juice**
- **2 teaspoons kosher salt**

1 Adjust oven rack 5 inches from broiler element and heat broiler. Using meat pounder or rolling pin, firmly but gently smash zucchini until flattened and cracked lengthwise. Trim and discard ends. Break each zucchini into 2 to 4 large pieces. Transfer zucchini pieces to large bowl, including any smaller pieces that have been created during smashing and breaking. Add oil and lemon juice and toss until zucchini is evenly coated.

2 Arrange zucchini, skin side down, on aluminum foil–lined rimmed baking sheet. Sprinkle with salt, making sure to season thicker pieces more heavily than thinner pieces. Broil until zucchini are lightly charred in spots, 9 to 12 minutes, rotating pan halfway through broiling. Drizzle with extra oil and serve.

WHACK ZUCCHINI good, then slide it under the broiler. Not only will you create a range of textures but you'll also unlock a surprising variety of flavors, all thanks to the oven char that develops on the craggy pieces.

NOTES

The zucchini don't need to be the same size, though it's best to use zucchini between 7 to 12 ounces each. If using a gas broiler, adjust the oven rack to 4 inches from the broiler element and use tongs to rearrange the zucchini pieces halfway through cooking instead of rotating the pan in step 2.

KITCHEN IMPROV

Sprinkle the zucchini with chopped toasted nuts, chopped scallions, and lots of fresh herbs. Drizzle with tahini or dollop with ricotta or Greek yogurt.

---

fastest-ever baked potatoes

Serves 4 • Total Time: 35 minutes

- **4 russet potatoes (8 ounces each), unpeeled**

1 Adjust oven rack to middle position and heat oven to 450 degrees. Poke each potato several times with fork. Microwave potatoes, uncovered, until slightly soft to the touch, 6 to 12 minutes, flipping over halfway through.

2 Place microwaved potatoes directly on oven rack and bake until skewer glides easily through flesh, about 20 minutes. Pierce top of each potato with fork several times to create dotted X. Press in at ends of potato to push flesh up and out and serve.

MICROWAVING POTATOES gives them a head start that cuts way down on baking time. Finishing them in the oven for just 20 minutes yields a fluffy interior ready for any fixings you like.

NOTES

Scrub and dry the potatoes thoroughly before poking them with a fork.

KITCHEN IMPROV

Substitute sweet potatoes for russets; start checking for doneness 5 minutes early. Top either variety with your choice of sour cream, scallions or chives, shredded cheese, crisp bacon, chopped hard-cooked eggs, or flaked smoked fish.

tilapia WITH harissa beurre monté AND bulgur salad

Serves 4 • Total Time: 45 minutes

- **1 cup medium-grind bulgur**
- **1½ cups boiling water plus 3 tablespoons tap water**
- **2 tablespoons currants**
- **1½ teaspoons table salt, divided**
- **8 tablespoons unsalted butter, cut into 8 pieces, chilled**
- **2 tablespoons harissa**
- **2 teaspoons lemon juice**
- **¼ teaspoon sugar**
- **4 (5- to 6-ounce) skinless tilapia fillets**
- **2 tablespoons vegetable oil**
- **¼ cup chopped fresh mint**
- **¼ cup chopped toasted pistachios**
- **2 tablespoons finely chopped pitted brine-cured green olives**
- **1 tablespoon finely chopped preserved lemon**
- **1 tablespoon minced fresh chives**

1. Combine bulgur, boiling water, currants, and 1 teaspoon salt in large bowl. Cover and let sit until water has been absorbed, about 25 minutes.

2. Meanwhile, bring 3 tablespoons water to simmer in small saucepan over medium-high heat; reduce heat to maintain very gentle simmer. Add 1 piece butter and cook, whisking constantly, until melted, 20 to 30 seconds. Continue to cook, whisking in butter 1 piece at a time, until all butter is incorporated and sauce has consistency of thin gravy, about 4 minutes. Whisk in harissa, lemon juice, and sugar. Season with salt to taste. Reduce heat to lowest possible setting and cover to keep warm until ready to serve.

3. Cut each tilapia fillet along seam running down middle to create 1 thick half and 1 thin half. Pat fillets dry with paper towels and sprinkle with remaining ½ teaspoon salt. Heat oil in 12-inch nonstick skillet over high heat until just smoking. Add thick fillets to skillet and cook until golden brown and tilapia registers 135 degrees, 2 to 3 minutes per side. Using 2 spatulas, transfer fillets to serving platter. Add thin fillets to now-empty skillet and cook until golden brown, about 1 minute per side; transfer to serving platter.

4. Add mint, pistachios, olives, and preserved lemon to bulgur and fluff with fork to combine. Whisk sauce vigorously to blend in any butterfat that has collected on surface. Serve tilapia with bulgur salad and sauce, sprinkling individual portions with chives.

BUTTER AND WATER is simmered and emulsified into an impressive French sauce that can be seasoned in myriad ways to enhance anything it touches. Spoon it liberally over browned fish fillets and a warm grain salad for easy weeknight elegance.

NOTES

Beurre monté can be covered and kept warm on your stove's lowest setting for up to 4 hours. It will break if simmered for an extended period of time, and it cannot be cooled and reheated.

KITCHEN IMPROV

This luscious meal would also be good with scallops, cod, or salmon. Use 1 teaspoon grated lemon zest if you don't have preserved lemon. Cilantro or parsley works in place of the mint or chives. You can swap almonds for pistachios. Beyond this, try other flavorful beurres montés: In place of harissa and lemon juice, add 1 tablespoon oyster sauce, ½ teaspoon orange zest, and 2 teaspoons orange juice for a savory orange version, or 1 tablespoon gochujang and 2 teaspoons lime juice for a gochujang version.

flounder WITH herbed asparagus rice AND salsa verde

Serves 4 • Total Time: 45 minutes

- **1 cup long-grain white rice, rinsed**
- **½ cup extra-virgin olive oil, divided**
- **3 garlic cloves, minced, divided**
- **1½ teaspoons table salt, divided**
- **1½ cups water**
- **1 cup minced fresh parsley**
- **2 tablespoons capers, minced**
- **1 tablespoon white wine vinegar**
- **1 pound asparagus, trimmed and sliced ¼ inch thick**
- **4 (5- to 6-ounce) skinless flounder fillets**

GARLIC-SCENTED asparagus rice shares equal billing with flounder in this springtime classic. The zesty green sauce is both stirred into the rice and spooned over the lightly browned fish, making both elements sparkle.

1 Cook rice, 1 tablespoon oil, two-thirds of garlic, and ½ teaspoon salt in large saucepan over medium-high heat, stirring frequently, until garlic is toasted and edges of rice are translucent, about 3 minutes. Stir in water and bring to boil. Cover, reduce heat to low, and cook until liquid is absorbed, about 20 minutes. Off heat, let rice rest, covered, for 10 minutes.

2 Meanwhile, combine remaining garlic, parsley, capers, vinegar, 5 tablespoons oil, and ¼ teaspoon salt in bowl; set aside.

3 Heat 1 tablespoon oil in 12-inch nonstick skillet over medium heat until shimmering. Add asparagus and ¼ teaspoon salt and cook until crisp-tender, about 3 minutes; transfer to plate.

4 Pat flounder dry with paper towels and sprinkle with remaining ½ teaspoon salt. Heat 1½ teaspoons oil in now-empty skillet over medium-high heat until just smoking. Place 2 fillets in skillet and cook until golden brown, about 2 minutes per side; transfer to serving platter. Repeat with remaining 1½ teaspoons oil and flounder; transfer to platter. Add asparagus and 2 tablespoons sauce to rice and fluff with fork to combine. Serve flounder with rice, passing remaining sauce separately.

NOTES

Try to purchase flounder fillets that are of similar size, and avoid those that weigh less than 5 ounces because they will cook too quickly.

KITCHEN IMPROV

Try sole instead of flounder. Use an equal weight of zucchini, quartered lengthwise and sliced ¼ inch thick, in place of asparagus. Change up the salsa verde by swapping in up to ½ cup of other leafy herbs for the parsley. Incorporate intensely flavored ingredients such as red pepper flakes, chopped olives, sun-dried tomatoes, or anchovies in addition to or in place of the capers.

THE BROILER is your shortcut to simultaneously produce perfectly cooked fish and char cherry tomatoes that dress up garlicky butter beans. You might want to double the pesto because it's seriously delicious on all kinds of vegetables, fish, and meat.

black cod WITH charred tomatoes, stewy beans AND tarragon-pistachio pesto

Serves 4 • Total Time: 45 minutes

- **1/3 cup plus 2 tablespoons extra-virgin olive oil, divided**
- **1/4 cup minced fresh parsley**
- **2 tablespoons minced fresh tarragon**
- **2 tablespoons finely chopped pistachios**
- **2 teaspoons lemon juice**
- **1/4 teaspoon minced garlic, plus 4 cloves, sliced thin**
- **Pinch table salt plus 1 teaspoon, divided**
- **Vegetable oil spray**
- **2 (15-ounce) cans butter beans, undrained**
- **4 (6- to 8-ounce) skin-on black cod fillets, 3/4 to 1 inch thick**
- **1 tablespoon honey, warmed**
- **1 pound cherry tomatoes on the vine**

1 Combine 1/3 cup oil, parsley, tarragon, pistachios, lemon juice, minced garlic, and pinch salt in bowl; set pesto aside.

2 Adjust oven rack 8 inches from broiler element and heat broiler. Line rimmed baking sheet with aluminum foil and spray with oil spray. Heat remaining 2 tablespoons oil and sliced garlic in medium saucepan over medium heat until garlic is fragrant and pale golden brown, 3 to 5 minutes. Stir in beans and their canning liquid and 1/4 teaspoon salt. Bring to brief simmer, then remove from heat and cover to keep warm.

3 Pat cod dry with paper towels and arrange skin side down on half of prepared sheet. Sprinkle with 1/2 teaspoon salt and brush with honey. Place tomatoes on empty side of prepared sheet, spray with oil spray, and sprinkle with remaining 1/4 teaspoon salt. Broil until tomatoes are shriveled and cod is spotty brown and registers 130 to 135 degrees, 7 to 12 minutes, rotating sheet halfway through broiling and shielding fillets or tomatoes with foil if they begin to get too dark. Serve cod with beans and tomatoes, drizzling individual portions with pesto.

NOTES

Black cod (which may be labeled as sablefish) often contains a row of small pin bones; they are difficult to remove from the raw fillets but can be easily removed once the fillets are cooked. To warm the honey and make it easier to brush onto the cod, gently heat in the microwave for a few seconds. Pesto can be refrigerated for up to 24 hours; bring to room temperature before using.

KITCHEN IMPROV

Salmon can be substituted for the black cod; reduce broiling time by about 2 minutes and cook until the fish registers 125 degrees (for farmed) or 120 degrees (for wild). Cherry tomatoes on the vine add an impressive-looking touch to the plated dish, but loose tomatoes work just as well. Feel free to substitute other canned beans, such as cannellini or pinto, for the butter beans.

seared tilapia WITH olive vinaigrette AND warm chickpea salad

Serves 4 • Total Time: 30 minutes

- 1 red bell pepper, stemmed, seeded, and chopped fine
- 1 small red onion, chopped fine
- 2 tablespoons red wine vinegar, divided
- 1 teaspoon table salt, divided
- 3/4 teaspoon pepper, divided
- 2 (15-ounce) cans chickpeas, rinsed
- 1/2 cup extra-virgin olive oil, divided
- 4 (5- to 6-ounce) skinless tilapia fillets
- 1 tablespoon chopped fresh oregano
- 1 cup pitted Castelvetrano olives, chopped coarse

A VIBRANT VINAIGRETTE made with meaty Castelvetrano olives jazzes up blank-canvas tilapia that's been sautéed to golden brown perfection. A chickpea and bell pepper salad makes a hearty pairing for a one-skillet dinner.

1. Combine bell pepper, onion, 1 tablespoon vinegar, 1/4 teaspoon salt, and 1/2 teaspoon pepper in large bowl. Cook chickpeas and 1/4 cup oil in 12-inch nonstick skillet over medium heat until heated through, about 3 minutes, coarsely mashing about one-quarter of chickpeas with back of spatula. Stir chickpea mixture into vegetable mixture. Season with salt and pepper to taste; set salad aside.

2. Wipe skillet clean with paper towels. Cut each tilapia fillet along seam running down middle to create 1 thick half and 1 thin half. Pat fillets dry with paper towels and sprinkle with 1/2 teaspoon salt. Heat 2 tablespoons oil in now-empty skillet over high heat until just smoking. Add thick fillets to skillet and cook until golden brown and tilapia registers 135 degrees, 2 to 3 minutes per side. Using 2 spatulas, transfer fillets to serving platter. Add thin fillets to now-empty skillet and cook until golden brown, about 1 minute per side; transfer to serving platter.

3. Whisk oregano, remaining 2 tablespoons oil, remaining 1 tablespoon vinegar, remaining 1/4 teaspoon salt, and remaining 1/4 teaspoon pepper together in bowl, then stir in olives. Serve tilapia with chickpea salad, passing olive topping separately.

NOTES

There's no need to take the temperature of the thin halves of the fillets; they will be cooked through by the time they are golden brown.

KITCHEN IMPROV

Try other fresh herbs, such as parsley or mint, in place of the oregano. Mild, buttery Castelvetrano olives are really good here. If you go with a more robustly flavored olive, use just 1/2 cup. Consider adding some crunch to the olive topping by including 1/4 cup chopped toasted nuts or toasted seeds.

DEEP CARAMELIZATION and browning come from simply broiling orange slices and swordfish together—no flipping, no splatter, just rich flavor. Tossing a salad while the fish and orange broil means the whole dish comes together fast, with bold contrast from the smoky citrus, crisp greens, and punchy vinaigrette.

swordfish WITH charred orange AND radicchio salad

Serves 4 • Total Time: 30 minutes

- 4 oranges
- 4 (6- to 8-ounce) skinless swordfish steaks, 1 to 1½ inches thick
- 5 tablespoons extra-virgin olive oil, divided
- ¾ teaspoon table salt, divided
- ¼ teaspoon pepper
- 2 scallions, white parts minced, green parts cut into 1-inch pieces
- 1½ tablespoons white wine vinegar
- 1 tablespoon honey
- 1 tablespoon Dijon mustard
- 2 small heads radicchio (6 ounces each), halved, cored, and cut into 2-inch pieces
- 1 fennel bulb, stalks discarded, bulbs halved, cored, and sliced thin

1 Adjust oven rack 4 inches from broiler element and heat broiler. Line rimmed baking sheet with aluminum foil and lightly spray with oil spray. Zest 1 orange to yield 2 teaspoons zest and set aside. Cut away peel and pith from all oranges, then slice crosswise into ¾-inch-thick rounds. Place orange slices on half of prepared sheet.

2 Pat swordfish dry with paper towels, brush with 1 tablespoon oil, and sprinkle with ½ teaspoon salt and pepper. Arrange swordfish on other half of sheet. Broil until oranges are charred and swordfish flakes apart when gently prodded with paring knife and registers 130 to 135 degrees, about 8 minutes; remove oranges from oven if they begin to get too dark.

3 Meanwhile, whisk reserved orange zest, scallion whites, vinegar, honey, mustard, and remaining ¼ teaspoon salt together in large bowl. Whisking constantly, slowly drizzle in remaining ¼ cup oil until emulsified. Add radicchio, fennel, and scallion greens and toss to combine. Season with salt and pepper to taste. Arrange salad on serving platter and top with oranges. Serve swordfish with salad.

NOTES

Look for swordfish steaks with as minimal a bloodline as possible. (The bloodline is the swordfish's dark, myoglobin-rich muscle, which can have an unpleasant mineral taste.) And ditch the skin: Rubbery swordfish skin tightens up more than the flesh during cooking and can cause the meat to buckle. It's easy to trim off with a sharp knife.

KITCHEN IMPROV

Add toasted pistachios, hazelnuts, or almonds to the salad for extra crunch. You can substitute mahi-mahi or halibut for the swordfish. Any variety of orange will work in this recipe. You can also substitute 2 grapefruit, quartering the rounds before arranging them on the salad.

lemony halibut WITH roasted fingerling potatoes

Serves 4 • Total Time: 45 minutes

- **1½ pounds fingerling potatoes, unpeeled, halved lengthwise**
- **2 tablespoons extra-virgin olive oil, divided**
- **1 teaspoon table salt, divided**
- **¾ teaspoon pepper, divided**
- **8 ounces grape tomatoes, halved**
- **4 (6- to 8-ounce) skinless halibut fillets, 1 to 1½ inches thick**
- **½ teaspoon dried oregano or thyme**
- **8 thin slices lemon**
- **2 tablespoons minced fresh parsley**

1 Adjust oven rack to lower-middle position and heat oven to 450 degrees. Toss potatoes with 2 teaspoons oil, ½ teaspoon salt, and ½ teaspoon pepper. Arrange potatoes cut side down on rimmed baking sheet in even layer. Roast until cut sides begin to brown, about 10 minutes.

2 Meanwhile, lay four 16-by-12-inch rectangles of aluminum foil on counter with short sides parallel to counter edge. Divide tomatoes evenly among foil rectangles, arranging in center of lower half of each sheet of foil, then place 1 fillet on each tomato pile. Sprinkle halibut with oregano, remaining ½ teaspoon salt, and remaining ¼ teaspoon pepper, then top each with 2 lemon slices and 1 teaspoon oil. Fold top half of foil over halibut and tomatoes, then tightly crimp edges into rough 9-by-6-inch packets.

3 Place packets on top of potatoes on sheet and bake until fish registers 130 to 135 degrees, about 15 minutes. Carefully open packets, allowing steam to escape away from you. Divide potatoes among 4 individual serving plates. Using thin metal spatula, gently slide halibut and tomatoes onto plates, then pour accumulated juices over top. Sprinkle with parsley and serve.

NOTES

Try to find fingerlings that are similar in size and no thicker than 1 inch. To test for doneness without opening the packets, use a marker to mark an "X" on the outside of the foil where the fillet is the thickest, then insert an instant-read thermometer through the "X" into the fish to measure its temperature. Assemble and refrigerate the packets up to 24 hours in advance.

KITCHEN IMPROV

You can use Yukon Gold potatoes, cut into ¾-inch pieces, instead of fingerlings. You can also substitute mahi-mahi or swordfish for the halibut. If you want, add a flavor boost to the packets by topping each portion of fish with up to 1 tablespoon of a prepared sauce or paste such as olive tapenade, zhoug, harissa, or chili crisp.

SHEET-PAN DINNERS are wonderfully efficient. Here, fingerling potatoes turn creamy and golden on a baking sheet while foil packets of fish and tomatoes steam right on top. The fish stays deliciously moist and creates a lemony broth to pour over everything.

one-pan cod AND green rice

Serves 4 • Total Time: 45 minutes

- **1 cup fresh cilantro leaves and tender stems**
- **1 ounce (1 cup) baby spinach**
- **1 jalapeño chile, stemmed, seeded, and chopped**
- **1 cup water**
- **½ cup mayonnaise**
- **2 teaspoons lime juice, plus lime wedges for serving**
- **2 teaspoons table salt, divided**
- **4 (6- to 8-ounce) skinless cod fillets, 1 to 1½ inches thick**
- **1 teaspoon chili powder**
- **2 tablespoons vegetable oil, divided**
- **1½ cups long-grain white rice, rinsed**
- **2 scallions, white and green parts separated and sliced thin**
- **2 garlic cloves, minced**
- **2 poblano chiles, stemmed, seeded, and chopped**
- **1½ cups chicken or vegetable broth**

BRILLIANT GREEN rice, flaky cod, and a zesty, herby sauce make this one-skillet supper dressy enough for company but simple enough for any night. Browning the presentation side of the fish elevates the dish in 2 minutes. And the trick to perfect fish and rice in one skillet? Staggered cooking.

1 Process cilantro, spinach, jalapeño, and water in blender until smooth, about 2 minutes, scraping down sides of blender jar as needed. Transfer 1 tablespoon cilantro mixture to small bowl and whisk in mayonnaise, lime juice, and ¼ teaspoon salt; set sauce aside. Reserve remaining cilantro mixture.

2 Pat cod dry with paper towels and sprinkle with chili powder and 1 teaspoon salt. Heat 1 tablespoon oil in 12-inch nonstick skillet over medium-high heat until just smoking. Place cod in skillet and cook until well browned on first side, about 2 minutes. Using 2 spatulas, carefully transfer cod to plate, browned side up.

3 Heat remaining 1 tablespoon oil in now-empty skillet over medium-high heat until shimmering. Stir in rice, scallion whites, and garlic and cook, stirring often, until edges of rice are translucent, about 2 minutes. Stir in poblanos, broth, reserved cilantro mixture, and remaining ¾ teaspoon salt and bring to boil. Cover, reduce heat to medium-low, and simmer for 10 minutes.

4 Carefully place cod browned side up on top of rice mixture. Cover skillet and cook until remaining liquid has been absorbed and cod flakes apart when gently prodded with paring knife and registers 135 degrees, 8 to 10 minutes. Off heat, drizzle cod with sauce and sprinkle with scallion greens. Serve cod and rice with lime wedges.

NOTES

For a spicier dish, add the jalapeño seeds to the rice.

KITCHEN IMPROV

Haddock, black sea bass, and hake all work in place of cod. The green sauce is cilantro-forward; if you prefer, use an equal amount of parsley leaves (but not stems, which can be bitter). To level up this dish, sprinkle with toasted slivered almonds.

poached halibut WITH pearl couscous AND spicy tomato zhoug

Serves 4 • Total Time: 35 minutes

- **½ cup plus 1 tablespoon extra-virgin olive oil, divided**
- **8 ounces cherry tomatoes, halved**
- **½ cup minced fresh cilantro**
- **6 garlic cloves (3 minced, 3 smashed and peeled)**
- **2 serrano chiles, stemmed, seeded, and chopped fine**
- **1½ teaspoons grated lemon zest plus 2 teaspoons juice**
- **½ teaspoon ground coriander**
- **½ teaspoon ground cumin**
- **1¼ teaspoons table salt, divided**
- **1½ cups pearl couscous**
- **2¾ cups chicken broth or water, divided**
- **¼ cup pistachios, toasted and chopped**
- **4 (6- to 8-ounce) skinless halibut fillets, 1 to 1½ inches thick**

ZHOUG, A SPICY, herbaceous Middle Eastern sauce, is tempered with juicy tomatoes to supercharge gently poached halibut. The bright herb sauce mingles beautifully with the fish and a side of pearl couscous studded with pistachios to create a dinner with satisfying textural appeal.

1 Combine ½ cup oil, tomatoes, cilantro, minced garlic, serranos, lemon juice, coriander, cumin, and ½ teaspoon salt in bowl. Season with salt to taste; set zhoug aside.

2 Cook couscous and remaining 1 tablespoon oil in large saucepan over medium heat, stirring frequently, until about half of grains are golden brown, about 6 minutes. Stir in 1¾ cups broth, ¼ teaspoon salt, and lemon zest and bring to boil. Reduce heat to medium-low, cover, and simmer, stirring occasionally, until broth has been absorbed, 9 to 12 minutes. Off heat, let couscous rest, covered, for 3 minutes. Add pistachios and fluff with fork to combine.

3 Meanwhile, bring remaining 1 cup broth and smashed garlic to simmer in 12-inch skillet over medium heat. Sprinkle halibut with remaining ½ teaspoon salt and place skinned side down in skillet. Cover and cook, adjusting heat to maintain gentle simmer, until halibut flakes apart when gently prodded with paring knife and registers 130 to 135 degrees, 10 to 15 minutes.

4 Using 2 spatulas, transfer halibut to serving platter and spoon zhoug over top. Serve with couscous.

NOTES

For a spicier version of the zhoug, include the serrano seeds. You can make the sauce up to 2 hours ahead.

KITCHEN IMPROV

You can substitute jalapeños for the serranos and almonds for the pistachios. Swordfish or mahi-mahi will work in place of halibut. If you have preserved lemon on hand, add 1 tablespoon, finely chopped, to the couscous in place of the lemon zest. For a sweet note, add 2 tablespoons chopped dried apricots, golden raisins, or figs to the couscous.

moroccan fish tagine

Serves 4 • Total Time: 35 minutes

- **1½ pounds skinless cod fillets, 1 to 1½ inches thick, cut into 2-inch pieces**
- **¾ teaspoon table salt, divided**
- **½ cup fresh whole cilantro leaves, plus ¼ cup chopped**
- **4 garlic cloves, peeled**
- **1¼ teaspoons ground cumin**
- **1¼ teaspoons paprika**
- **¼ teaspoon cayenne pepper**
- **1½ tablespoons lemon juice**
- **6 tablespoons extra-virgin olive oil, divided**
- **1 onion, halved and sliced ¼ inch thick**
- **1 green bell pepper, stemmed, seeded, and cut into ¼-inch-wide strips**
- **1 carrot, peeled and sliced ¼ inch thick on bias**
- **1 (14.5-ounce) can diced tomatoes**
- **⅓ cup pitted brine-cured green olives, quartered lengthwise**
- **2 tablespoons finely chopped preserved lemon**

HAPPINESS IS a saucy pot of fish—and there's nothing shy about this vibrant, punchy dish. Versatile cod is coated with an herb-spice paste before braising in a mix of vegetables, green olives, and preserved lemon. Serve with couscous to soak up the sauce and mellow the bold flavors.

1. Toss cod with ½ teaspoon salt in bowl; set aside. Pulse cilantro leaves, garlic, cumin, paprika, and cayenne in food processor until cilantro and garlic are finely chopped, about 12 pulses. Add lemon juice and pulse briefly to combine. Transfer mixture to small bowl and stir in 2 tablespoons oil; set aside.

2. Heat remaining ¼ cup oil in Dutch oven over medium heat until shimmering. Add onion, bell pepper, carrot, and remaining ¼ teaspoon salt and cook until softened, 5 to 7 minutes. Stir in tomatoes and their juice, olives, and preserved lemon. Spread mixture in even layer on bottom of pot.

3. Toss cod with cilantro mixture until evenly coated, then arrange over vegetables in single layer. Cover pot and cook until cod starts to turn opaque and juices released from cod are simmering vigorously, 3 to 5 minutes. Remove pot from heat and let sit, covered, until cod is opaque and just cooked through (cod should register 135 degrees), 3 to 5 minutes. Sprinkle with chopped cilantro and serve.

NOTES

Picholine or Cerignola olives are nice options here. Instead of couscous, serve with quinoa or crusty bread.

KITCHEN IMPROV

You can substitute haddock, black sea bass, or hake for the cod. If you don't have preserved lemon, you can use 2 teaspoons grated lemon zest instead.

chraime

Serves 4 • Total Time: 45 minutes

- **3 tablespoons extra-virgin olive oil, plus extra for drizzling**
- **1 onion, chopped fine**
- **1 red bell pepper, stemmed, seeded, and chopped**
- **1 jalapeño chile, stemmed, seeded, and minced**
- **3/4 teaspoon table salt**
- **1/4 cup tomato paste**
- **6 garlic cloves, minced**
- **1 tablespoon ground dried Aleppo pepper**
- **2 teaspoons paprika**
- **1½ teaspoons ground coriander**
- **1 teaspoon ground caraway**
- **½ teaspoon ground cumin**
- **¼ teaspoon pepper**
- **1½ cups water**
- **1½ pounds skinless haddock fillets, ½ to ¾ inch thick, cut into 3-inch pieces**
- **10 ounces cherry tomatoes**
- **½ cup chopped fresh cilantro**
- **Lemon wedges**

WHITE FISH fillets braised in a cherry tomato sauce heady with North African spices traces back to Jewish cooks in Libya and Morocco. Often eaten on Friday night Shabbat and at holidays, this elegant dinner is easy enough to enjoy any night.

1 Heat oil in 12-inch skillet over medium heat until shimmering. Add onion, bell pepper, jalapeño, and salt and cook until vegetables are softened, 5 to 7 minutes. Stir in tomato paste, garlic, Aleppo pepper, paprika, coriander, caraway, cumin, and pepper and cook until fragrant, about 30 seconds. Stir in water, scraping up any browned bits, and bring to simmer. Reduce heat to low, cover, and cook until flavors meld, about 10 minutes.

2 Nestle haddock into sauce and spoon some sauce over fish. Sprinkle tomatoes around fish and return to simmer. Reduce heat to low, cover, and cook until fish flakes apart when gently prodded with paring knife and registers 135 degrees, 5 to 7 minutes. Season with salt and pepper to taste. Sprinkle with cilantro, drizzle with extra oil, and serve with lemon wedges.

NOTES

Thin tail-end fillets can be folded to achieve the proper thickness. This dish is typically spicy; for a milder version, reduce the Aleppo pepper to 1 or 2 teaspoons. If you don't have Aleppo, use 1 tablespoon ancho chile powder and a pinch of cayenne.

KITCHEN IMPROV

You can substitute cod, black sea bass, or hake for the haddock. You can use ground fennel instead of the caraway. Serve with challah or couscous.

seared tuna steaks WITH wilted frisée AND mushroom salad

Serves 4 • Total Time: 45 minutes

- **3 tablespoons harissa, divided**
- **1 tablespoon lemon juice plus lemon wedges for serving**
- **6 tablespoons extra-virgin olive oil, divided**
- **1–3 tablespoons hot water (110 degrees)**
- **1 shallot, halved and sliced thin**
- **1¼ pounds cremini mushrooms, trimmed and halved if small or quartered if large**
- **12 ounces shiitake mushrooms, stemmed and sliced ½ inch thick**
- **1 teaspoon table salt, divided**
- **1 head frisée (6 ounces), cut into 1-inch pieces**
- **2 teaspoons sugar**
- **¼ teaspoon pepper**
- **4 (6- to 8-ounce) tuna steaks, 1 to 1½ inches thick**
- **2 tablespoons chopped fresh mint**

1. Whisk 2 tablespoons harissa, lemon juice, and 1 tablespoon oil together in bowl. Whisk in hot water, 1 tablespoon at a time, until sauce is pourable; set harissa sauce aside.

2. Heat 2 tablespoons oil in 12-inch nonstick skillet over medium heat until shimmering. Add shallot and cook until softened, about 2 minutes. Add cremini mushrooms, shiitake mushrooms, and ½ teaspoon salt. Cover and cook, stirring occasionally, until mushrooms have released their liquid, 8 to 10 minutes.

3. Uncover skillet, add 2 tablespoons oil, and cook, stirring occasionally, until mushrooms are deep golden brown and tender, 10 to 12 minutes. Add remaining 1 tablespoon harissa and cook until fragrant, about 30 seconds. Transfer mushrooms to large bowl, add frisée, and toss to combine; set aside. Wipe skillet clean with paper towels.

4. Combine sugar, pepper, and remaining ½ teaspoon salt in separate bowl. Pat tuna dry with paper towels and sprinkle with sugar mixture. Heat remaining 1 tablespoon oil in now-empty skillet over medium-high heat until just smoking. Cook steaks, flipping every 1 to 2 minutes, until centers are translucent red when checked with tip of paring knife and steaks register 110 degrees (for rare), or until steaks are opaque at perimeter and reddish-pink at center and register 125 degrees (for medium-rare), 2 to 5 minutes.

5. Transfer steaks to cutting board and slice ½ inch thick. Sprinkle mint over mushroom-frisée salad and season with salt and pepper to taste. Drizzle tuna with reserved harissa sauce and serve with salad and lemon wedges.

MODERN BISTRO vibes define this casually sophisticated dinner. Layers of flavor are created by pairing harissa-sauced seared tuna with a salad of golden sautéed mushrooms and delicate frisée. Pro tip: Adding the hot mushrooms (seasoned with more harissa) to the greens wilts them gently.

NOTES

Harissa is available in both mild and spicy versions; use whichever you prefer. If you want your tuna cooked medium, cook the steaks to 125 degrees, then tent with aluminum foil for 5 minutes.

KITCHEN IMPROV

Try another mildly bitter green, such as escarole or chicory, in place of the frisée. Feel free to swap in other herbs, such as dill, parsley, or tarragon, for the mint.

EASY UPGRADES elevate this pantry-friendly meal: Choose rich, oil-packed tuna. Warm the beans so they absorb more flavor. Mix a quick aioli to top toasted baguette. And cut up a watermelon radish for dazzling color.

NOTES

While any oil-packed tuna will work (don't substitute water-packed), this is a great time to use a jar of oil-packed tuna fillets that flake into large, silky-textured pieces. Two 6½-ounce jars of tuna yield about 8 ounces when drained. A rasp-style grater makes quick work of turning the garlic into a paste.

KITCHEN IMPROV

Substitute another type of tinned fish; try smoked mackerel fillets, smoked salmon, or smoked trout. Watermelon radish brings striking color, but you can substitute 6 ounces of another type of radish.

warm white beans WITH tuna, fennel AND herbs

Serves 4 • Total Time: 45 minutes

- **1 shallot, sliced thin**
- **2 teaspoons grated lemon zest, divided, plus 3 tablespoons juice, divided**
- **¼ cup mayonnaise**
- **¼ teaspoon garlic minced to paste**
- **3 tablespoons extra-virgin olive oil, divided, plus extra for drizzling**
- **¼ teaspoon red pepper flakes**
- **2 (15-ounce) cans cannellini beans, 2 tablespoons canning liquid reserved, beans rinsed**
- **¼ teaspoon plus ⅛ teaspoon table salt, divided**
- **¼ teaspoon pepper, divided**
- **2 tablespoons capers, rinsed**
- **1 (8-inch) piece baguette, cut on bias into 8 slices**
- **¼ teaspoon Dijon mustard**
- **½ fennel bulb, stalks discarded, bulb cored and sliced thin**
- **1 watermelon radish, trimmed, halved, and sliced thin (1½ cups)**
- **½ cup chopped fresh dill and/or parsley**
- **2 (6½-ounce) jars olive oil–packed tuna, drained and broken into 1½-inch pieces**

1. Combine shallot and 2 tablespoons lemon juice in small bowl; set aside, tossing shallot occasionally. Whisk mayonnaise, garlic, and ½ teaspoon lemon zest and 1 teaspoon lemon juice together in small bowl. Season with salt and pepper to taste; set garlic mayonnaise aside.

2. Heat 2 tablespoons oil in medium saucepan over medium heat until shimmering. Add pepper flakes and remaining 1½ teaspoons lemon zest and cook until fragrant, about 30 seconds. Add beans, reserved bean liquid, ¼ teaspoon salt, and ⅛ teaspoon pepper and cook until warmed through, about 3 minutes, stirring occasionally. Off heat, stir in capers and remaining 2 teaspoons lemon juice; let sit until flavors meld, about 15 minutes.

3. Meanwhile, adjust oven rack 4 inches from broiler element and heat broiler. Place bread on rimmed baking sheet and broil until golden, 1 to 2 minutes per side. Let cool slightly, then spread garlic mayonnaise over slices.

4. Drain reserved shallots in fine-mesh strainer, reserving lemon juice. In medium bowl, whisk to combine 2 teaspoons strained lemon juice (discard the rest), mustard, remaining 1 tablespoon oil, remaining ⅛ teaspoon salt, and remaining ⅛ teaspoon pepper. Add drained shallot, fennel, radish, and dill and toss to combine. Arrange beans on serving platter, top with fennel mixture and tuna, and drizzle with extra oil. Serve with toasted bread.

tuna-quinoa bowl WITH tahini

Serves 4 • Total Time: 35 minutes

- **1 cup white quinoa**
- **1 teaspoon table salt, divided, plus salt for cooking quinoa**
- **1/3 cup tahini**
- **5 tablespoons lemon juice (2 lemons), divided**
- **1 1/2 teaspoons garlic powder**
- **2 (6 1/2-ounce) jars olive oil–packed tuna, drained, with 2 tablespoons oil reserved**
- **1/4 cup shelled pistachios, chopped fine, divided**
- **1/4 cup minced fresh parsley, divided**
- **1 English cucumber, quartered lengthwise and sliced 1/2 inch thick**
- **10 ounces cherry tomatoes, halved**

SMOOTH, NUTTY tahini makes a rich-tasting dressing base for both the tuna and quinoa in this novel bowl. And nothing could be more refreshing than the cucumber-tomato salad that garnishes the dish.

1 Bring 2 quarts water to boil in large saucepan over medium-high heat. Add quinoa and 1 1/2 teaspoons salt, return to boil, and cook until quinoa is tender, 10 to 12 minutes. Drain quinoa, return to now-empty saucepan, and cover to keep warm.

2 Meanwhile, stir 1/3 cup water, tahini, 3 tablespoons lemon juice, garlic powder, and 1/2 teaspoon salt together in 1-cup liquid measuring cup.

3 Combine tuna and reserved oil in medium bowl and flake tuna with fork. Add 1/2 cup dressing, 2 tablespoons pistachios, and 2 tablespoons parsley and stir until well combined; set aside. Combine cucumber, tomatoes, remaining 2 tablespoons parsley, remaining 2 tablespoons lemon juice, and remaining 1/2 teaspoon salt in second medium bowl.

4 Spoon quinoa into 4 shallows bowls. Drizzle with remaining dressing. Spoon tuna into center of quinoa. Scatter cucumber-tomato salad around tuna. Divide remaining pistachios evenly among bowls, sprinkling around edges. Serve.

NOTES

This recipe uses oil-packed tuna; do not substitute water-packed tuna. Look for two 6 1/2-ounce jars of tuna, which yield about 8 ounces tuna when drained.

KITCHEN IMPROV

Substitute another type of tinned fish, such as smoked mackerel fillets, smoked salmon, or smoked trout. If the fish is not packed in oil, substitute 2 tablespoons extra-virgin olive oil in step 3. You can switch up the nuts and fresh herbs; try almonds or walnuts and cilantro or basil. Add olives to the cucumber-tomato salad. For extra protein, add wedges of hard-cooked egg to each bowl.

kedgeree

Serves 4 • Total Time: 35 minutes

- **4 large eggs**
- **4 tablespoons unsalted butter**
- **1 large onion, chopped**
- **4 teaspoons curry powder**
- **1½ teaspoons table salt, divided**
- **6 cups cooked basmati rice, room temperature**
- **2 (4- to 5-ounce) tins oil-packed smoked trout, drained and flaked into 1-inch pieces**
- **1 cup frozen peas, thawed**
- **½ cup chopped fresh parsley**
- **1 teaspoon grated lemon zest plus 3 tablespoons juice, plus lemon wedges for serving**
- **1 jalapeño chile, stemmed and sliced thin (optional)**

TRANSFORM LEFTOVER rice into a sophisticated Anglo-Indian comfort food through the magic of curry powder, smoked fish, and fudgy soft-cooked eggs. Though traditionally a breakfast dish, this pantry-friendly favorite makes an even more satisfying "brinner"—that is, breakfast for dinner.

1 Bring 1 inch water to rolling boil in medium saucepan over high heat. Using tongs, place eggs in water. Cover, reduce heat to medium (small wisps of steam should escape from beneath lid), and cook eggs for 8 minutes. Remove cover, transfer saucepan to sink, and place under cold running water for 1 minute. Let eggs sit in water.

2 Meanwhile, melt butter in 12-inch nonstick skillet over medium heat. Add onion, curry powder, and ½ teaspoon salt and cook until softened, 7 to 9 minutes. Add rice and remaining 1 teaspoon salt and increase heat to medium-high. Cook, stirring and pressing on rice with spatula to break up clumps, until rice mixture is well combined and heated through, about 5 minutes. Remove skillet from heat.

3 Peel and halve eggs. Add smoked trout, peas, parsley, and lemon zest and juice to rice and toss to combine. Season with salt and pepper to taste. Top with eggs and sliced jalapeño, if using. Serve with lemon wedges.

NOTES

Basmati rice boasts a delicate fragrance, but any long-grain white rice will work. This recipe works best with day-old rice; alternatively, cook the rice a couple hours ahead, spread it on a rimmed baking sheet, and let it cool completely before using.

KITCHEN IMPROV

A variety of tinned fish can work here. Try smoked mackerel fillets, smoked salmon, or good-quality oil-packed tuna.

seared scallops WITH polenta, bacon AND poblano chiles

Serves 4 • Total Time: 45 minutes

- **3 cups water**
- **¾ cup instant polenta**
- **2 tablespoons unsalted butter**
- **1 teaspoon table salt, divided**
- **¾ teaspoon pepper, divided**
- **4 ounces sharp cheddar cheese, shredded (1 cup)**
- **2 poblano chiles, stemmed, seeded, and chopped**
- **4 slices bacon, chopped fine**
- **4 scallions, white and green parts separated and sliced thin**
- **1 tablespoon Worcestershire sauce**
- **2 garlic cloves, minced**
- **1½ pounds large sea scallops, tendons removed**
- **2 tablespoons vegetable oil, divided**

1 Bring water to boil in large saucepan. Whisk in polenta, butter, ½ teaspoon salt, and ¼ teaspoon pepper and cook until thickened, about 2 minutes. Off heat, stir in cheese; cover to keep warm.

2 Cook poblanos, bacon, and ¼ teaspoon pepper in 12-inch nonstick skillet over medium-high heat until bacon is rendered and browned and poblanos are softened, about 8 minutes. Stir in scallion whites, Worcestershire, and garlic and cook until fragrant, about 30 seconds. Transfer to bowl and wipe skillet clean with paper towels.

3 Pat scallops dry with paper towels and sprinkle with remaining ½ teaspoon salt and remaining ¼ teaspoon pepper. Heat 1 tablespoon oil in now-empty skillet over high heat until just smoking. Add half of scallops, flat side down, and cook, without moving them, until well browned, about 1½ minutes. Flip and cook until browned on second sides, about 1½ minutes. Transfer to plate and tent with aluminum foil. Wipe skillet clean with paper towels; repeat with remaining 1 tablespoon oil and remaining scallops. Serve polenta topped with bacon mixture and scallops and sprinkled with scallion greens.

NOTES

You can use old-fashioned polenta, but you'll need to increase the simmering time by 25 minutes and cover the pan; you may also need to add more water. Look for "dry" scallops, which don't have chemical additives and taste better than "wet." For the best browning, don't move the scallops once you've added them to the skillet, except to flip them.

KITCHEN IMPROV

Use another semisoft cheese, such as smoked gouda or Monterey Jack. Other mild chiles, such as Anaheim or cubanelle, would work well here; you can also substitute 1 bell pepper.

DECISIVE HIGH-HEAT cooking is the secret to achieving a great sear on scallops. Adding flavors that accentuate their sweetness is the secret to turning the mollusks into a memorable dinner. Quick-cooking instant polenta frees up time to sauté a savory bacon-poblano topping.

shrimp WITH black bean sauce

Serves 4 • Total Time: 35 minutes

- **1 pound extra-large shrimp (21 to 25 per pound), peeled, deveined, and tails removed**
- **1 tablespoon soy sauce**
- **1 tablespoon Shaoxing wine**
- **3/4 cup chicken broth**
- **1 tablespoon oyster sauce**
- **1 tablespoon sugar**
- **2 teaspoons toasted sesame oil**
- **1½ teaspoons cornstarch**
- **2 tablespoons vegetable oil**
- **5 tablespoons fermented black beans (dau si), rinsed, drained, and chopped coarse**
- **2 scallions, white and green parts separated and sliced thin**
- **4 garlic cloves, minced**
- **1½ teaspoons minced fresh ginger**
- **1 red bell pepper, stemmed, seeded, and cut into 1/4-inch-wide strips**

BELOVED FOR their savory, nuanced funk, China's fermented black beans (dau si) are pantry friendly to boot. The beans infuse this quick weeknight stir-fry—inspired by classic Cantonese dishes—with complex, salty savor.

1 Toss shrimp with soy sauce and Shaoxing wine in bowl; let sit for 10 minutes. Meanwhile, whisk broth, oyster sauce, sugar, sesame oil, and cornstarch together in second bowl; set aside.

2 Heat vegetable oil in 14-inch flat-bottomed wok or 12-inch nonstick skillet over high heat until just smoking. Add fermented black beans, scallion whites, garlic, and ginger and cook, stirring constantly, until fragrant, about 30 seconds. Move bean mixture up side of wok and add bell pepper. Cook, stirring constantly, until pepper is warmed through, about 30 seconds.

3 Move pepper to sides of wok. Add shrimp in even layer (some overlapping is OK) and cook, without stirring, until undersides of shrimp turn pink, about 30 seconds. Stir to combine shrimp, bean mixture, and pepper and continue to cook, stirring occasionally, until shrimp are just shy of being cooked through, about 30 seconds.

4 Stir broth mixture to recombine, add to wok, and cook, stirring frequently, until shrimp are opaque throughout and sauce has thickened to consistency of heavy cream, about 1 minute. Off heat, stir in scallion greens. Serve.

NOTES

This dish is highly seasoned, so make sure to serve it with plain rice or another unseasoned grain or noodles. Find fermented black beans in Asian markets or online. Don't use jarred fermented black bean sauce, as brands can vary widely in flavor and saltiness. Have all the ingredients prepared so that you're equipped for fast cooking.

KITCHEN IMPROV

Replace the bell pepper with sliced asparagus or snow peas. Since the stir-fry will require your attention on the stovetop, you could consider pairing this with a simple oven-roasted vegetable such as cabbage wedges or broccoli.

seared shrimp WITH tomato, lime AND avocado

Serves 4 • Total Time: 30 minutes

- 1½ **pounds extra-large shrimp (21 to 25 per pound), peeled, deveined, and tails removed**
- ½ **teaspoon chipotle chile powder**
- ½ **teaspoon table salt, divided**
- ¼ **teaspoon pepper**
- 2 **tablespoons extra-virgin olive oil, divided, plus extra for drizzling**
- 1 **pound tomatoes, cored and cut into ½-inch pieces**
- 3 **scallions, white and green parts separated and sliced thin**
- ¼ **cup chopped fresh cilantro**
- 1 **tablespoon lime juice, plus lime wedges for serving**
- 3 **garlic cloves, minced**
- 1 **avocado, halved, pitted, and cut into ½-inch pieces**

SUMMER COOKING doesn't get any better than this ridiculously simple recipe that shows off the season's best ripe tomatoes. Smoky chipotle, creamy avocado, juicy tomatoes, and bright lime become a near-instant sauce for perfectly seared shrimp.

1 Pat shrimp dry with paper towels, then toss with chile powder, ¼ teaspoon salt, and pepper. Heat 1 tablespoon oil in 12-inch nonstick skillet over medium-high heat until just smoking. Add half of shrimp in single layer and cook, without stirring, until spotty brown and edges turn pink on bottom side, about 1 minute. Flip shrimp and continue to cook until all but very center is opaque, about 30 seconds. Transfer shrimp to large plate. Repeat with remaining 1 tablespoon oil and remaining shrimp.

2 Return now-empty skillet to medium-high heat. Add tomatoes, scallion whites, cilantro, lime juice, garlic, and remaining ¼ teaspoon salt. Cook until tomatoes soften slightly, about 1 minute. Stir in shrimp and cook until shrimp are opaque throughout, about 1 minute. Transfer shrimp and tomatoes to serving platter, sprinkle with scallion greens, top with avocado, and drizzle with extra oil. Serve with lime wedges.

NOTES

Don't be tempted to sear all the shrimp at once; the extra space in the skillet ensures the shrimp brown, not steam. Serve with couscous, quinoa, rice, or lightly charred tortillas.

KITCHEN IMPROV

Halved cherry tomatoes make a great alternative to regular tomatoes (especially outside of peak season). If you don't have chipotle chile powder, use classic chili powder or equal amounts of paprika and ground cumin.

fried rice WITH shrimp, lime AND peanuts

Serves 4 • Total Time: 35 minutes

- **¼ cup vegetable oil, divided**
- **¼ cup fish sauce**
- **2 tablespoons lime juice, plus lime wedges for serving**
- **2 tablespoons packed brown sugar**
- **2 tablespoons sambal oelek**
- **4 garlic cloves, minced**
- **4 large eggs, lightly beaten**
- **8 ounces extra-large shrimp (21 to 25 per pound), peeled, deveined, tails removed, and cut into 1-inch pieces**
- **4 cups coarsely chopped green cabbage**
- **4 cups cooked long-grain white rice, room temperature**
- **½ cup chopped unsalted dry-roasted peanuts**
- **½ cup fried shallots**
- **½ cup torn Thai basil, cilantro, and/or mint leaves**
- **1 Thai chile, stemmed and sliced thin (optional)**

BOLD AND TANGY (thanks to fish sauce and lime juice) and made hearty with the addition of cabbage, this satisfying stir-fry comes together quickly with leftover rice. Packaged crispy shallots—a tasty shortcut for busy nights—and chopped peanuts add a crunchy topping.

1 Combine 1 tablespoon oil, fish sauce, lime juice, sugar, sambal oelek, and garlic in bowl; set aside.

2 Heat 1 tablespoon oil in 14-inch flat-bottomed wok or 12-inch nonstick skillet over medium-high heat until just smoking. Add eggs and cook, stirring frequently with stiff rubber spatula, until eggs are set but still soft, about 15 seconds; transfer to bowl.

3 Heat 1 tablespoon oil in now-empty wok over medium-high heat until shimmering. Add shrimp and cook, tossing slowly but constantly, until opaque throughout, about 1 minute; transfer to bowl with eggs. Heat remaining 1 tablespoon oil in again-empty wok over medium-high heat until shimmering. Add cabbage and cook, tossing slowly but constantly, until bright green and beginning to soften, about 2 minutes; transfer to bowl with eggs and shrimp.

4 Add fish sauce mixture to again-empty wok and cook over medium-high heat, stirring frequently, until slightly thickened, about 2 minutes. Add rice and cook, stirring and pressing on rice with spatula to break up clumps, until rice is evenly coated and most of sauce has been absorbed, about 4 minutes. Add eggs, shrimp, and cabbage and cook, tossing constantly, until heated through, about 2 minutes. Transfer fried rice to serving platter and top with peanuts, shallots, basil, and Thai chile, if using. Serve with lime wedges.

NOTES

You can find packaged crispy shallots in Asian markets or online. Plan ahead for day-old rice for this recipe. Alternatively, cook your rice 2 hours ahead, spread on a rimmed baking sheet, and let cool completely before chilling for 30 minutes. This stir-fry moves quickly, so have all the ingredients prepped and ready to go.

KITCHEN IMPROV

Can't find sambal oelek? Chile-garlic sauce works just as well. Green cabbage has a nice crunch, but napa cabbage is great too—its leaves are more delicate, so stir-fry for only about 30 seconds in step 3.

red curry shrimp WITH coconut rice AND cucumber relish

Serves 4 • Total Time: 45 minutes

- **1½ cups jasmine rice, rinsed**
- **1½ cups water**
- **1 cup plus 6 tablespoons canned coconut milk, divided**
- **2 tablespoons plus 1 teaspoon sugar, divided**
- **2¼ teaspoons table salt, divided**
- **¼ cup distilled white vinegar**
- **¼ teaspoon red pepper flakes**
- **1 English cucumber, cut into ½-inch pieces**
- **½ cup coarsely chopped salted dry-roasted peanuts**
- **2 tablespoons chopped fresh cilantro**
- **1½ pounds jumbo shrimp (16 to 20 per pound), peeled, deveined, and tails removed**
- **2 tablespoons Thai red curry paste**

1 Combine rice, water, 1 cup coconut milk, 1 tablespoon sugar, and ¾ teaspoon salt in large saucepan. Bring to boil over high heat. Reduce heat to low, cover, and gently simmer until liquid has been absorbed, about 20 minutes. Remove saucepan from heat and let sit, covered, for 10 minutes. Mix rice gently but thoroughly with rubber spatula.

2 Meanwhile, whisk vinegar, pepper flakes, 1 tablespoon sugar, and 1 teaspoon salt in bowl until sugar has dissolved. Add cucumber, peanuts, and cilantro and toss to combine; set relish aside.

3 Pat shrimp dry with paper towels. Cook curry paste, 1 tablespoon coconut milk, remaining 1 teaspoon sugar, and remaining ½ teaspoon salt in 12-inch nonstick skillet over medium-high heat until mixture is dry, about 3 minutes. Add shrimp and cook, stirring occasionally, until shrimp are opaque throughout, about 5 minutes. Stir in remaining 5 tablespoons coconut milk and bring to brief simmer. Serve shrimp with coconut rice and cucumber relish.

COOLING CONTRAST comes from coconut rice in this bold shrimp dish with Thai flavors. While the rice simmers, pull together a sweet-sour-spicy cucumber relish (basically a salad) with peanuts and cilantro. The fiery shrimp pair beautifully with the crunchy salad and creamy rice.

NOTES

Make sure to use full-fat canned coconut milk; Aroy-D is a good brand. The rice can be cooked in a rice cooker instead of on the stovetop.

KITCHEN IMPROV

Fragrant and flavorful jasmine rice is great here, but any long-grain white rice will work, including basmati or Texmati. Extra-large shrimp (21 to 25 per pound) can be substituted for jumbo shrimp. If you use them, reduce the cooking time in step 3 by 1 to 2 minutes.

mussels WITH white wine AND parsley

Serves 4 • Total Time: 45 minutes

- **3 tablespoons extra-virgin olive oil**
- **1 large onion, halved and sliced thin**
- **3 garlic cloves, minced**
- **Pinch red pepper flakes**
- **1 cup dry white wine**
- **3 sprigs fresh thyme**
- **2 bay leaves**
- **4 pounds mussels, scrubbed and debearded**
- **¼ teaspoon table salt**
- **2 tablespoons unsalted butter, cut into 4 pieces**
- **2 tablespoons chopped fresh parsley**
- **Lemon wedges for serving**

THERE'S SOMETHING so sophisticated about mussels for dinner, even though you're eating with your hands. Bathed in wine with aromatics and oven-steamed for even cooking, these mussels will transport you to a French bistro.

1 Adjust oven rack to lowest position and heat oven to 500 degrees. Heat oil, onion, garlic, and pepper flakes in large roasting pan over medium heat (over 2 burners, if possible) and cook, stirring constantly, until onion is softened, about 5 minutes. Stir in wine, thyme sprigs, and bay leaves and boil until wine is slightly reduced, about 1 minute.

2 Stir in mussels and salt. Cover pan tightly with aluminum foil and transfer to oven. Roast until most mussels have opened (a few may remain closed), 15 to 18 minutes.

3 Remove pan from oven. Push mussels to sides of pan. Being careful of hot pan handles, add butter to center and whisk until melted. Discard thyme sprigs and bay leaves and stir in parsley. Serve with lemon wedges.

NOTES

Before cooking, discard any mussel with an unpleasant odor or with a cracked shell or a shell that won't close. Brothy mussels call out for crusty bread (or garlic toast if you want to up your game) and a bottle of nice wine (already open for cooking).

KITCHEN IMPROV

It's easy to gussy up this dish; start by simply rendering a few slices of chopped bacon in the roasting pan before adding the onion and garlic. Or for an even more refined dish, substitute 1 pound thinly sliced leeks for the onion, ½ cup Pernod plus ½ cup water for the wine, and ¼ cup crème fraîche for the butter.

mostly vegetables and beans

chapter 4

roasted cauliflower AND chickpeas WITH romesco AND sumac onions

Serves 4 • Total Time: 45 minutes

- **1 red onion, halved and cut through root end into 1/4-inch-thick slices**
- **3 tablespoons sherry vinegar, divided**
- **2 tablespoons lemon juice**
- **1/2 cup extra-virgin olive oil, divided**
- **1 tablespoon ground sumac**
- **1 1/2 teaspoons table salt, divided**
- **1/2 teaspoon sugar**
- **1 head cauliflower (2 pounds), cored and cut into 2-inch florets**
- **1 (15-ounce) can chickpeas, rinsed**
- **2/3 cup jarred roasted red peppers, patted dry**
- **1/4 cup slivered almonds, toasted**
- **6 tablespoons fresh parsley leaves, divided**
- **1 garlic clove, minced**
- **8 ounces Belgian endive, leaves separated**

NUTTY ROMESCO sauce unites roasted cauliflower and chickpeas with crisp, slightly bitter endive and tangy, quick-pickled red onion for a sheet-pan meal that's a study in contrasts. High-heat roasting yields soft, burnished cauliflower and crispy chickpeas.

1 Adjust oven rack to middle position and heat oven to 475 degrees. Combine onion, 2 tablespoons vinegar, lemon juice, 1 tablespoon oil, sumac, 1/4 teaspoon salt, and sugar in bowl and microwave until steaming, about 2 minutes; set aside for serving.

2 Toss cauliflower, chickpeas, 1/4 cup oil, and 1 teaspoon salt together on rimmed baking sheet, then spread into even layer over sheet. Roast until cauliflower is golden in spots, about 20 minutes. Stir, then redistribute evenly over sheet. Continue to roast until lightly charred throughout, 8 to 10 minutes.

3 Meanwhile, process red peppers, almonds, 1/4 cup parsley, garlic, remaining 1 tablespoon vinegar, remaining 3 tablespoons oil, and remaining 1/4 teaspoon salt in food processor until smooth, about 1 minute. Season romesco with salt and pepper to taste.

4 Arrange endive leaves in even layer over serving platter, then top with cauliflower and chickpeas. Dollop with romesco, sprinkle with sumac onions and remaining 2 tablespoons parsley, and serve.

NOTES

The sumac-pickled onion and romesco sauce can be refrigerated separately for up to 3 days; bring them to room temperature before serving. The sumac adds tartness and fruitiness, but you can omit it. Use red wine vinegar if you don't have sherry vinegar.

KITCHEN IMPROV

Other bitter greens, such as escarole, frisée, and chicory, can be used in place of the endive.

BLANK-CANVAS EGGPLANT is neutral on its own but readily absorbs whatever flavors you cook it with. Gently braising eggplant wedges turns them meltingly tender and creamy while imbuing them with the aromatic flavors of the sauce. Serve with plenty of rice.

braised eggplant WITH soy, garlic AND ginger

Serves 4 • Total Time: 45 minutes

- 1½ cups water
- ¼ cup Shaoxing wine
- 2 tablespoons soy sauce
- 4 teaspoons sugar
- 2 teaspoons doubanjiang (broad bean chile paste)
- 1 teaspoon cornstarch
- 1 pound Chinese or Japanese eggplants
- 1 tablespoon vegetable oil
- 1 garlic clove, minced
- 1 teaspoon grated fresh ginger
- ½ teaspoon toasted sesame oil
- 2 scallions, sliced thin on bias

1 Whisk water, Shaoxing wine, soy sauce, sugar, doubanjiang, and cornstarch in medium bowl until sugar has dissolved; set aside. Trim ½ inch from top and bottom of one eggplant, then halve crosswise. Cut each half lengthwise into 2 pieces. Cut each piece into ¾-inch-thick wedges. Repeat with remaining eggplant.

2 Heat vegetable oil in 12-inch nonstick skillet over medium heat until shimmering. Add garlic and ginger and cook, stirring constantly, until fragrant, about 30 seconds. Spread eggplant evenly in skillet (pieces will not form single layer). Pour Shaoxing wine mixture over eggplant. Increase heat to high and bring to boil. Reduce heat to maintain gentle boil. Cover and cook until eggplant is soft and has decreased in volume enough to form single layer on bottom of skillet, about 15 minutes, gently shaking skillet to settle eggplant halfway through cooking (some pieces will remain opaque).

3 Uncover and continue to cook, swirling skillet occasionally, until liquid is thickened and reduced to just a few tablespoons, 12 to 14 minutes. Transfer to serving platter, drizzle with sesame oil, sprinkle with scallions, and serve.

NOTES

Two 8- to 10-ounce globe or Italian eggplants may be substituted for the Chinese eggplant; prepare as directed in step 1. (Don't use larger eggplants; they will disintegrate when braised.) Be sure to cut the eggplant so that each piece has some skin attached; this keeps them intact as they cook. You can substitute dry sherry for the Shaoxing wine and 1 teaspoon chili-garlic sauce or sriracha for the doubanjiang.

KITCHEN IMPROV

Add some crunch with chopped toasted peanuts, toasted sesame or pepitas, or crispy shallots. Instead of rice, try serving the eggplant over Chinese wheat noodles, ramen, or another grain, such as pearl barley or oat berries.

roasted mushrooms AND escarole WITH couscous AND lemon vinaigrette

Serves 4 • Total Time: 40 minutes

- **2½ pounds wild mushrooms, trimmed and torn into 2-inch pieces**
- **1 onion, chopped fine**
- **¼ cup plus 5 teaspoons extra-virgin olive oil, divided**
- **3 garlic cloves, sliced thin**
- **1 tablespoon plus ⅛ teaspoon plus pinch kosher salt, divided**
- **1 head escarole (1 pound), cut into 2-inch wedges through core**
- **1 cup boiling water**
- **1 cup couscous**
- **3 tablespoons minced fresh parsley, divided**
- **1 tablespoon lemon juice, plus lemon wedges for serving**
- **¾ teaspoon Dijon mustard**
- **¼ cup dry white wine**

1 Adjust oven racks to upper-middle and lower-middle positions and heat oven to 450 degrees. Toss mushrooms, onion, 2 tablespoons oil, garlic, and 2 teaspoons salt together on rimmed baking sheet, then spread into even layer over sheet. Place escarole wedges on second rimmed baking sheet, then brush all over with 2 tablespoons oil and sprinkle with 1 teaspoon salt. Roast mushrooms on lower rack for 5 minutes, then place sheet with escarole on upper rack. Roast until mushrooms are browned and escarole is tender and slightly browned, 10 to 15 minutes.

2 Meanwhile, combine boiling water, couscous, and ⅛ teaspoon salt in bowl. Cover and let sit until couscous is tender and all liquid has been absorbed, about 7 minutes. Add 2 tablespoons parsley and fluff with fork to combine; cover and set aside until ready to serve.

3 Whisk lemon juice, mustard, remaining pinch salt, and remaining 1 tablespoon parsley together in bowl. Whisking constantly, slowly drizzle in remaining 5 teaspoons oil until emulsified; set aside until ready to serve, whisking to recombine if needed.

4 Transfer escarole to serving platter and set aside. Transfer sheet with mushrooms to wire rack. Immediately drizzle wine evenly over mushrooms on sheet and toss until most of liquid is evaporated, about 1 minute, scraping up any browned bits on sheet. Add mushrooms and couscous to platter with escarole and drizzle with reserved vinaigrette. Serve with lemon wedges.

SAVORY, MEATY mushrooms and slightly bitter escarole are roasted on separate sheet pans, then paired with easy-to-prepare couscous to create this satisfying supper flavored with garlic, white wine, and a lemon-mustard dressing.

NOTES

A combination of wild mushrooms is great here, but using just cremini or white button mushrooms is also perfectly fine. If using shiitakes, be sure to remove the stems. If you have dry vermouth on hand, consider using it in place of the wine.

KITCHEN IMPROV

Boost the seasoning on the mushrooms by including up to 2 teaspoons pantry spices such as paprika, ground coriander, or ground fennel seed. Substitute another delicate fresh herb for the parsley, such as dill, tarragon, or basil.

PAIR CARAMELIZED sweet potato wedges with spiced tempeh crumbles and a variety of fresh toppings to make a hearty dinner. The avocado-yogurt sauce is bright and cooling.

NOTES

Buy potatoes that are the same size so they will cook at the same rate. Small potatoes, about 8 ounces each, are best for this recipe. Be sure to scrub and dry the whole potatoes thoroughly before cutting them into wedges.

KITCHEN IMPROV

This dish is great as is, but it's also good topped with sliced radishes and jalapeños. You can also add quick-pickled red onion, which has countless uses: Combine 1 thinly sliced red onion, 1 cup wine vinegar, ⅓ cup sugar, and 1 tablespoon table salt in a medium bowl. Cover and microwave until steaming, about 2 minutes; let sit for 10 minutes before straining and using.

loaded sweet potato wedges WITH tempeh

Serves 4 • Total Time: 45 minutes

- **2 pounds sweet potatoes, unpeeled, cut lengthwise into 2-inch-wide wedges**
- **5 tablespoons extra-virgin olive oil, divided**
- **3/4 teaspoon plus 1/8 teaspoon table salt, divided**
- **1 ripe avocado, halved, pitted, and cut into 1/2-inch pieces**
- **1/4 cup plain yogurt, plus extra for serving**
- **1 teaspoon lime juice, plus lime wedges for serving**
- **1 1/2 teaspoons ground cumin, divided**
- **1/8 teaspoon pepper**
- **8 ounces tempeh, crumbled into pea-size pieces**
- **1 teaspoon ground coriander**
- **1 teaspoon smoked paprika**
- **1/8 teaspoon ground cinnamon**
- **4 ounces cherry tomatoes, halved**
- **3/4 cup chopped fresh cilantro**
- **3 scallions, sliced thin**

1. Adjust oven rack to middle position and heat oven to 450 degrees. Line rimmed baking sheet with aluminum foil and spray with vegetable oil spray. Toss potato wedges with 1 tablespoon oil and 1/2 teaspoon salt in bowl, then arrange cut sides down in single layer on prepared sheet. Roast until tender and sides in contact with sheet are well browned, 25 to 30 minutes.

2. Meanwhile, using sturdy whisk, mash and stir avocado, yogurt, lime juice, 1/2 teaspoon cumin, pepper, and 1/8 teaspoon salt together in bowl until as smooth as possible. Season with salt and pepper to taste; set aside for serving.

3. Heat remaining 1/4 cup oil in 12-inch skillet over medium heat until shimmering. Add tempeh, coriander, paprika, cinnamon, remaining 1 teaspoon cumin, and remaining 1/4 teaspoon salt and cook until well browned, 8 to 12 minutes, stirring often; remove from heat and cover to keep warm.

4. Transfer sweet potatoes to individual serving plates and top with crispy tempeh, tomatoes, cilantro, and scallions. Serve, passing avocado sauce, extra yogurt, and lime wedges separately.

stuffed delicata squash

Serves 4 • Total Time: 45 minutes

- **2 delicata squash (about 1 pound each), halved lengthwise and seeded**
- **1¾ teaspoons table salt, divided, plus salt for cooking bulgur**
- **½ teaspoon pepper**
- **1 cup medium-grind bulgur**
- **4 tablespoons unsalted butter, plus 2 tablespoons melted**
- **10 ounces cremini mushrooms, trimmed and chopped**
- **1 onion, chopped**
- **5 ounces (5 cups) baby spinach, chopped coarse**
- **1 teaspoon minced fresh thyme**
- **½ cup chopped toasted pecans**
- **2 ounces sharp cheddar cheese, shredded (½ cup)**

1 Sprinkle cut sides of squash with 1 teaspoon salt and pepper. Microwave in large covered bowl until tender, 12 to 15 minutes. Bring 2 quarts water to boil in large saucepan. Add bulgur and 1 teaspoon salt. Reduce heat to medium-low and simmer until tender, 5 to 8 minutes; drain and set aside.

2 Meanwhile, melt 4 tablespoons butter in 12-inch nonstick skillet over medium-high heat. Add mushrooms, onion, and remaining ¾ teaspoon salt and cook, stirring occasionally, until vegetables are browned, about 10 minutes. Stir in spinach and thyme and cook until wilted, about 3 minutes. Off heat, stir in bulgur, pecans, and cheddar.

3 Adjust oven rack 8 inches from broiler element and heat broiler. Transfer squash, cut side up, to rimmed baking sheet. Tightly pack bulgur mixture into squash halves, mounding bulgur mixture up over squash rims. Brush filling with remaining 2 tablespoons melted butter. Broil until lightly browned, about 5 minutes. Serve.

DELICATA SQUASH offers earthy sweetness similar to acorn or butternut, but with far less elbow grease required. Halving the squash creates boats ideal for holding a hearty bulgur filling studded with mushrooms and spinach.

NOTES

To ensure that the flesh cooks evenly, choose squash that are similar in size and shape. Delicata have thin, edible skin that needn't be removed; simply use a vegetable peeler to pare away any tough brown blemishes.

KITCHEN IMPROV

Any combination of mushrooms will work; if using shiitakes, remove the stems. You can substitute an equal weight of thawed frozen spinach or kale for the fresh spinach (just be sure to thoroughly squeeze it dry after weighing). You can substitute rosemary or sage for thyme. Other semisoft cheeses such as Monterey Jack, fontina, or Swiss can be used in place of the cheddar.

buttery summer squash WITH caramelized lemon AND burrata

Serves 4 • Total Time: 40 minutes

- **5 tablespoons unsalted butter, divided**
- **2 ounces rustic bread, torn into rough ½-inch pieces (2 cups)**
- **1 teaspoon table salt, divided**
- **¼ teaspoon red pepper flakes**
- **1 teaspoon grated lemon zest plus ½ lemon**
- **3 yellow summer squash or zucchini (8 ounces each), cut into ¾-inch pieces**
- **8 ounces burrata cheese, room temperature**
- **2 tablespoons torn fresh dill**

1 Melt 2 tablespoons butter in 12-inch nonstick skillet over medium heat. Add bread pieces, ¼ teaspoon salt, and pepper flakes and cook, stirring frequently, until bread is golden brown, about 5 minutes; transfer croutons to bowl and wipe skillet clean with paper towels.

2 Trim end of lemon half, then slice into thin rounds, discarding any seeds. Working with a few stacked lemon rounds at a time, slice into thin strips, then cut strips crosswise into very small pieces (you should have ½ cup finely chopped lemon pieces). Melt 1 tablespoon butter in now-empty skillet over medium heat. Add minced lemon and ¼ teaspoon salt and cook, stirring occasionally, until well browned and soft, about 8 minutes. Transfer lemon pieces to small bowl.

3 Add remaining 2 tablespoons butter to any butter left in skillet and melt over medium heat. Add squash and remaining ½ teaspoon salt and cook until lightly browned and softened, 10 to 12 minutes. Stir lemon pieces and grated lemon zest into squash in skillet, then transfer to serving platter; let cool slightly. Tear burrata into bite-size pieces over squash, then sprinkle with croutons and dill and serve.

SAUTÉING LEMON pieces transforms the fruit from sharp and acidic to floral and aromatic—all the better to elevate humble summer squash for a light summery meal. Cooking the squash and lemon in butter adds needed richness; torn burrata and toasty pieces of bread bring creaminess and texture.

NOTES

After zesting the lemon, you should chop the lemon half, pith and all. You can use sourdough, ciabatta, or any rustic bread for the croutons.

KITCHEN IMPROV

Dollops of ricotta cheese or torn fresh mozzarella are nice alternatives to the burrata. Torn fresh basil or minced fresh chives work well in place of the dill.

broccoli AND feta frittata

Serves 4 • Total Time: 35 minutes

- **12 large eggs**
- **1/3 cup whole milk**
- **3/4 teaspoon table salt, divided**
- **1 tablespoon extra-virgin olive oil**
- **12 ounces broccoli florets, cut into 1/2-inch pieces (4 cups)**
- **Pinch red pepper flakes (optional)**
- **1/2 teaspoon grated lemon zest plus 1/2 teaspoon juice**
- **4 ounces feta cheese, crumbled into 1/2-inch pieces (1 cup)**

FORGIVINGLY EASY and improvisational by nature, frittatas are sort of an Italian homestyle version of the filled omelet. This one starts with adding broccoli and feta, but the possibilities are endless.

1 Adjust oven rack to middle position and heat oven to 350 degrees. Whisk eggs, milk, and 1/2 teaspoon salt in bowl until well combined.

2 Heat oil in 12-inch ovensafe nonstick skillet over medium-high heat until shimmering. Add broccoli, pepper flakes (if using), and remaining 1/4 teaspoon salt and cook, stirring frequently, until broccoli is crisp-tender and spotty brown, 7 to 9 minutes. Add 3 tablespoons water and lemon zest and juice and continue to cook, stirring constantly, until broccoli is just tender and no water remains in skillet, about 1 minute longer.

3 Add feta and egg mixture and cook, using silicone spatula to stir and scrape bottom of skillet, until large curds form and spatula leaves trail through eggs but eggs are still very wet, about 30 seconds. Smooth curds into even layer and transfer skillet to oven. Bake until frittata is slightly puffy and surface bounces back when lightly pressed, 6 to 9 minutes.

4 Using silicone spatula, loosen frittata from skillet and transfer to cutting board. Let sit for 5 minutes before slicing and serving.

NOTES

You will need a 12-inch ovensafe nonstick skillet. This frittata is equally good served warm or at room temperature.

KITCHEN IMPROV

Swapping in other vegetables for the broccoli is easy. Start by trying 1 pound of asparagus, zucchini, bell peppers, or mushrooms, cut into 1/2-inch pieces. You can also use another crumbly or shredded semisoft cheese instead of feta: Goat cheese, queso fresco, cheddar, or Monterey Jack all work well.

CHICKPEAS BRING hearty richness to this spiced, veggie-loaded frittata. Steaming the chickpeas in their liquid gives them a creamy texture for a protein-packed frittata that stays tender.

chickpea AND spinach frittata WITH cumin AND paprika

Serves 4 • Total Time: 40 minutes

- **1 (15-ounce) can chickpeas, undrained**
- **8 large eggs**
- **1¼ teaspoons table salt, divided**
- **3 tablespoons extra-virgin olive oil, divided**
- **1 small red onion, halved and sliced thin**
- **1 teaspoon pepper**
- **1 teaspoon smoked paprika**
- **1 teaspoon ground cumin**
- **10 ounces frozen chopped spinach, thawed and squeezed dry**

1 Adjust oven rack to middle position and heat oven to 350 degrees. Transfer chickpeas and their canning liquid to medium bowl and microwave, covered, until chickpeas are steaming and have softened, 6 to 7 minutes. Drain and rinse chickpeas; set aside.

2 Whisk eggs and 1 teaspoon salt in large bowl until well combined. Whisking constantly, drizzle in 2 tablespoons olive oil until incorporated.

3 Heat remaining 1 tablespoon oil in 10-inch ovensafe nonstick skillet over medium heat until shimmering. Add onion and remaining ¼ teaspoon salt and cook until beginning to soften, about 2 minutes. Stir in pepper, paprika, and cumin and cook until fragrant, about 30 seconds. Stir in spinach and chickpeas and cook until heated through, about 3 minutes.

4 Add egg mixture and cook, using silicone spatula to stir and scrape bottom of skillet until large curds form and spatula leaves trail through eggs but eggs are still wet, about 30 seconds. Smooth curds into even layer and transfer skillet to oven. Bake until frittata is just set, 8 to 10 minutes.

5 Using silicone spatula, loosen frittata from skillet and transfer to cutting board. Let sit for 5 minutes before slicing and serving.

NOTES

You will need a 10-inch ovensafe nonstick skillet. This frittata is equally good served warm or at room temperature.

KITCHEN IMPROV

Swapping in frozen chopped kale or collard greens for the spinach is an easy sub. You can also include 2 ounces of crumbly or shredded semisoft cheese such as feta, goat, cheddar, or Monterey Jack in the egg mixture. Consider serving with a simple yogurt sauce: Combine ½ cup plain yogurt, 2 tablespoons chopped fresh leafy herbs (such as parsley, basil, or tarragon), and 2 teaspoons lemon juice or wine vinegar; season with salt and pepper to taste.

savory dutch baby WITH portobellos, roasted red peppers, walnuts AND feta

Serves 4 • Total Time: 45 minutes

- **1¾ cups (8¾ ounces) all-purpose flour**
- **1 tablespoon plus ¼ teaspoon sugar, divided**
- **1¼ teaspoons table salt, divided**
- **1½ cups milk**
- **6 large eggs**
- **3 tablespoons unsalted butter**
- **3 tablespoons extra-virgin olive oil, divided**
- **1¼ pounds portobello mushroom caps, gills removed, sliced thin**
- **½ teaspoon grated lemon zest plus 2 teaspoons juice**
- **½ cup chopped jarred roasted red peppers**
- **2 ounces feta cheese, cut into ¼-inch cubes (½ cup)**
- **½ cup fresh parsley leaves**
- **¼ cup walnuts, toasted and chopped**

SOME DRAMA at dinner can be a good thing. This lofty, custardy pancake graced with savory toppings will elicit oohs and aahs. Starting the batter in a cold oven lets it warm slowly before the sides puff, ensuring that the pancake is sturdy enough for the toppings.

1 Adjust oven rack to lower-middle position. Whisk flour, 1 tablespoon sugar, and ½ teaspoon salt together in large bowl. Whisk milk and eggs together in second bowl. Whisk two-thirds of milk mixture into flour mixture until no lumps remain, then slowly whisk in remaining milk mixture until smooth.

2 Melt butter in 12-inch ovensafe nonstick skillet over medium-low heat. Add batter to skillet, immediately transfer to oven, and set oven to 375 degrees. Bake until edges are deep golden brown and center is beginning to brown, 30 to 35 minutes. Gently transfer Dutch baby to cutting board. Let cool for at least 5 minutes. (Dutch baby will deflate.)

3 Meanwhile, heat 1 tablespoon oil in 12-inch skillet over medium-high heat until shimmering. Add mushrooms and ½ teaspoon salt and cook, stirring frequently, until mushrooms are tender, 4 to 6 minutes.

4 Whisk lemon zest and juice, remaining ¼ teaspoon sugar, and remaining ¼ teaspoon salt together in bowl. Whisking constantly, slowly drizzle in remaining 2 tablespoons oil. Add red peppers, feta, and parsley and stir to combine. Spread mushrooms over Dutch baby, followed by red pepper mixture and walnuts. Cut into wedges and serve.

NOTES

You will need a 12-inch ovensafe nonstick skillet. The look and texture of the mushrooms will be better if you take the time to remove the gills.

KITCHEN IMPROV

Use any combination of mushrooms (shiitakes should be stemmed). Or switch up the toppings entirely: Brightly dressed greens or thinly sliced raw vegetables such as celery or fennel make a good base. From there add diced fresh fruit, thinly sliced or crumbled cheeses, sliced deli meats or cubed cooked proteins, briny olives or pickled vegetables, and/or toasted nuts or seeds.

lavash flatbreads WITH romesco, tomatoes AND spinach

Serves 4 • Total Time: 30 minutes

- 2/3 cup jarred roasted red peppers, patted dry
- 1/4 cup slivered almonds, toasted
- 1/4 cup fresh parsley leaves
- 7 tablespoons extra-virgin olive oil, divided
- 1 tablespoon sherry vinegar
- 2 garlic cloves, minced, divided
- 1/2 teaspoon table salt, divided
- 10 ounces frozen spinach, thawed, squeezed dry, and chopped
- 5 ounces cherry or grape tomatoes, halved
- 1/2 cup pitted green olives, chopped
- 1/4 teaspoon red pepper flakes
- 2 (12 by 9-inch) lavash breads
- Grated Parmesan cheese

1 Adjust oven racks to upper-middle and lower-middle positions and heat oven to 475 degrees. Process red peppers, almonds, parsley, 3 tablespoons oil, vinegar, half of garlic, and 1/4 teaspoon salt in food processor until smooth, about 1 minute, scraping down sides of bowl as needed. Season with salt and pepper to taste; set romesco aside.

2 Combine spinach, tomatoes, olives, pepper flakes, 2 tablespoons oil, remaining garlic, and remaining 1/4 teaspoon salt in bowl. Brush both sides of lavash with remaining 2 tablespoons oil and lay on 2 baking sheets. Bake until crisp and golden brown, about 4 minutes, switching and rotating sheets and flipping lavash halfway through baking.

3 Spread romesco evenly over each lavash, then top with spinach mixture. Bake until warmed through, about 4 minutes, switching and rotating sheets halfway through baking. Sprinkle with Parmesan, slice, and serve.

STORE-BOUGHT LAVASH has a crisp, cracker-like texture that makes a convenient and delicious base for vegetables. A bright homemade romesco sauce adds big flavors and anchors the toppings.

NOTES

The romesco sauce can be refrigerated for up to 2 days; bring to room temperature before using.

KITCHEN IMPROV

Try other nuts in your romesco, like cashews, pistachios, and walnuts. You can also swap in red or white wine vinegar for the sherry vinegar and frozen chopped kale for the spinach. For cheesier flatbreads, sprinkle up to 2 ounces shredded fontina, Gruyère, or Monterey Jack onto the flatbreads before baking.

corn, tomato AND arugula pizza

Serves 4 to 6 • Total Time: 45 minutes

- **2 tablespoons extra-virgin olive oil, divided**
- **½ cup crème fraîche**
- **¼ cup chopped fresh basil**
- **¼ teaspoon red pepper flakes**
- **1 pound pizza dough, room temperature**
- **8 ounces fontina cheese, shredded (2 cups)**
- **6 ounces cherry tomatoes, quartered**
- **1 ear corn, kernels cut from cob**
- **1 shallot, sliced thin**
- **¼ teaspoon table salt**
- **2 ounces (2 cups) baby arugula**

1 Adjust oven rack to middle position and heat oven to 500 degrees. Brush rimmed baking sheet with 1 tablespoon oil. Combine crème fraîche, basil, and pepper flakes in bowl.

2 Press and roll dough into 15 by 11-inch rectangle on lightly floured counter. Transfer dough to prepared sheet and brush edges with 2 teaspoons oil. Spread crème fraîche mixture over dough, leaving ½-inch border, then sprinkle evenly with fontina, tomatoes, corn, shallot, and salt. Bake until cheese is spotty brown and crust is golden, 15 to 20 minutes, rotating sheet halfway through baking.

3 Transfer pizza to wire rack and let cool for 5 minutes. Toss arugula with remaining 1 teaspoon oil and season with salt and pepper to taste. Top pizza with arugula, slice, and serve.

NOTES

Make sure the dough is at room temperature or it will be difficult to stretch. If the dough springs back while shaping, let it rest for a few minutes before rolling it again.

KITCHEN IMPROV

If fresh corn isn't in season, you can substitute ¾ cup thawed frozen corn. Crème fraîche is really nice here, but you can substitute sour cream. Consider swapping in other summer produce for the tomatoes. An equal weight of zucchini or summer squash, eggplant, or bell pepper, cut into ½-inch pieces, are all good choices. Other bitter salad greens such as frisée, watercress, or endive can be used in place of the arugula; you may want to chop the greens into bite-size pieces depending on their size.

SUMMER PIZZA should make the most of summer ingredients, and this one bursts with flavor from sweet corn and cherry tomatoes. Velvety crème fraîche lets the bright flavors shine, and fontina cheese brings a little more pizzazz than mozzarella.

SARDINIAN FLAVORS of fennel, Pecorino, and tomatoes inspire this rustic, risotto-like meal made with fregula, a nutty toasted spherical pasta much-used in the local cuisine. Chickpeas echo the fregula's shape and add heartiness.

fregula WITH chickpeas, tomatoes AND fennel

Serves 4 to 6 • Total Time: 45 minutes

- 3 tablespoons extra-virgin olive oil, plus extra for drizzling
- 1 fennel bulb, 1/4 cup fronds minced, stalks discarded, bulb halved, cored, and sliced thin
- 1 onion, chopped fine
- 3 garlic cloves, minced
- 2 teaspoons minced fresh rosemary or 3/4 teaspoon dried
- 1 teaspoon fennel seeds
- 1/2 teaspoon table salt
- 1/2 teaspoon pepper
- 1/4 teaspoon red pepper flakes
- 4 cups water
- 2 (15-ounce) cans chickpeas, undrained
- 10 ounces cherry or grape tomatoes
- 8 ounces fregula
- 1 tablespoon lemon juice
- Grated Pecorino Romano cheese

1 Heat oil in Dutch oven over medium heat until shimmering. Add sliced fennel and onion and cook until vegetables are softened, 5 to 7 minutes. Stir in garlic, rosemary, fennel seeds, salt, pepper, and pepper flakes and cook until fragrant, about 30 seconds.

2 Stir in water, chickpeas and their liquid, tomatoes, and fregula and bring to boil. Reduce heat to medium-low and simmer until fregula is tender, about 20 minutes, stirring occasionally. Stir in lemon juice and fennel fronds and season with salt and pepper to taste. Serve, drizzling individual portions with extra oil and passing Pecorino separately.

NOTES

If fregula is unavailable, swap in pearl couscous or fideos and toast the pasta in a dry skillet over medium heat until fragrant, about 5 minutes, before using. Couscous and fideos will cook more quickly, so in step 2, begin checking for doneness after 12 minutes.

KITCHEN IMPROV

Use other canned beans, such as great northern or cannellini, in place of the chickpeas. Add extra richness with a dollop of mascarpone or Greek yogurt, or add crunch by sprinkling with toasted pine nuts or slivered almonds before serving. Fresh or dried thyme can be used in place of the rosemary.

risotto WITH asparagus, mushrooms AND peas

Serves 4 • Total Time: 45 minutes

- 5 tablespoons unsalted butter, divided
- 8 ounces cremini mushrooms, trimmed and sliced thin
- 1 teaspoon table salt, divided
- 6 cups vegetable or chicken broth
- 1½ cups water
- 1 onion, chopped fine
- 2 cups arborio rice
- 6 ounces asparagus, trimmed and cut into ½-inch pieces
- 2 ounces Parmesan or Pecorino Romano cheese, grated (1 cup)
- 1 cup frozen peas, thawed
- 1 teaspoon lemon juice

WEEKNIGHT RISOTTO?
You're not dreaming. Traditionally, risotto can demand over 30 minutes of stovetop stirring for creamy results. This hands-off version, studded with spring veggies, can simmer mostly on its own and requires 5 minutes of stirring, tops.

1. Melt 1 tablespoon butter in Dutch oven over medium heat. Add mushrooms and ¼ teaspoon salt and cook, covered, until softened, about 5 minutes. Using slotted spoon, transfer mushrooms to bowl. Discard any liquid left in pot and wipe dry with paper towels.

2. Microwave broth and water in 8-cup liquid measuring cup or large bowl until hot, about 5 minutes. Meanwhile, melt 2 tablespoons butter in now-empty pot over medium heat. Add onion and remaining ¾ teaspoon salt and cook until onion is softened, about 5 minutes. Stir in rice and cook, stirring often, until edges begin to turn translucent, about 3 minutes.

3. Stir in 6 cups hot broth. Reduce heat to medium-low, cover, and simmer until almost all liquid has been absorbed, about 12 minutes. Stir in asparagus, cover, and cook for 2 minutes.

4. Add ¾ cup hot broth and stir gently and constantly until risotto becomes creamy, about 3 minutes. Stir in Parmesan, mushrooms, peas, lemon juice, and remaining 2 tablespoons butter. Season with salt and pepper to taste. Before serving, stir in remaining hot broth as needed to loosen consistency of risotto.

NOTES

The consistency of risotto is largely a matter of preference, so if you like a brothy risotto, add extra broth in step 4. This is a great place to use homemade broth if you have it.

KITCHEN IMPROV

Swap in frozen corn or fava beans for the peas. Stir in up to ¼ cup chopped fresh herbs such as parsley, tarragon, chives, or basil just before serving. Make an even heartier meal by stirring in up to 1 cup shredded or diced cooked chicken or ham or sautéed shrimp with the Parmesan.

spicy polenta WITH white beans AND kale

Serves 4 • Total Time: 30 minutes

- **6 tablespoons extra-virgin olive oil, divided, plus extra for drizzling**
- **1 onion, chopped**
- **12 ounces lacinato kale, stemmed and chopped**
- **1 (15-ounce) can white beans, rinsed**
- **1 (14.5-ounce) can fire-roasted diced tomatoes**
- **1 teaspoon table salt, divided**
- **3 garlic cloves, minced**
- **½ teaspoon red pepper flakes, plus extra for serving**
- **4 cups vegetable or chicken broth**
- **1 cup instant polenta**
- **8 ounces fresh mozzarella cheese, torn into 1-inch pieces**

NO-FUSS INSTANT POLENTA makes a versatile base for an equally easy vegetable-forward topping. Canned tomatoes turn kale and white beans into a proper hearty sauce. Using fire-roasted tomatoes, along with garlic and red pepper flakes, kicks up the flavor.

1 Heat 3 tablespoons oil in 12-inch nonstick skillet over medium-high heat until shimmering. Add onion and cook until softened and lightly browned, 5 to 7 minutes. Stir in kale, beans, tomatoes and their juice, and ¾ teaspoon salt. Cover and cook, stirring occasionally, until kale is very tender and sauce is thickened, 8 to 10 minutes.

2 Meanwhile, cook garlic, pepper flakes, and remaining 3 tablespoons oil in large saucepan over medium heat, stirring frequently, until garlic begins to turn straw-colored, about 4 minutes. Add broth and bring to boil. Whisk in polenta and remaining ¼ teaspoon salt and cook until thickened, about 2 minutes. Season with salt and pepper to taste.

3 Divide polenta evenly among serving bowls and top with bean mixture and mozzarella. Drizzle with extra oil, sprinkle with extra pepper flakes, and serve.

NOTES

Instant polenta expedites this dinner. You can certainly use old-fashioned, but you will need to increase the simmering time by 25 minutes and may need to add more water during simmering.

KITCHEN IMPROV

Curly kale can be used in place of the lacinato. Any variety of white bean will work; consider large butter beans for their impressive appearance. Instead of fresh mozzarella, you can use a shredded semisoft cheese such as fontina, cheddar, or pepper Jack. Toasted nuts sprinkled on top add crunch (pine nuts are a great choice).

wild mushroom ragout WITH farro

Serves 4 • Total Time: 45 minutes

- **3½ cups vegetable or chicken broth**
- **1½ cups whole farro, rinsed**
- **1 pound portobello mushroom caps, halved and sliced ½ inch wide**
- **18 ounces assorted mushrooms, trimmed and halved if small or quartered if large**
- **2 tablespoons extra-virgin olive oil**
- **1 onion, chopped fine**
- **½ ounce dried porcini mushrooms, rinsed and minced**
- **3 garlic cloves, minced**
- **1 teaspoon minced fresh thyme or ¼ teaspoon dried**
- **¼ cup dry Madeira**
- **1 (14.5-ounce) can petite diced tomatoes, drained**
- **2 tablespoons minced fresh parsley**

1 Combine broth and farro in large saucepan and bring to simmer over medium heat. Cook until farro is tender and creamy, 20 to 25 minutes. Season with salt and pepper to taste; cover and keep warm.

2 Meanwhile, microwave portobello and assorted mushrooms in covered bowl until tender, 6 to 8 minutes. Drain, reserving mushroom juices.

3 Heat oil in Dutch oven over medium-high heat until shimmering. Add onion and porcini and cook until onion is softened and lightly browned, 5 to 7 minutes. Stir in drained mushrooms and cook, stirring often, until mushrooms are dry and lightly browned, about 5 minutes.

4 Stir in garlic and thyme and cook until fragrant, about 30 seconds. Stir in Madeira and reserved mushroom juices, scraping up any browned bits. Stir in tomatoes and simmer gently until sauce is slightly thickened, about 8 minutes. Off heat, stir in parsley and season with salt and pepper to taste. Portion farro into individual serving bowls, top with mushroom mixture, and serve.

MEATY PORTOBELLOS, combined with other fresh mushrooms and dried porcini, make a rich, intensely flavorful stew to top nutty, delicately chewy farro. Whole-grain farro is not only incredibly nutritious, it also cooks quickly.

NOTES

Don't use pearl, quick-cooking, or presteamed farro (check the ingredient list on the package to determine this). We love a mix of white or cremini, shiitake, and oyster mushrooms, but you can choose just one or two varieties if you like. Remove any shiitake stems, which are woody and unpleasant.

KITCHEN IMPROV

Dry sherry or red wine can be substituted for the Madeira. Feel free to swap hearty herbs such as rosemary or oregano for the thyme, and tender herbs such as basil or tarragon for the parsley. Drizzle portions with good balsamic vinegar and/or sprinkle with grated Parmesan cheese before serving.

bean sides TO match (OR EAT ON THEIR OWN)

easy cuban black beans

Serves 4 • Total Time: 20 minutes

- **2 tablespoons extra-virgin olive oil**
- **2 large shallots, minced**
- **1 green bell pepper, stemmed, seeded, and chopped fine**
- **4 garlic cloves, minced**
- **½ teaspoon dried oregano**
- **½ teaspoon ground cumin**
- **¼ teaspoon pepper**
- **2 (15-ounce) cans black beans, drained with liquid reserved, divided**

1 Heat oil in large saucepan over medium heat until shimmering. Add shallots and bell pepper and cook until softened and beginning to brown, 6 to 8 minutes. Stir in garlic, oregano, cumin, and pepper and cook until fragrant, about 30 seconds.

2 Off heat, add ½ cup beans and all reserved bean liquid and mash with potato masher until mostly smooth. Stir in remaining beans. Cook over medium heat until warmed through, about 3 minutes. Season with salt and pepper to taste and serve.

CANNED BEANS don't sacrifice quality for convenience. But to do a little more than simply open a can, draw flavor inspiration from Cuba, where spiced black beans are a staple.

NOTES

These beans are even better the next day—leftovers make an excellent breakfast when tucked into a soft taco with a fried egg and salsa.

KITCHEN IMPROV

Level up the beans by sprinkling them with chopped cilantro, thinly sliced scallions, shredded cheese, chopped tomatoes, and/or pickled jalapeños. Make them a meal by serving with rice, quinoa, or other grains; or with plantain chips, sliced avocado, lime wedges, sour cream, or hot sauce.

---

curried lentils

Serves 4 • Total Time: 25 minutes

- **2 tablespoons extra-virgin olive oil**
- **1 large shallot, minced**
- **4 garlic cloves, minced**
- **1 tablespoon curry powder**
- **2 (15-ounce) cans brown lentils, rinsed**
- **¾ cup vegetable or chicken broth**

Heat oil in large saucepan over medium heat until shimmering. Add shallot and cook until softened and lightly browned, 3 to 5 minutes. Stir in garlic and curry powder and cook until fragrant, about 30 seconds. Stir in lentils and broth and bring to simmer. Reduce heat to medium and cook, stirring occasionally, until flavors meld and lentils just begin to break down, about 5 minutes. Season with salt and pepper to taste and serve.

COMFORTING CURRIED lentils are easy to pull together, can make a meal with a grain or roasted vegetable, and reheat beautifully.

NOTES

While dried lentils don't take that long to cook, using canned lentils is a no-brainer for time-pressed meals.

KITCHEN IMPROV

Drizzle with yogurt, or sprinkle with fresh herbs, scallions, tomatoes, or goat or feta cheese. To make the lentils a meal, stir in cubed tofu or a cooked protein and serve with rice or naan.

stewed chickpeas AND spinach WITH dill AND lemon

Serves 4 to 6 • Total Time: 20 minutes

- 2 tablespoons extra-virgin olive oil, plus extra for drizzling
- 3 garlic cloves, sliced thin
- 1/4 teaspoon red pepper flakes
- 2 (15-ounce) cans chickpeas (1 can drained and rinsed, 1 can undrained)
- 10 ounces (10 cups) baby spinach
- 1/2 cup vegetable or chicken broth
- 1/4 teaspoon table salt
- 1/4 cup chopped fresh dill
- 1 tablespoon lemon juice

Cook oil, garlic, and pepper flakes in Dutch oven over medium heat until garlic is golden brown, 3 to 5 minutes. Stir in chickpeas and their liquid, spinach, broth, and salt. Increase heat to medium-high and cook, stirring occasionally, until spinach is wilted and liquid is slightly thickened, about 5 minutes. Off heat, stir in dill and lemon juice. Season with salt and pepper to taste, drizzle with extra oil, and serve.

A LEMONY DILLED broth anchors this Greek-inspired side dish featuring convenient canned chickpeas that are tossed with a tangle of wilted spinach.

NOTES

Don't be alarmed by the volume of spinach—it will cook down significantly.

KITCHEN IMPROV

Any fresh delicate greens you have will work here, including chopped escarole, baby kale, arugula, or a mix. Any canned beans can be used. Substitute other delicate fresh herbs for the dill, such as tarragon or basil. You can make this dish heartier by cooking some crumbled sausage in the pot before adding the oil, or turn it into a ribollita-style dish by folding in cubes of stale bread following the spinach.

---

easy white bean gratin

Serves 4 • Total Time: 25 minutes

- 1 onion, chopped fine
- 2 tablespoons extra-virgin olive oil
- 3 garlic cloves, minced
- 1 teaspoon minced fresh rosemary or 1/4 teaspoon dried
- 2 (15-ounce) can cannellini beans, rinsed, divided
- 1/2 cup vegetable or chicken broth
- 2 ounces Parmesan or Pecorino Romano cheese, grated (1 cup)

1. Microwave onion, oil, garlic, and rosemary in medium bowl, stirring occasionally, until onion is softened, about 5 minutes.
2. Adjust oven rack to upper middle position and heat broiler. Add 2/3 cup beans to bowl with onion mixture and mash with potato masher until smooth. Stir in broth and remaining whole beans until combined. Transfer mixture to 8-inch square broiler-safe baking dish or pan and sprinkle evenly with Parmesan. Broil until mixture is bubbling around edges and cheese is golden brown, 5 to 7 minutes. Transfer dish to wire rack and let cool slightly before serving.

CREAMY, BUBBLY bean gratins are a supremely satisfying way to utilize pantry ingredients.

NOTES

You will need an 8-inch square broiler-safe baking dish or pan.

KITCHEN IMPROV

Any beans work here: Try pinto or small white beans. Any melty cheese works as well; for extra cheesiness, use cheddar or Monterey Jack. Thyme or sage can be substituted for the rosemary. A red onion or 3 large shallots can be substituted for the onion. Bulk up the gratin by including thawed frozen spinach or kale. Top with crispy bacon or arrange croutons under the cheese before broiling.

ful medames

Serves 4 • Total Time: 25 minutes

- 3 tablespoons extra-virgin olive oil, divided, plus extra for drizzling
- 2 teaspoons ground cumin
- 2 (15-ounce) cans fava beans, undrained
- 3 tablespoons lemon juice
- 4 garlic cloves, minced
- 3 tablespoons tahini
- 1 tomato, cored and cut into ½-inch pieces
- ¼ cup finely chopped onion
- 2 tablespoons minced fresh parsley
- 1 serrano chile, stemmed, seeded, and minced
- 2 hard-cooked large eggs, quartered
- 4 (8-inch) pitas

RUSTIC MASHED FAVA beans are flavored with cumin and garlic and topped with a host of fresh ingredients for one of Egypt's most beloved breakfast dishes. It also happens to make an excellent quick weeknight dinner.

1 Combine 1 tablespoon oil and cumin in medium saucepan and cook over medium heat until fragrant, about 2 minutes. Stir in beans and their liquid. Bring to simmer and cook until liquid thickens slightly, 8 to 10 minutes.

2 Off heat, mash beans to coarse consistency using potato masher. Stir in lemon juice, garlic, and remaining 2 tablespoons oil and season with salt to taste.

3 Spread bean mixture evenly over serving platter. Drizzle with tahini, then top with tomato, onion, parsley, serrano, and eggs. Drizzle with extra oil and serve with pitas.

NOTES

The bean mixture can be prepared through step 2 and refrigerated for up to 4 days; when ready to serve, bring to room temperature and adjust the consistency with warm water as needed.

KITCHEN IMPROV

Fava beans are traditional, but other creamy canned beans such as butter, pinto, or cannellini will also work well. You can substitute other fresh herbs (such as basil or cilantro) for the parsley and use ½ medium jalapeño in place of the serrano. You can also serve this with a variety of flatbreads, crackers, or even crudités.

palak dal

Serves 4 • Total Time: 45 minutes

- 4½ cups water
- 1½ cups (10½ ounces) dried red lentils, picked over and rinsed
- 1 tablespoon grated fresh ginger
- ¾ teaspoon ground turmeric
- 3 tablespoons ghee
- 1½ teaspoons brown or yellow mustard seeds
- 1½ teaspoons cumin seeds
- 1 large onion, chopped
- 15 curry leaves, coarsely torn (optional)
- 6 garlic cloves, sliced
- 4 whole dried arbol chiles
- 1 serrano chile, halved lengthwise
- 6 ounces (6 cups) baby spinach
- 1½ teaspoons table salt
- 1½ teaspoons lemon juice, plus extra for seasoning
- ⅓ cup chopped fresh cilantro

1 Bring water, lentils, ginger, and turmeric to boil in large saucepan over medium-high heat. Reduce heat to maintain vigorous simmer. Cook, uncovered and stirring occasionally, until lentils are soft and starting to break down, 18 to 20 minutes.

2 Meanwhile, melt ghee in 10-inch skillet over medium-high heat. Add mustard seeds and cumin seeds and cook, stirring constantly, until seeds sizzle and pop, about 30 seconds. Add onion and cook, stirring frequently, until onion is just starting to brown, about 5 minutes. Add curry leaves (if using), garlic, arbols, and serrano and cook, stirring frequently, until onion and garlic are golden brown, 3 to 4 minutes. Set skillet aside.

3 Whisk lentils vigorously until coarsely pureed, about 30 seconds. Continue to cook until lentils have consistency of loose polenta or oatmeal, up to 5 minutes. Stir in spinach and salt and continue to cook until spinach is fully wilted, 30 to 60 seconds. Add lemon juice to lentils and stir to incorporate. (Dal should have consistency of loose polenta. If too thick, loosen with hot water, adding 1 tablespoon at a time.) Season with salt and extra lemon juice to taste. Transfer dal to individual serving bowls and spoon onion mixture on top. Sprinkle with cilantro and serve.

NOTES

You can substitute browned butter for the ghee; discard browned butter solids before using. Fresh curry leaves add a wonderful aroma (store extra leaves in the freezer), but you can omit them. You can substitute ½ teaspoon cayenne pepper for arbols and ½ jalapeño for the serrano. Monitor the spices and aromatics carefully during frying, and reduce the heat if needed to prevent them from scorching.

KITCHEN IMPROV

You can substitute an equal weight of thawed frozen spinach or kale for the fresh spinach (just be sure to thoroughly squeeze it dry after weighing). Bulk up on fresh herbs by including torn mint leaves. Drizzle with yogurt before serving or bring lemon wedges to the table.

SPICES SIZZLED in ghee with onion, garlic, chiles, and optional curry leaves makes a flavorful, textural, altogether scene-stealing garnish for an otherwise simple dal of red lentils and spinach. Serve with naan and/or rice.

chana masala

Serves 4 • Total Time: 45 minutes

- 1 small red onion, quartered, divided
- 10 sprigs fresh cilantro, stems and leaves separated
- 1 (1½-inch) piece ginger, peeled and chopped coarse
- 2 garlic cloves, chopped coarse
- 2 serrano chiles, stemmed, halved, seeded, and sliced thin crosswise, divided
- 3 tablespoons vegetable oil
- 1 (14.5-ounce) can diced tomatoes
- 1 teaspoon Kashmiri chile powder
- 1 teaspoon ground cumin
- ½ teaspoon ground turmeric
- ½ teaspoon fennel seeds
- 2 (15-ounce) cans chickpeas, undrained
- 1½ teaspoons garam masala
- ½ teaspoon table salt
- Lime wedges

PANTRY-FRIENDLY CANNED chickpeas anchor this version of one of North India's most popular dishes. The fragrantly spiced, tangy tomato-ginger sauce (made easy with the help of a food processor) turns chickpeas into a dinnertime hero. Serve with naan and/or rice.

1 Coarsely chop three-quarters of onion; reserve remaining quarter for garnish. Cut cilantro stems into 1-inch lengths. Process chopped onion, cilantro stems, ginger, garlic, and half of serranos in food processor until finely chopped, scraping down sides of bowl as needed, about 20 seconds. Cook oil and onion mixture in large saucepan over medium-high heat, stirring frequently, until onion is fully softened and beginning to stick to saucepan, 5 to 7 minutes.

2 While onion mixture cooks, process tomatoes and their juice in now-empty food processor until smooth, about 30 seconds. Add chile powder, cumin, turmeric, and fennel seeds to onion mixture and cook, stirring constantly, until fragrant, about 1 minute. Stir in chickpeas and their liquid and processed tomatoes and bring to boil. Adjust heat to maintain simmer, cover, and simmer for 15 minutes. While mixture cooks, finely chop reserved onion quarter.

3 Stir garam masala and salt into chickpea mixture and continue to cook, uncovered and stirring occasionally, until chickpeas are softened and sauce is thickened, 8 to 12 minutes. Season with salt to taste. Transfer to wide, shallow serving bowl. Sprinkle with finely chopped onion, cilantro leaves, and remaining serranos and serve, passing lime wedges separately.

NOTES

If you prefer a spicier chana masala, leave the seeds in the serranos. Kashmiri chile powder should have a brilliant red hue, a fruity flavor, and a slightly tannic edge—but very little heat. If you can't find it, substitute sweet paprika.

KITCHEN IMPROV

Add a bit more complexity by using canned fire-roasted diced tomatoes. You can swap in 1 medium jalapeño for the serranos. The intensely flavored sauce makes any canned beans taste amazing, so if you don't have chickpeas on hand you can easily swap in other varieties.

sicilian white beans AND escarole

Serves 4 • Total Time: 30 minutes

- **1 tablespoon extra-virgin olive oil, plus extra for serving**
- **2 onions, chopped fine**
- **½ teaspoon table salt**
- **4 garlic cloves, minced**
- **⅛ teaspoon red pepper flakes**
- **1 head escarole (1 pound), trimmed and sliced 1 inch thick**
- **1 (15-ounce) can cannellini beans, rinsed**
- **1 cup vegetable broth**
- **1 cup water**
- **2 teaspoons lemon juice**

BUTTERY WHITE BEANS and slightly bitter escarole combine in this speedy but comforting dish. Cranking up the heat after the escarole wilts reduces the liquid quickly before the beans can become mushy.

1 Heat oil in Dutch oven over medium heat until shimmering. Add onions and salt and cook until softened and lightly browned, 5 to 7 minutes. Stir in garlic and pepper flakes and cook until fragrant, about 30 seconds.

2 Stir in escarole, beans, broth, and water and bring to simmer. Cook, stirring occasionally, until escarole is wilted, about 5 minutes. Increase heat to high and cook until liquid is nearly evaporated, 10 to 15 minutes. Stir in lemon juice and season with salt and pepper to taste. Drizzle with extra oil and serve.

NOTES

With such a simple dish, every ingredient plays a big role. This is a good time to pull out your best olive oil for drizzling at the end.

KITCHEN IMPROV

This beans-and-greens formula is beautiful in its simplicity but takes well to customization. Cook some sausage in the pot first and use the rendered fat to sauté the onions. Use chickpeas instead of cannellini beans. Swap out escarole for chicory if you love the flavor of bitter greens (you might want to add a bit more lemon and olive oil at the end). Add chopped preserved lemon or toasted pine nuts for a flavor boost.

calabrian chile white beans WITH almond romesco

Serves 4 • Total Time: 45 minutes

- 1 red bell pepper, stemmed, seeded, and halved lengthwise
- 8 ounces cherry or grape tomatoes, halved
- 1/4 cup extra-virgin olive oil, divided
- 1 cup fresh basil leaves plus 2 tablespoons chopped
- 1 1/2 ounces Parmesan cheese, grated (3/4 cup), plus extra for serving
- 2/3 cup sliced almonds
- 2 tablespoons jarred crushed Calabrian chiles, plus extra for serving
- 2 tablespoons tomato paste
- 2 tablespoons cider vinegar
- 2 garlic cloves, chopped
- 3/4 teaspoon table salt, divided
- 1 onion, chopped fine
- 2 (15-ounce) cans cannellini beans, rinsed
- 2 cups vegetable or chicken broth

1 Adjust oven rack 6 inches from broiler element and heat broiler. Toss bell pepper and cherry tomatoes with 2 tablespoons oil in bowl, then spread in even layer, skin side up, on rimmed baking sheet. Broil until well charred, 8 to 12 minutes. Transfer vegetables and any juices to food processor.

2 Add whole basil leaves, Parmesan, almonds, Calabrian chiles, tomato paste, vinegar, garlic, and 1/2 teaspoon salt and process to coarse paste, 15 to 20 seconds, scraping down sides of bowl once halfway through processing. Season romesco with salt to taste.

3 Heat remaining 2 tablespoons oil in Dutch oven over medium heat until shimmering. Add onion and remaining 1/4 teaspoon salt and cook until softened, about 5 minutes. Stir in romesco, beans, and broth, increase heat to medium-high, and bring to boil. Reduce heat to medium-low and simmer until thickened slightly, about 10 minutes. Season with salt to taste, then sprinkle with chopped basil. Serve with extra Parmesan and extra Calabrian chiles.

BOLDLY FLAVORED ingredients bring spice and rustic texture to canned cannellini beans in this amazing vegetarian meal. Broiling the red pepper and tomatoes before whizzing them in a food processor imbues the vibrant romesco with lightly smoky flavor.

NOTES

Jarred crushed Calabrian chiles are available in the condiment section of some specialty markets and online. You can prepare the romesco through step 2 and refrigerate it for up to 24 hours.

KITCHEN IMPROV

This flexible recipe is a good choice when you're working with limited supplies: Use other beans such as great northern or chickpeas. Substitute crushed hot red peppers or chili-garlic sauce for the chiles. Go with walnuts instead of almonds. Or stir in baby spinach or kale for a dose of greens.

cacio e pepe beans with squash, sage and walnuts

Serves 4 • Total Time: 45 minutes

- 2 pounds butternut squash, peeled, seeded, and cut into 1-inch pieces (6 cups)
- 2 tablespoons extra-virgin olive oil, divided
- ½ teaspoon table salt, divided
- 1½ teaspoons pepper, divided, plus extra for serving
- 4 tablespoons unsalted butter
- ⅓ cup chopped walnuts
- ¼ cup fresh sage leaves
- ½ teaspoon lemon juice
- 2 (15-ounce) cans navy beans (1 can rinsed, 1 can undrained)
- ¼ cup water
- 2 ounces Pecorino Romano cheese, grated (1 cup), plus extra for serving
- 2 garlic cloves, minced to paste (1 teaspoon)

NAVY BEANS become ultracreamy when you take advantage of their starchy canning liquid and stir in lots of Pecorino Romano cheese. Roasted squash adds sweetness, and a browned butter, sage, and walnut drizzle makes humble beans feel downright luxurious.

1 Adjust oven rack to middle position and heat oven to 450 degrees. Toss squash with 1 tablespoon oil, ¼ teaspoon salt, and ⅛ teaspoon pepper and spread in even layer on rimmed baking sheet. Roast until tender and sides touching sheet are well browned, about 25 minutes.

2 Meanwhile, melt butter in large saucepan over medium heat. Add walnuts, sage leaves, ⅛ teaspoon pepper, and remaining ¼ teaspoon salt and cook, stirring frequently, until nuts are lightly toasted and butter is browned, about 3 minutes. Stir in lemon juice, then transfer to bowl and cover to keep warm.

3 Heat remaining 1 tablespoon oil in now-empty saucepan over medium heat until shimmering. Add remaining 1¼ teaspoons pepper and cook until fragrant, about 30 seconds. Add beans and bean liquid and water and bring to simmer. Reduce heat to low, cover, and simmer gently for 5 minutes.

4 Off heat, stir in Pecorino and garlic, stirring in 1 to 2 tablespoons hot water if sauce begins to overthicken. Transfer beans and squash to platter or divide among individual serving bowls, then drizzle with walnut mixture. Sprinkle with additional pepper and Pecorino and serve.

NOTES

For the best texture, it's important to remove the fibrous flesh just below the squash's skin. You can also skip the peeling and buy prepeeled squash halves; you will need about 1½ pounds to yield 6 cups.

KITCHEN IMPROV

Feel free to swap in other creamy beans such as cannellini, great northern, or pinto for the navy beans. You can swap in unpeeled delicata squash for the butternut; quarter it lengthwise and slice it 1 inch thick. Other nuts, like almonds, hazelnuts, and pine nuts, also work here.

east african coconut curry WITH tofu AND squash

Serves 4 to 6 • Total Time: 45 minutes

- 3 tablespoons extra-virgin olive oil, divided
- 1 pound butternut squash, peeled, seeded, and cut into 1/2-inch pieces (3 cups)
- 1 1/2 teaspoons table salt, divided
- 1 onion, chopped fine
- 2 tablespoons curry powder
- 2 cinnamon sticks
- 1/4 cup tomato paste
- 2 tablespoons grated fresh ginger
- 2 garlic cloves, minced
- 1 1/2 teaspoons sugar
- 1 (15-ounce) can coconut milk
- 1 cup water
- 14 ounces firm tofu, cut into 1-inch pieces
- 1 tablespoon lime juice
- 1 cup fresh mint leaves
- 1/4 cup chopped roasted cashews

SILKY COCONUT curries are popular throughout East Africa. This weeknight-friendly version features butternut squash and tofu, which plumps and tenderizes as it braises in the spiced coconut milk. Serve with rice noodles or steamed rice.

1 Heat 1 tablespoon oil in 12-inch nonstick skillet over medium-high heat until shimmering. Add squash and 1/4 teaspoon salt and cook until spotty brown and beginning to soften, 7 to 10 minutes; transfer to bowl.

2 Add onion, 1 tablespoon oil, and 1/4 teaspoon salt to now-empty skillet and cook over medium heat until softened, about 5 minutes. Add curry powder and cinnamon sticks and cook until fragrant, about 30 seconds. Stir in tomato paste, ginger, garlic, sugar, remaining 1 tablespoon oil, and remaining 1 teaspoon salt and cook until fragrant, about 1 minute. Whisk in coconut milk and water and bring to simmer. Stir in squash and tofu. Reduce heat to medium-low, cover, and cook, stirring occasionally, until squash is tender, about 10 minutes.

3 Off heat, discard cinnamon sticks. Stir in lime juice and season with salt and pepper to taste. Top with mint and cashews and serve.

NOTES

It's important to remove the fibrous flesh just below the squash's skin. Or skip the peeling and purchase prepeeled butternut squash halves; you'll need about 12 ounces to yield 3 cups. Firm or extra-firm tofu works best; avoid soft tofu. You will need a 12-inch nonstick skillet with a tight-fitting lid.

KITCHEN IMPROV

You can swap in unpeeled delicata squash for the butternut; quarter it lengthwise and slice it 1 inch thick. Bulk up on the fresh herbs; basil, cilantro, and parsley are all great additions. Other nuts, including almonds and hazelnuts, work well, too.

chickpea curry

Serves 4 • Total Time: 40 minutes

- **2 tablespoons vegetable oil**
- **2 green bell peppers, stemmed, seeded, and cut into 1-inch pieces**
- **1½ teaspoons table salt**
- **½ teaspoon pepper**
- **1 jalapeño chile, stemmed, seeded, and minced**
- **4 garlic cloves, minced**
- **1 tablespoon grated fresh ginger**
- **1 tablespoon curry powder**
- **2 (15-ounce) cans chickpeas, rinsed**
- **1 (14.5-ounce) can diced tomatoes**
- **1 (14-ounce) can coconut milk**

1 Heat oil in Dutch oven over medium-high heat until shimmering. Add bell peppers, salt, and pepper and cook until bell peppers are beginning to brown, 5 to 7 minutes. Add jalapeño, garlic, ginger, and curry powder and cook until fragrant, about 30 seconds.

2 Add chickpeas, tomatoes and their juice, and coconut milk and bring to boil. Cover, reduce heat to medium-low, and simmer until bell peppers are tender and flavors meld, stirring occasionally, about 20 minutes. Serve.

SIMPLE, SPEEDY, and pantry-friendly, this curry punches far above its weight in terms of flavor payoff. Jalapeño, garlic, ginger, and curry powder bloom in hot oil to provide a flavor base that becomes a savory broth with the addition of coconut milk and diced canned tomatoes. Serve with rice.

NOTES

To make this curry spicier, add the seeds from the jalapeño.

KITCHEN IMPROV

This is a great use-it-up curry for whatever vegetables you have on hand. Cauliflower, sweet potatoes, eggplant, or cabbage (up to 3 cups) would all work well in place of the green bell peppers. Add baby kale, spinach, or arugula during the last couple minutes of simmering. Sprinkle with fresh cilantro or parsley.

chickpea shakshuka

Serves 4 • Total Time: 35 minutes

- 2 tablespoons extra-virgin olive oil, plus extra for drizzling
- 1 onion, chopped fine
- 1 cup jarred roasted red peppers, patted dry and chopped coarse
- 1 teaspoon table salt
- ½ teaspoon pepper
- 1 (15-ounce) can chickpeas, rinsed
- 1½ teaspoons smoked paprika
- 1 teaspoon ground cumin
- 1 (28-ounce) can crushed tomatoes
- 4 large eggs
- 2 ounces goat cheese, crumbled (½ cup)

ADDING CHICKPEAS to shakshuka nudges this dish of eggs in a tomato-pepper sauce firmly into dinner territory. (In North Africa, it's enjoyed at any time of day.) Using jarred roasted red peppers makes this as pantry-friendly as it is speedy.

1 Heat oil in 12-inch nonstick skillet over medium-high heat until shimmering. Add onion, red peppers, salt, and pepper and cook until onion is softened, about 5 minutes. Add chickpeas, paprika, and cumin and cook until fragrant, about 1 minute. Stir in tomatoes and bring to simmer. Cover, reduce heat to medium-low, and cook until flavors meld, about 5 minutes. Remove skillet from heat.

2 Using back of spoon, make 4 shallow indentations (about 1 inch wide) in surface of vegetable mixture. Crack 1 egg into each indentation (which will hold yolk in place but not fully contain egg). Bring to simmer over medium-low heat. Cover and cook until yolks film over, 3 to 6 minutes, adjusting heat to maintain gentle simmer. Continue to cook, covered, until whites are softly but uniformly set (if skillet is shaken lightly, each egg should jiggle as single unit), 1 to 3 minutes.

3 Sprinkle with goat cheese, drizzle with extra oil, and serve.

NOTES

You will need a 12-inch nonstick skillet with a tight-fitting lid.

KITCHEN IMPROV

You can swap in cannellini or great northern beans for the chickpeas. Make this dish heartier by using 8 eggs: Create 8 divots (7 around the perimeter and 1 in the center) in step 2. You can also top each serving with yogurt. Level up the presentation by sprinkling the shakshuka with fresh herbs (parsley, mint, and/or cilantro) in addition to the goat cheese.

always craveable noodles

chapter 5

mezzi rigatoni WITH spicy gochujang tomato sauce

Serves 4 to 6 ▪ Total Time: 35 minutes

- **5 tablespoons unsalted butter, divided**
- **1/3 cup panko bread crumbs**
- **3 garlic cloves, minced, divided**
- **2 shallots, minced**
- **3 tablespoons gochujang**
- **1 tablespoon tomato paste**
- **1 cup passata**
- **1/2 cup heavy cream**
- **1/2 teaspoon table salt, plus salt for cooking pasta**
- **1 pound mezzi rigatoni or rigatoni**
- **1 tablespoon chopped fresh chives**
- **Grated or shaved Parmesan cheese**

OPPOSITE CORNERS of the world come together in this vibrant pasta sauce, which is powered by Italian passata, an uncooked strained tomato puree, and Korean gochujang, a deeply savory fermented chile paste that has deep umami and just a hint of heat.

1 Bring 4 quarts water to boil in large pot. While water comes to boil, melt 1 tablespoon butter in 12-inch nonstick skillet over medium heat. Add panko and cook, stirring frequently, until evenly browned and fragrant, 2 to 4 minutes. Transfer panko to small bowl and stir in one-third of garlic.

2 Melt remaining 4 tablespoons butter in now-empty skillet over medium heat. Add shallots and cook until beginning to brown, 3 to 5 minutes. Stir in remaining garlic and cook until fragrant, about 30 seconds. Stir in gochujang and tomato paste and cook until fragrant, about 1 minute. Stir in passata, heavy cream, and salt. Season with salt and pepper to taste. Cover to keep warm.

3 Meanwhile, add pasta and 1 tablespoon salt to boiling water and cook, stirring often, until pasta is al dente. Reserve 1 cup cooking water, then drain pasta and return it to pot. Add sauce and 1/2 cup reserved cooking water and toss to combine. Adjust consistency with additional reserved cooking water as needed. Serve, sprinkling individual portions with seasoned panko, chives, and Parmesan.

NOTES

Pomì is a good brand of passata to look for. If you can't find it, use canned tomato puree (which is cooked). For the gochujang paste, don't substitute gochujang sauce, which contains additional ingredients.

KITCHEN IMPROV

Other short or tubular pasta shapes such as fusilli, farfalle, orecchiette, ziti, or penne work in place of the rigatoni. Use sliced scallions in place of the chives; parsley and basil are also good alternatives.

COMPLEX FLAVOR from a few humble ingredients is a hallmark of one of Rome's most iconic pasta dishes. Adding a touch of cream ensures that this luscious sauce doesn't separate and perfectly coats each pasta strand.

cacio e pepe

Serves 4 to 6 • Total Time: 30 minutes

- **6 ounces Pecorino Romano cheese, 4 ounces grated fine (2 cups) and 2 ounces grated coarse (1 cup)**
- **1 pound spaghetti**
- **Table salt for cooking pasta**
- **2 tablespoons heavy cream**
- **2 teaspoons extra-virgin olive oil**
- **1½ teaspoons pepper**

1. Place finely grated Pecorino in medium bowl. Set colander in large serving bowl.

2. Bring 4 quarts water to boil in large pot. Add spaghetti and 1 tablespoon salt and cook, stirring often, until al dente. Drain spaghetti into prepared colander, reserving cooking water. Pour 1½ cups cooking water into 2-cup liquid measuring cup and discard remainder. Return drained spaghetti to now-empty bowl.

3. Slowly whisk 1 cup reserved cooking water into finely grated Pecorino until smooth, then whisk in heavy cream, oil, and pepper. Gradually pour cheese mixture over spaghetti and toss to combine. Let spaghetti rest for 1 to 2 minutes, tossing frequently and adding remaining cooking water as needed to adjust consistency. Serve, passing coarsely grated Pecorino separately.

NOTES

Seek out imported Pecorino Romano. Use the small holes on a box grater to grate the cheese finely and the large holes to grate it coarsely. (Alternatively, use a food processor to grate it finely: Cut the cheese into 2-inch pieces and process until finely ground, about 45 seconds.) For a slightly less rich dish, you can substitute half-and-half for the heavy cream. Don't skip the brief rest before serving; this allows the flavors to develop and the sauce to thicken to just the right consistency.

KITCHEN IMPROV

Linguine will also work well in this dish; avoid tubular pasta shapes. Add minced fresh parley, basil, oregano, or tarragon to the pasta just before serving. To make this pasta heartier, top with sliced cooked chicken or poached shrimp.

pasta WITH creamy lemon–sichuan peppercorn sauce

Serves 4 to 6 • Total Time: 35 minutes

- **4 teaspoons Sichuan peppercorns**
- **1 pound spaghetti**
- **Table salt for cooking pasta**
- **3 tablespoons extra-virgin olive oil**
- **2 garlic cloves, minced**
- **1 cup chicken or vegetable broth**
- **1 cup crème fraîche**
- **3 tablespoons white miso**
- **2 teaspoons grated lemon zest plus 2 tablespoons juice**
- **1 teaspoon pepper**
- **2 tablespoons chopped fresh parsley**

BRIGHT LEMON, umami-packed miso, and tangy crème fraîche combine with tingly Sichuan peppercorns (added in two stages to showcase their unique flavor) to create an unexpected and utterly delicious creamy pasta dish.

1 Bring 4 quarts water to boil in large pot. While water comes to boil, heat dry medium saucepan over medium heat for 1 minute. Add peppercorns and toast until fragrant, about 1 minute, stirring frequently. Transfer peppercorns to mortar and pestle, let cool to room temperature, then coarsely grind.

2 Add pasta and 1 tablespoon salt to boiling water and cook, stirring often, until al dente. Reserve 1 cup cooking water, then drain pasta and return it to pot.

3 Meanwhile, cook oil, garlic, and half of ground peppercorns over medium heat in now-empty saucepan until fragrant, about 1 minute. Stir in broth and bring to boil. Reduce heat to medium-low and simmer until reduced by half, about 5 minutes. Whisk in crème fraîche, miso, lemon zest and juice, and pepper. Increase heat to medium-high and return to brief simmer. Season with salt and pepper to taste. Cover and keep warm.

4 Add sauce and ½ cup reserved cooking water to pasta and toss to combine. Adjust consistency with remaining reserved cooking water as needed. Stir in remaining ground peppercorns and season with salt and pepper to taste. Sprinkle with parsley and serve immediately.

NOTES

A mortar and pestle is good for grinding the peppercorns, but you could also use a spice grinder.

KITCHEN IMPROV

Spaghetti or linguine is great for this dish, but short or tubular pasta shapes such as penne, fusilli, farfalle, ziti, or rigatoni also work. Serve with extra lemon juice for a very punchy sauce.

AMP UP THE FLAVOR big-time with chili crisp in this streamlined Sichuan supper. This spicy, fragrant condiment is a smart shortcut to flavoring a rich and tangy sauce for springy noodles, savory pork, and tender bok choy.

NOTES

You can substitute dry sherry and balsamic vinegar for theShaoxing wine and Chinese black vinegar, respectively. Use a neutral chili crisp that has onion or garlic but does not include fermented black beans. A mortar and pestle is the best tool for grinding a small amount of Sichuan peppercorns. (If you want to use a spice grinder, grind a larger amount and measure out a heaping ¼ teaspoon.) You can make the chili crisp sauce ahead and refrigerate it for up to 1 week; bring it to room temperature before using.

KITCHEN IMPROV

Fresh (or frozen) noodles have the best texture, but 12 ounces dried Chinese wheat noodles or even spaghetti will also work.

chili crisp noodles

Serves 4 to 6 • Total Time: 45 minutes

- **1/3 cup plus 2 tablespoons soy sauce, divided**
- **1/3 cup unsweetened natural peanut butter**
- **3 tablespoons Chinese black vinegar**
- **1/4 cup chili crisp, plus extra for serving**
- **2 tablespoons plus 1/2 teaspoon sugar, divided**
- **2 garlic cloves, minced to paste**
- **1 teaspoon grated fresh ginger**
- **1/2 teaspoon Sichuan peppercorns, finely ground**
- **1 tablespoon vegetable oil**
- **8 ounces ground pork**
- **1 pound baby bok choy, stalks sliced thin crosswise, greens cut into 3/4-inch pieces**
- **2 scallions, white and green parts separated and sliced thin**
- **2 tablespoons Shaoxing wine**
- **1 pound fresh Chinese wheat noodles**

1. Whisk 1/3 cup soy sauce and peanut butter in medium bowl until fully incorporated, then whisk in vinegar until combined. Add chili crisp, 2 tablespoons sugar, garlic, ginger, and peppercorns and whisk to combine. (Sauce should be thick enough to coat a spoon; adjust consistency with 1 to 2 tablespoons water as needed.)

2. Bring 4 quarts water to boil in large pot. While water comes to boil, heat oil in 12-inch nonstick skillet over medium-high heat until shimmering. Add pork and cook, breaking up meat with wooden spoon, until browned, 5 to 7 minutes. Add bok choy stalks and scallion whites and cook, stirring constantly, for 1 minute. Stir in bok choy greens, Shaoxing wine, remaining 2 tablespoons soy sauce, and remaining 1/2 teaspoon sugar, stirring to coat pork and bok choy. Reduce heat to medium and cook until bok choy greens are wilted, about 1 minute; set aside.

3. Add noodles to boiling water. Reduce heat to maintain very gentle simmer and cook, stirring occasionally, until almost tender (center of noodles should be firm with slightly opaque dot). Drain noodles very well in colander and rinse with warm running water. Drain well. Gently toss noodles with 3/4 cup sauce in separate bowl.

4. Divide noodles among individual serving bowls. Top with pork mixture, then sprinkle with scallion greens. Serve with remaining chili crisp sauce and extra chili crisp, mixing each bowl well before eating.

san francisco–style garlic noodles

Serves 4 • Total Time: 40 minutes

- **8 tablespoons unsalted butter, cut into 4 pieces**
- **2 teaspoons garlic powder**
- **1½ ounces Parmesan cheese, shredded (½ cup)**
- **5 teaspoons minced garlic, divided**
- **½ teaspoon kosher salt**
- **1 pound fresh lo mein noodles**
- **1 tablespoon Maggi Seasoning**
- **3 scallions, sliced thin**
- **¼ teaspoon sugar**

1 Microwave butter, covered, in 1-cup liquid measuring cup at 50 percent power until melted, about 1 minute. Let sit until whey and yellow butterfat separate, 3 to 5 minutes. Combine garlic powder and 1½ teaspoons water in small bowl and stir until smooth paste forms. Stir in additional 1½ teaspoons water and set aside. Crumble Parmesan into approximately ¼-inch pieces and set aside.

2 Bring 4 quarts water to boil in large pot. While water comes to boil, transfer 3 tablespoons butterfat to 10-inch skillet (it's OK if a small amount of whey ends up in skillet). Add 4 teaspoons garlic and salt and cook over medium-low heat, stirring occasionally, until garlic is pale golden brown, 7 to 10 minutes. Add remaining 1 teaspoon garlic, stir well, and remove skillet from heat.

3 Add noodles to boiling water and reduce heat to maintain very gentle simmer. Cook, stirring occasionally, until almost tender (center of noodles should be firm with slightly opaque dot). Drain well.

4 Add noodles and Maggi to skillet. Cook over medium-high heat, tossing with tongs, until Maggi is absorbed and any large garlic clumps are broken up, about 30 seconds. Add scallions, sugar, remaining 5 tablespoons butter (whey and butterfat), and garlic powder mixture and toss until well combined, about 30 seconds. Off heat, season with pepper to taste. Add 2 tablespoons Parmesan and toss to combine. Serve immediately, passing remaining Parmesan separately.

NOTES

Using only the butterfat to cook the garlic prevents milk solids in the butter from browning, which would alter this dish's iconic flavor. Use the large holes of a box grater to shred the Parmesan. Don't substitute granulated garlic for garlic powder, as it will clump. Fresh (or frozen) noodles will give the best texture, but 12 ounces dried lo mein noodles or spaghetti will also work. You can substitute liquid soy aminos if Maggi is unavailable; don't use soy sauce or coconut aminos.

KITCHEN IMPROV

To make these noodles heartier, top them with cooked ground chicken, pork, or beef. Roasted Asparagus or Broiled Smashed Zucchini (pages 142–143) also make great additions.

BUTTER-GLOSSED, CHEWY, and flecked with Parmesan and scallions, San Francisco's beloved and historic noodle dish is simple to make, taking advantage of the microwave to clarify the butter and using garlic in three different ways to achieve deep flavor.

NUTTY, FRAGRANT, and soothing, liang mian is a fresh, easy option for summer dining. Every bite manages to be both hearty and refreshing, thanks to the chewy noodles coated in a satisfyingly sweet-hot dressing and the cool cucumber garnish.

liang mian (CHILLED SESAME NOODLES)

Serves 4 • Total Time: 45 minutes

- **1 pound fresh Chinese wheat noodles**
- **2 teaspoons toasted sesame oil, divided**
- **¼ cup Chinese sesame paste**
- **1 tablespoon mayonnaise**
- **1 tablespoon chili oil, divided**
- **3 tablespoons soy sauce**
- **5 teaspoons Chinese black vinegar**
- **4 teaspoons sugar**
- **1½ teaspoons minced garlic, divided**
- **1 teaspoon grated fresh ginger**
- **1 Persian cucumber, cut into 3-inch-long matchsticks**
- **1 scallion, sliced thin**
- **Toasted sesame seeds (optional)**

1 Bring 4 quarts water to boil in large pot. Add noodles and reduce heat to maintain very gentle simmer. Cook, stirring occasionally, until almost tender (center of noodles should be firm with slightly opaque dot). Meanwhile, place 1 teaspoon sesame oil in large bowl.

2 Drain noodles very well in colander. Transfer noodles to bowl with oil and toss with tongs until lightly coated. Transfer noodles to rimmed baking sheet and spread into even layer. Refrigerate until cold, about 20 minutes.

3 Whisk sesame paste, mayonnaise, 2 teaspoons chili oil, and remaining 1 teaspoon sesame oil together in now-empty bowl. Add soy sauce, vinegar, 4 teaspoons water, sugar, 1 teaspoon garlic, and ginger and whisk until smooth. Season dressing to taste with remaining 1 teaspoon chili oil and remaining ½ teaspoon garlic. Add cold noodles and toss until well combined. Divide noodles evenly among serving bowls and top with cucumber, scallion, and sesame seeds, if using. Serve immediately.

NOTES

Look for sesame paste that isdark and smooth, and stir well before using. If Chinese sesame paste or black vinegar is unavailable, use unsalted, unsweetened natural peanut butter or balsamic vinegar, respectively. You can also sub in one-quarter of an English cucumber for the Persian cucumber.

KITCHEN IMPROV

Fresh (or frozen) noodles have the best texture, but you can use 12 ounces of dried Chinese wheat noodles or spaghetti. It's easy to personalize each serving: You might spice it up with a dollop of chili crisp, make it more filling with shredded chicken or bits of ham, add extra freshness with cilantro or basil leaves, and/or counter the rich dressing with more thinly sliced vegetables such as bell peppers, radishes, snow peas, or carrots.

easy side salads

mixed green salad WITH miso-honey vinaigrette

Serves 4 • Total Time: 20 minutes

- **1 tablespoon white miso**
- **1½ tablespoons mayonnaise**
- **1 teaspoon honey**
- **2 tablespoons rice vinegar**
- **⅛ teaspoon table salt**
- **¼ cup extra-virgin olive oil, divided**
- **2 tablespoons vegetable oil**
- **4 cups mixed baby lettuce (4 ounces)**
- **½ English cucumber, halved lengthwise and sliced thin**
- **1 cup snow peas, strings removed and cut in half**
- **1 tablespoon toasted sesame seeds (optional)**

1 Using fork, stir miso, mayonnaise, and honey in 1-cup jar until well combined. Add vinegar and salt. Seal jar and shake until smooth, about 10 seconds. Add 2 tablespoons olive oil, seal jar, and shake until combined, about 10 seconds. Add remaining 2 tablespoons olive oil and repeat shaking. Add vegetable oil and shake until smooth and thickened.

2 Combine lettuce, cucumber, and snow peas in large bowl. Measure out ¼ cup dressing and drizzle over salad. Use tongs to toss until salad is well coated with dressing. Sprinkle salad with sesame seeds, if using. Serve.

TENDER GREENS, juicy cucumber, and crisp snow peas (or other favorite veggies) are tossed with a mellow "shake-ahead" dressing for a versatile green salad.

NOTES

The dressing makes about ½ cup, enough for a second salad. Refrigerate it for up to 1 week; shake briefly before using.

KITCHEN IMPROV

You could use green leaf lettuce, baby arugula, or romaine lettuce hearts in place of the mixed baby lettuce. Swap in or add extra veggies: Sliced bell pepper, thinly sliced celery, shaved carrot ribbons, and thawed frozen peas are all great options. Add chopped toasted nuts or seeds. Make a Dijon-honey vinaigrette by swapping in 1 tablespoon Dijon mustard for the miso and white wine vinegar for the rice vinegar.

---

arugula salad WITH grapes, fennel AND blue cheese

Serves 4 • Total Time: 20 minutes

- **4 teaspoons apricot jam**
- **3 tablespoons white wine vinegar**
- **1 small shallot, minced**
- **¼ teaspoon table salt**
- **¼ teaspoon pepper**
- **3 tablespoons extra-virgin olive oil**
- **½ small fennel bulb, halved, cored, and sliced thin**
- **5 ounces (5 cups) baby arugula**
- **6 ounces seedless red grapes, halved lengthwise (1 cup)**
- **3 ounces blue cheese, crumbled (¾ cup)**
- **½ cup pecans or walnuts, toasted and chopped**

1 Whisk jam and vinegar in large bowl until smooth. Add shallot, salt, and pepper and whisk until combined. Whisking constantly, slowly drizzle in oil until emulsified. Stir in fennel and let sit for 10 minutes.

2 Add arugula and grapes and toss gently to coat. Season with salt and pepper to taste. Sprinkle with blue cheese and pecans and serve.

SWEET GRAPES and salty blue cheese are strong supporting players to peppery arugula and anise-y fennel. Chopped pecans add a toasty crunch.

NOTES

Any mild blue cheese will work here.

KITCHEN IMPROV

Try other types of fruit jams, such as seedless raspberry or fig. Swap in other types of vinegar and crumbly cheese, like goat or feta. Use green leaf lettuce, mixed baby greens, or romaine lettuce hearts in place of the arugula. Mince and add some of the fennel fronds, or add minced fresh dill or parsley.

zucchini ribbon salad

Serves 4 • Total Time: 15 minutes

- **1½ pounds zucchini or summer squash**
- **2 tablespoons extra-virgin olive oil**
- **½ teaspoon grated lime zest plus 1 tablespoon juice**
- **1 garlic clove, minced**
- **¾ teaspoon table salt**
- **¼ teaspoon pepper**
- **½ cup chopped fresh cilantro or parsley**
- **2 ounces queso fresco, crumbled (½ cup)**
- **¼ cup pepitas or sunflower seeds, toasted**

Using vegetable peeler, shave zucchini lengthwise into very thin ribbons. Whisk oil, lime zest and juice, garlic, salt, and pepper together in large bowl. Add zucchini, cilantro, and queso fresco and toss to combine. Season with salt and pepper to taste. Sprinkle with pepitas and serve immediately.

WHEN LIFE gives you zucchini, make zucchini ribbon salad. Shave it into long ribbons with a vegetable peeler, creating ample surface area for the flavorful dressing to cling to. Toss in tangy queso fresco, crunchy toasted pepitas, and fresh cilantro for textural contrast.

NOTES

Using in-season zucchini and good-quality olive oil makes a big difference here. Look for small zucchini, which are younger and have thinner skins.

KITCHEN IMPROV

Sub feta for the queso fresco. Or swap in lemon for lime juice, shaved Parmesan for the queso fresco, and chopped nuts for the seeds.

---

pai huang gua (SICHUAN SMASHED CUCUMBERS)

Serves 4 • Total Time: 25 minutes

- **2 English cucumbers**
- **1½ teaspoons kosher salt**
- **4 teaspoons Chinese black vinegar**
- **1 teaspoon garlic, minced to paste**
- **1 tablespoon soy sauce**
- **2 teaspoons toasted sesame oil**
- **1 teaspoon sugar**
- **1 teaspoon sesame seeds, toasted**

1 Trim and discard ends from cucumbers. Cut cucumbers crosswise into 3 equal lengths. Place pieces in large zipper-lock bag and seal bag. Using small skillet or rolling pin, firmly but gently smash cucumber pieces until flattened and split lengthwise into 3 to 4 spears each. Tear spears into rough 1- to 1½-inch pieces and transfer to colander set in large bowl. Toss pieces with salt and let sit for at least 15 minutes or up to 30 minutes.

2 While cucumbers sit, whisk vinegar and garlic together in small bowl; let sit for at least 5 minutes or up to 15 minutes.

3 Whisk soy sauce, oil, and sugar into vinegar mixture until sugar has dissolved. Transfer cucumbers to medium bowl and discard any extracted liquid. Add dressing and sesame seeds to cucumbers and toss to combine. Serve immediately.

SMASHING CUCUMBERS is a classic Chinese technique that creates lots of crags and crevices—which both helps the cucumbers shed excess liquid and also helps them hold onto the sesame-soy dressing.

NOTES

Seek out Chinese Chinkiang (or Zhenjiang) black vinegar for this dish. If you can't find it, you can substitute 2 teaspoons unseasoned rice vinegar plus 1 teaspoon balsamic vinegar. A rasp grater makes quick work of turning the garlic into a paste.

KITCHEN IMPROV

Spice things up by drizzling the salad with chili oil or chili crisp.

bucatini WITH charred zucchini, mint AND lemon

Serves 4 to 6 • Total Time: 35 minutes

- **1½ pounds zucchini, sliced into ½-inch-thick rounds**
- **1 teaspoon table salt, divided, plus salt for cooking pasta**
- **2 tablespoons unsalted butter, divided**
- **¼ cup extra-virgin olive oil, plus extra for drizzling**
- **3 garlic cloves, sliced thin**
- **1 tablespoon coriander seeds, cracked**
- **½ teaspoon red pepper flakes**
- **1 pound bucatini**
- **¼ cup grated Parmesan cheese, plus extra for serving**
- **1 cup torn fresh mint leaves**
- **3 tablespoons capers, rinsed**
- **2 teaspoons grated lemon zest plus 3 tablespoons juice**
- **4 ounces (½ cup) whole-milk ricotta cheese, room temperature (optional)**
- **3 tablespoons toasted pine nuts**

1 Bring 4 quarts water to boil in large pot. While water comes to boil, sprinkle zucchini with ¼ teaspoon salt. Melt 1 tablespoon butter in 12-inch nonstick skillet over medium-high heat. Arrange half of zucchini in skillet in single layer and cook until well browned on both sides, 3 to 5 minutes per side; transfer to paper towel–lined plate. Repeat with remaining 1 tablespoon butter and remaining zucchini; transfer to plate.

2 Off heat, add oil, garlic, and coriander to now-empty skillet and cook, using residual heat, until fragrant and just beginning to brown, about 2 minutes. Stir in pepper flakes.

3 Meanwhile, add pasta and 1 tablespoon salt to boiling water and cook, stirring often, until al dente. Reserve 1½ cups cooking water, then drain pasta and return to pot. Add 1 cup reserved cooking water, oil mixture, Parmesan, and remaining ¾ teaspoon salt and stir constantly until most of water has been absorbed but still pools slightly in bottom of pot. Gently stir in zucchini, mint, capers, and lemon zest and juice. Adjust consistency with remaining reserved cooking water as needed.

4 Dollop individual portions with ricotta, if using. Sprinkle with pine nuts and extra Parmesan and drizzle with extra oil before serving.

NOTES

Look for zucchini that are 2 inches in diameter or smaller for the best flavor. If using larger zucchini, halve them lengthwise before slicing; you may need to brown the zucchini in three batches, using an additional tablespoon of butter. To crack coriander seeds, place them on a cutting board and use the back of a heavy saucepan and a rocking motion.

KITCHEN IMPROV

Bucatini, with its hollow center, is great for absorbing the sauce, but other strand pastas like spaghetti and linguine also work. Swap in summer squash for some or all of the zucchini. Add fresh basil in combination with the mint. Use chopped toasted walnuts, almonds, or pistachios instead of pine nuts.

ZUCCHINI BROWNED in butter is the star of this upgraded aglio e olio. Lemon, capers, pine nuts, and citrusy coriander seeds bring complexity, while an optional dollop of ricotta adds creaminess and richness.

viet-cajun garlic-butter rice noodles WITH corn AND shrimp

Serves 4 • Total Time: 45 minutes

- **6 ounces rice vermicelli**
- **8 tablespoons unsalted butter**
- **1 shallot, minced**
- **4 garlic cloves, minced to paste (2 teaspoons)**
- **2 teaspoons grated fresh ginger**
- **¼ teaspoon red pepper flakes, plus extra for sprinkling**
- **5 teaspoons fish sauce**
- **2 teaspoons Cajun seasoning**
- **2 teaspoons sugar**
- **1 teaspoon grated lime zest plus 2 tablespoons juice**
- **1 pound extra-large shrimp (21 to 25 per pound), peeled, deveined, and tails removed**
- **3 ears corn, kernels cut from cobs**
- **3 celery ribs, sliced thin on bias**
- **½ cup chopped fresh cilantro, divided**

VIET-CAJUN FUSION cuisine (created by Vietnamese immigrants who settled in the Gulf Coast region of Louisiana and Texas) inspires these umami-rich rice noodles coated with a flavor-packed butter sauce and topped with a mixture of juicy shrimp, sweet corn, and crunchy celery.

1. Place vermicelli in large bowl and cover with boiling water. Let sit until noodles are just tender, about 10 minutes. Drain noodles and rinse under cold running water until cool. Drain noodles very well, then spread in even layer on rimmed baking sheet and set aside.

2. Melt butter in Dutch oven over medium heat. Add shallot and cook, stirring frequently, until softened, about 3 minutes. Stir in garlic, ginger, and pepper flakes and cook until fragrant, about 30 seconds. Stir in fish sauce, Cajun seasoning, sugar, and lime zest and juice, then reduce heat to lowest setting to keep butter sauce warm.

3. Combine shrimp, corn, celery, and ⅓ cup butter sauce in 12-inch nonstick skillet. Cook over medium heat, stirring frequently, until shrimp are opaque throughout and celery is crisp-tender, 5 to 7 minutes. Off heat, stir in ¼ cup cilantro.

4. Add noodles to remaining butter sauce and gently toss to coat. Divide noodles among individual serving bowls, then top with shrimp mixture. Sprinkle with remaining ¼ cup cilantro and extra pepper flakes. Serve.

NOTES

If fresh corn isn't in season, substitute 2 cups thawed frozen corn. A rasp grater makes quick work of turning the garlic into a paste.

KITCHEN IMPROV

You can swap in Creole or Old Bay seasonings for the Cajun seasoning (or simply use paprika). This recipe also works well with 8 ounces lump crabmeat instead of shrimp; add the crab to the corn and celery mixture during the last few minutes of cooking to heat through. Instead of cilantro, use Thai basil or mint. Sprinkle with crispy shallots if you have them.

rigatoni WITH marinated tomatoes AND burrata

Serves 4 to 6 • Total Time: 45 minutes

- **1½ pounds ripe tomatoes, cored and cut into ½-inch pieces**
- **1½ teaspoons table salt, plus salt for cooking pasta**
- **¼ teaspoon pepper**
- **¼ teaspoon sugar**
- **5 tablespoons extra-virgin olive oil, divided**
- **3 garlic cloves, minced**
- **1 pound rigatoni**
- **8 ounces burrata cheese, room temperature**
- **½ cup fresh basil leaves, torn**

WARM GARLIC oil turns chopped tomatoes and their juices into a cohesive and flavorful sauce after 20 minutes of marinating—conveniently, the time it takes to cook the pasta.

1 Bring 4 quarts water to boil in large pot. While water comes to boil, combine tomatoes, salt, pepper, and sugar in bowl. Heat 1 tablespoon oil and garlic in 8-inch nonstick skillet over medium heat until garlic just begins to turn golden, 3 to 5 minutes. Pour hot oil mixture over tomatoes and toss to combine. Let sit for at least 20 minutes.

2 Meanwhile, add pasta and 1 tablespoon salt to boiling water and cook, stirring often, until al dente. Drain pasta and return it to pot.

3 Drain tomatoes in colander set over bowl. Add tomatoes and ½ cup drained tomato juice to pasta and toss vigorously until liquid is mostly absorbed. Adjust consistency with extra tomato juice as needed. Transfer pasta to serving bowls. Cut burrata into 1-inch pieces, collecting creamy liquid. Sprinkle burrata over pasta and drizzle with creamy liquid. Drizzle with remaining ¼ cup oil. Season with pepper to taste and sprinkle with basil. Serve.

NOTES

This dish is best made with ripe, in-season tomatoes. If those are not available, opt for ripe tomatoes on the vine that are tender to the touch.

KITCHEN IMPROV

Try other short or tubular pasta shapes such as penne, fusilli, or ziti in place of the rigatoni. Dollops of ricotta cheese or torn fresh mozzarella are a good substitute for the burrata. Fresh mint is a great alternative to basil here. The flavorful sauce is liquidy, so sop up any extra with crusty bread.

SMALL BUT mighty cherry tomatoes are wonderful in quick pasta sauces, especially when paired with fried caper panko bread crumbs, which you'll want to put on everything (fish, roasted veggies, scrambled eggs, and more).

NOTES

Use cherry tomatoes because grape tomatoes won't break down as much and will produce a drier sauce. Adjust the amount of red pepper flakes to suit your palate.

KITCHEN IMPROV

Try other short or tubular pasta shapes such as fusilli, farfalle, orecchiette, ziti, or rigatoni in place of the penne.

pasta WITH burst cherry tomato sauce AND fried caper crumbs

Serves 4 to 6 • Total Time: 45 minutes

- **¼ cup plus 2 tablespoons extra-virgin olive oil, divided**
- **¼ cup capers, rinsed and patted dry**
- **3 anchovy fillets, rinsed, patted dry, and minced, divided**
- **½ cup panko bread crumbs**
- **1½ teaspoons plus ⅛ teaspoon table salt, divided, plus salt for cooking pasta**
- **⅛ teaspoon pepper**
- **¼ cup minced fresh parsley**
- **1 teaspoon grated lemon zest**
- **2 garlic cloves, sliced thin**
- **2 pounds cherry tomatoes**
- **¼ teaspoon sugar**
- **⅛–¼ teaspoon red pepper flakes**
- **12 ounces penne**
- **2 tablespoons unsalted butter, cut into 2 pieces and chilled**
- **1 cup fresh basil leaves, torn if large**

1 Bring 4 quarts water to boil in large pot. While water comes to boil, heat 2 tablespoons oil in 10-inch skillet over medium heat until shimmering. Add capers and one-third of anchovies and cook, stirring frequently, until capers have darkened and shrunk, 3 to 4 minutes. Using slotted spoon, transfer caper mixture to paper towel–lined plate.

2 Leave oil in skillet and return skillet to medium heat. Add panko, ⅛ teaspoon salt, and pepper to oil left in skillet and cook over medium heat, stirring constantly, until panko is golden brown, 4 to 5 minutes. Transfer panko to medium bowl and stir in parsley, lemon zest, and reserved caper mixture.

3 Cook remaining ¼ cup oil, remaining anchovies, and garlic in large saucepan over medium heat, stirring occasionally, until anchovies break down and garlic is lightly browned, about 5 minutes. Add tomatoes, remaining 1½ teaspoons salt, sugar, and pepper flakes to saucepan and stir to combine. Cover, increase heat to medium-high, and cook, without stirring, for 10 minutes.

4 Meanwhile, add pasta and 1 tablespoon salt to boiling water and cook, stirring often, until al dente. Reserve ½ cup cooking water, then drain pasta and return it to pot. Add tomato mixture and butter and stir gently until oil, butter, and tomato juices combine to form light sauce, about 15 seconds. Adjust consistency with reserved cooking water as needed, adding 2 tablespoons at a time. Stir in basil and season with salt to taste. Serve, passing caper crumb topping separately.

spaghetti AL tonno

Serves 4 to 6 • Total Time: 45 minutes

- **2 (5- to 7-ounce) jars/cans olive oil–packed tuna, drained**
- **1 tablespoon lemon juice**
- **1 teaspoon table salt, divided, plus salt for cooking pasta**
- **½ teaspoon pepper, divided**
- **¼ cup extra-virgin olive oil, divided, plus extra for drizzling**
- **1½ tablespoons minced garlic, divided**
- **3 anchovy fillets, rinsed, patted dry, and minced**
- **¼–½ teaspoon red pepper flakes**
- **1 (14.5-ounce) can whole peeled tomatoes, drained with juice reserved, crushed by hand into small pieces**
- **1 pound spaghetti**
- **6 tablespoons chopped fresh parsley, divided**

1. Bring 4 quarts water to boil in large pot. While water comes to boil, gently stir tuna, lemon juice, ¼ teaspoon salt, and ¼ teaspoon pepper together in small bowl.
2. Heat 2 tablespoons oil, 1 tablespoon garlic, anchovies, and pepper flakes in large saucepan over medium heat, stirring occasionally, until oil sizzles gently and anchovies break down, about 2 minutes. Stir in tomatoes and their juice and ½ teaspoon salt. Bring to gentle simmer and cook, stirring occasionally, until slightly thickened, 6 to 7 minutes. Cover and keep warm.
3. Add pasta and 1 tablespoon salt to boiling water and cook, stirring often, until barely al dente. Reserve ½ cup cooking water. Drain pasta and return it to pot. Off heat, add tomato mixture, remaining ¼ teaspoon salt, remaining ¼ teaspoon pepper, and remaining 1½ teaspoons garlic and toss until pasta is well coated. Add tuna mixture and toss gently. Cover and set aside for 3 minutes so flavors can meld and pasta can finish cooking.
4. Adjust consistency of sauce with reserved cooking water as needed. Add ¼ cup parsley and remaining 2 tablespoons oil and toss to combine. Season with salt and pepper to taste. Drizzle individual portions with extra oil and sprinkle with remaining 2 tablespoons parsley. Serve.

OIL-PACKED TUNA is the star of this gutsy weeknight savior, supported by anchovies, garlic, and canned tomatoes. You'll want to keep this recipe in heavy rotation since the ingredient list is almost all pantry staples.

NOTES

Crushing the whole peeled tomatoes by hand creates great texture and feels so satisfying. Adjust the amount of red pepper flakes to suit your palate. Toss gently at the end to preserve some decent-size chunks of tuna.

KITCHEN IMPROV

Instead of strand pasta, you can use short or tubular pasta shapes such as penne, fusilli, farfalle, ziti, or rigatoni. If you happen to only have water-packed tuna or diced tomatoes on hand, don't let that stop you. Top with toasted bread crumbs, if you like. Or, add capers or chopped olives.

penne WITH pancetta AND asparagus

Serves 4 to 6 • Total Time: 45 minutes

- **4 ounces pancetta, cut into ½-inch pieces**
- **1 pound asparagus, trimmed and cut into 2-inch lengths on bias**
- **⅛ teaspoon table salt, plus salt for cooking pasta**
- **1 garlic clove, minced**
- **1 pound penne**
- **4 ounces (½ cup) mascarpone cheese**
- **1 ounce Pecorino Romano cheese, grated (½ cup), plus extra for serving**
- **1 tablespoon lemon juice**
- **1 teaspoon pepper**
- **⅓ cup chopped fresh basil**

1 Bring 4 quarts water to boil in large pot. While water comes to boil, cook pancetta in 12-inch nonstick skillet over medium heat until lightly browned and crispy, about 10 minutes. Using slotted spoon, transfer pancetta to paper towel–lined plate, leaving fat in skillet.

2 Heat fat over high heat until just smoking. Add asparagus and salt and cook, without stirring, until just starting to brown, about 3 minutes. Stir and continue to cook until asparagus is browned and tender, about 2 minutes longer. Off heat, stir in garlic.

3 Meanwhile, add pasta and 1 tablespoon salt to boiling water and cook, stirring often, until al dente. Reserve 1½ cups cooking water, then drain pasta and return it to pot over low heat.

4 Add mascarpone, Pecorino, lemon juice, pepper, pancetta, asparagus, and 1 cup reserved cooking water to pasta in pot and toss and stir vigorously to thoroughly combine, about 1 minute. Let pasta rest off heat for 3 minutes. Stir in basil. Adjust consistency with remaining reserved cooking water as needed. Season with salt and pepper to taste. Serve, passing extra Pecorino separately.

ASPARAGUS STARS in this creamy, porky pasta. Silky-smooth mascarpone provides a luxurious creamy element, making this weeknight-friendly pasta feel restaurant quality.

NOTES

Buy asparagus spears that are between ¼ inch and ½ inch in diameter. Buy a hunk of pancetta from the deli counter rather than presliced pancetta.

KITCHEN IMPROV

Try other short or tubular pasta shapes such as fusilli, ziti, or rigatoni in place of the penne. You can use thick-cut bacon in place of the pancetta.

orecchiette WITH navy beans, brussels sprouts AND bacon

Serves 4 • Total Time: 35 minutes

- **2 teaspoons vegetable oil**
- **1/4 cup panko bread crumbs**
- **2 teaspoons Dijon mustard**
- **1/8 teaspoon plus 1/2 teaspoon table salt, divided, plus salt for cooking pasta**
- **Pinch cayenne pepper**
- **8 ounces orecchiette**
- **2 slices bacon, chopped fine**
- **10 ounces brussels sprouts, trimmed, halved, and sliced thin**
- **1 (15-ounce) can navy beans, undrained**
- **1 tablespoon cider vinegar**
- **1/2 teaspoon pepper**
- **1/3 cup sour cream**

PROTEIN-PACKED AND hearty, this pasta-and-bean combo is nutritious, economical, and satisfying. The mustardy panko crumb topping makes it feel just the right amount of special.

1. Bring 4 quarts water to boil in large saucepan. While water comes to boil, combine oil, panko, mustard, 1/8 teaspoon salt, and cayenne in 12-inch nonstick skillet. Cook over medium-high heat, stirring frequently, until panko is golden brown, about 5 minutes. Transfer to small bowl and let cool completely.
2. Add pasta and 1 tablespoon salt to boiling water and cook, stirring often, until al dente. Reserve 1 cup cooking water and drain pasta. Return pasta to pot and cover to keep warm.
3. Meanwhile, cook bacon in now-empty skillet over medium-high heat, stirring frequently, until crispy, 4 to 5 minutes. Using slotted spoon, transfer bacon to paper towel–lined plate to drain, leaving fat in skillet. Add brussels sprouts, 1 tablespoon water, and remaining 1/2 teaspoon salt and stir to coat. Cover and cook, stirring occasionally, until sprouts are crisp-tender and bright green, about 4 minutes. Stir in beans and their liquid, 1/4 cup reserved pasta cooking water, vinegar, and pepper and cook until bubbling.
4. Add brussels sprout mixture and sour cream to pasta and stir until all ingredients are combined. Adjust consistency with remaining reserved cooking water as needed. Season with salt and pepper to taste. Serve, sprinkling individual portions with bread crumbs and bacon.

NOTES

To maximize efficiency when trimming, halving, and slicing the brussels sprouts, complete one task at a time on all of the sprouts.

KITCHEN IMPROV

Try other short or tubular pasta shapes such as penne, fusilli, ziti, or rigatoni in place of the orecchiette. You can also substitute cannellini or pinto beans for the navy beans.

mushroom yaki udon

Serves 4 • Total Time: 30 minutes

- **1 pound fresh or frozen udon**
- **3/4 teaspoon table salt, plus salt for cooking noodles**
- **3 tablespoons ketchup**
- **3 tablespoons oyster sauce**
- **1½ tablespoons Worcestershire sauce**
- **2 teaspoons sugar**
- **2 garlic cloves, minced**
- **1 tablespoon vegetable oil**
- **6 scallions, white and green parts separated and sliced thin**
- **8 ounces shiitake mushrooms, stemmed and sliced ½ inch thick**
- **8 ounces oyster mushrooms, trimmed and sliced ½ inch thick**

SAUCY NOODLES, quickly stir-fried with a variety of add-in ingredients and toppings, are a Japanese street-food favorite. Here's a weeknight-friendly homage, with a duo of umami-rich mushrooms, plenty of fragrant scallions, and an extremely savory sauce.

1 Bring 4 quarts water to boil in large pot. Add noodles and 1 tablespoon salt and cook, stirring often, until almost tender (center should still be firm with slightly opaque dot). Drain noodles and rinse under cold running water until water runs clear. Drain well and set aside.

2 Meanwhile, whisk ¼ cup water, ketchup, oyster sauce, Worcestershire, sugar, garlic, and salt together in small bowl. Heat oil in 14-inch flat-bottomed wok or 12-inch nonstick skillet over medium-high heat until just smoking. Add scallion whites and cook, stirring slowly and constantly until starting to brown, about 2 minutes. Add shiitake and oyster mushrooms and cook, stirring occasionally, until softened and liquid has mostly evaporated, 5 to 7 minutes.

3 Add ketchup mixture to mushrooms in wok and bring to simmer. Add udon and scallion greens and cook, tossing occasionally, until noodles are warmed through, about 2 minutes. Serve immediately.

NOTES

The texture of fresh or frozen udon is really nice here. If you can only find dried, reduce the amount to 12 ounces.

KITCHEN IMPROV

The mushroom combo is delicious, but you can use 1 pound of a single variety. Toppings can really elevate this meal: Garnish with drained benishoga (red pickled ginger), drizzle with Kewpie mayo, and sprinkle with katsuobushi (smoked bonito flakes) and seasoned toasted seaweed.

mapo eggplant pasta

Serves 4 • Total Time: 45 minutes

- **2 teaspoons Sichuan peppercorns**
- **1 pound Chinese eggplant**
- **8 ounces 80 percent lean ground beef**
- **2 tablespoons extra-virgin olive oil**
- **3 tablespoons doubanjiang (broad bean chile paste)**
- **4 garlic cloves, minced**
- **2 teaspoons minced fresh ginger**
- **4 scallions, white and green parts separated and sliced thin**
- **2 tablespoons Shaoxing wine**
- **2 cups chicken broth**
- **1 tablespoon soy sauce**
- **2 tablespoons cornstarch**
- **8 ounces rigatoni**
- **Table salt for cooking pasta**
- **2–3 tablespoons chili crisp**

1. Bring 2 quarts water to boil in large pot. While water comes to boil, grind Sichuan peppercorns using mortar and pestle until finely ground; set aside. Trim stem end of eggplant. Hold knife at about 45 degree angle relative to eggplant and cut 1½ inches from end. Roll eggplant 90 degrees toward you (quarter turn) and cut again 1½ inches from end at same angle. Repeat rolling and cutting. (Eggplant pieces should be roughly triangular in shape.)

2. Cook beef and oil in 12-inch skillet over medium heat until beef is no longer pink, about 6 minutes, breaking up meat with spoon. Stir in 1 teaspoon reserved ground Sichuan peppercorns, doubanjiang, garlic, ginger, and scallion whites and cook until fragrant, about 1 minute. Stir in Shaoxing wine, scraping up any brown bits. Stir in eggplant, chicken broth, and soy sauce. Bring to boil over high heat, then cover, reduce heat to medium, and simmer vigorously until eggplant is tender, 8 to 10 minutes.

3. Whisk cornstarch and 2 tablespoons water together in small bowl until fully dissolved. Stir into sauce in skillet and cook, uncovered and stirring constantly, until sauce has thickened, about 1 minute.

4. Meanwhile, add pasta and ½ tablespoon salt and cook, stirring occasionally, until al dente. Reserve 1 cup cooking water, then drain pasta and return it to pot. Add sauce along with chili crisp and remaining ground Sichuan peppercorns and toss to combine. Adjust consistency with reserved cooking water as needed. Sprinkle with scallion greens and serve.

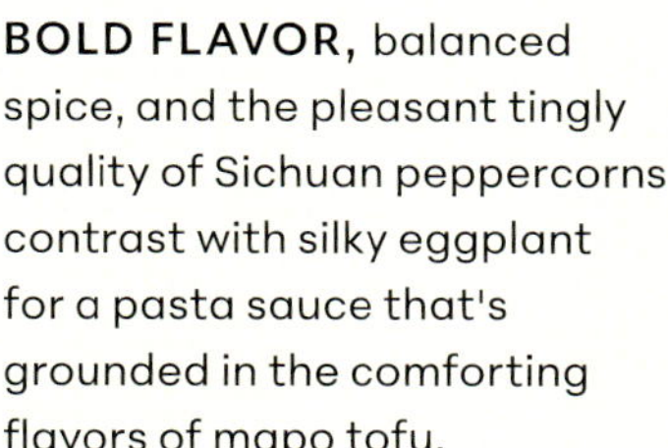

BOLD FLAVOR, balanced spice, and the pleasant tingly quality of Sichuan peppercorns contrast with silky eggplant for a pasta sauce that's grounded in the comforting flavors of mapo tofu.

NOTES

Use the larger or smaller amount of chili crisp based on your heat tolerance. Doubanjiang, a deep reddish-brown chili paste, is a Sichuan pantry staple. It's worth seeking out doubanjiang from Pixian (look for Pixian on the label), which has an assertive, rich flavor.

KITCHEN IMPROV

You can also use Japanese eggplant. You can substitute ground pork or lamb for the beef, or you could make this vegetarian by browning mushrooms instead, or simply leaving out the meat. Use another short or tubular pasta such as penne, fusilli, or ziti in place of the rigatoni.

creamy pumpkin ramen

Serves 4 • Total Time: 30 minutes

- **3 tablespoons unsalted butter, divided**
- **12 fresh sage leaves**
- **¼ cup roasted pepitas**
- **1 teaspoon sherry vinegar**
- **1 large shallot, finely chopped**
- **¾ teaspoon table salt, plus salt for cooking noodles**
- **¼ teaspoon ground nutmeg**
- **1 cup canned unsweetened pumpkin puree**
- **½ cup heavy cream**
- **2 ounces Parmesan cheese, grated (1 cup), plus extra for serving**
- **4 (3-ounce) packages ramen noodles, seasoning packets discarded**
- **Pepper**

SAGE AND PUMPKIN—a winning flavor pairing—dress up instant ramen to create serious comfort food. Using canned pumpkin, the sauce is quick to make but tastes sophisticated and lush, thanks to additions of cream, nutmeg, and plenty of Parmesan.

1 Bring 4 quarts water to boil in large pot. While water comes to boil, melt 2 tablespoons butter in 12-inch nonstick skillet over medium heat. Add sage and cook until crispy, about 3 minutes. Scrape butter and sage into small bowl, then stir in pepitas and vinegar.

2 Melt remaining 1 tablespoon butter in now-empty skillet over medium heat. Add shallot, salt, and nutmeg and cook, stirring occasionally, until shallot is softened, about 3 minutes. Stir in pumpkin and cream until well combined. Bring to simmer and cook until thickened slightly, 2 to 4 minutes. Off heat, stir in Parmesan. Cover sauce and keep warm.

3 Meanwhile, add noodles and 1 tablespoon salt to boiling water and cook, stirring often, until tender. Reserve 1 cup cooking water, then drain noodles and return them to pot. Add sauce to noodles and toss to combine. Adjust consistency with reserved cooking water as needed. Serve immediately, topping individual portions with sage mixture and sprinkling with pepper and extra Parmesan.

NOTES

Buy plain, unsweetened pumpkin puree.

KITCHEN IMPROV

The creamy sauce pairs especially well with starchy instant ramen, but you can also use spaghetti or linguine or short or tubular pasta such as penne, fusilli, ziti, or rigatoni. Trade pepitas for another seed or nut (hazelnuts are nice). Rosemary can be used in place of the sage; cook it until fragrant, about 30 seconds.

pea AND pistachio pesto pasta

Serves 4 to 6 • Total Time: 30 minutes

- 1 cup frozen peas, thawed
- 2/3 cup shelled pistachios
- 1/2 cup extra-virgin olive oil
- 1 ounce grated Parmesan cheese (1/2 cup), plus extra for serving
- 1/4 cup fresh mint leaves
- 2 teaspoons grated lemon zest
- 1 garlic clove, chopped
- 1 1/2 teaspoons table salt, plus salt for cooking pasta
- 1/4 teaspoon pepper
- 1 pound penne
- 1 pound Swiss chard, stemmed and chopped

ALTERNATIVE PESTO ALERT: Pistachios and green peas are enlivened with refreshing mint, lemon zest, Parmesan, and garlic and blitzed up in a food processor to make a light yet nutty and buttery pesto. Toss it with penne and Swiss chard for a vibrant, veg-forward pasta.

1. Bring 4 quarts water to boil in large pot. While water comes to boil, process peas, pistachios, oil, Parmesan, mint, lemon zest, garlic, salt, and pepper until smooth, about 1 minute, scraping down sides of processor bowl as needed.
2. Add pasta and 1 tablespoon salt to boiling water and cook, stirring often. One minute before pasta is finished cooking, add chard to pot, stirring to submerge. Reserve 3/4 cup cooking water, then drain pasta and chard and return them to pot.
3. Add pesto and 1/4 cup reserved cooking water to pasta-chard mixture in pot and toss to combine. Adjust consistency with remaining reserved cooking water as needed and season with salt to taste. Serve with extra Parmesan.

NOTES

The pesto can be made ahead and refrigerated for up to 3 days or frozen for up to 3 months. To prevent browning, press plastic wrap flush to the surface or top with a thin layer of olive oil. Bring to room temperature before using.

KITCHEN IMPROV

Instead of peas and pistachios, try thawed frozen fava beans and blanched almonds. You can also use other fresh herbs such as basil, parsley, or tarragon. Other short or tubular pasta shapes like fusilli, farfalle, orecchiette, ziti, or rigatoni work well. Swap in curly-leaf spinach for the Swiss chard.

All-Clad
All-Clad

ultracreamy spaghetti WITH zucchini

Serves 4 • Total Time: 45 minutes

- **2 pounds small zucchini, sliced 1/8 inch thick**
- **1 teaspoon table salt, plus salt for cooking pasta**
- **2 tablespoons extra-virgin olive oil**
- **1 pound spaghetti**
- **2 tablespoons unsalted butter**
- **2 tablespoons chopped fresh basil**
- **1/2 teaspoon pepper**
- **2 1/2 ounces mild provolone cheese, shredded (2/3 cup)**
- **1/3 cup grated Parmesan cheese**

SUMMER'S BOUNTY of squash finds its calling in this take on the Amalfi Coast's splendid spaghetti alla Nerano. Microwaving and then sautéing the zucchini is easier than the traditional frying—and nearly as effective at removing the squash's excess moisture.

1 Bring 4 quarts water to boil in large pot. While water comes to boil, stir zucchini, 1/4 cup water, and salt together in large bowl. Cover and microwave until zucchini is softened (some slices will curl at edges) and liquid is released, 10 to 12 minutes, stirring halfway through microwaving. Drain zucchini in colander and let cool slightly, about 5 minutes.

2 Heat oil in 12-inch nonstick skillet over medium-high heat until shimmering. Add zucchini and spread into even layer. Cook, stirring every 4 minutes and then reflattening into even layer, until zucchini is very tender and about half of slices have browned, 10 to 12 minutes (it is OK if some pieces fall apart).

3 Meanwhile, add pasta and 1 tablespoon salt to boiling water and cook, stirring often, until al dente. Reserve 1 1/2 cups cooking water, then drain pasta and return it to pot.

4 Add 1 cup reserved cooking water, zucchini, butter, basil, and pepper to pasta. Set pot over low heat and cook, stirring and tossing pasta constantly, until ingredients are evenly distributed and butter is melted, about 1 minute. Off heat, add provolone and Parmesan. Stir vigorously until cheeses are melted and pasta is coated in creamy, lightly thickened sauce, about 1 minute, adjusting consistency with remaining reserved cooking water as needed. Serve immediately.

NOTES

Be sure to use zucchini that are smaller than 8 ounces because they contain fewer seeds. Using a mandoline will make quick work of slicing the zucchini. Use a 2 1/2-ounce block of mild provolone from the deli counter rather than presliced cheese. The zucchini mixture in step 2 can be refrigerated for up to 2 days.

KITCHEN IMPROV

Linguine will also work well in this dish; avoid tubular shapes. To make this pasta heartier, serve it with sliced cooked chicken or poached shrimp.

creamy broccoli pasta WITH crispy panko

Serves 4 to 6 • Total Time: 45 minutes

- **½ cup plus 1 tablespoon extra-virgin olive oil, divided**
- **½ cup panko bread crumbs**
- **⅛ teaspoon plus 1 teaspoon table salt, divided, plus salt for cooking broccoli and pasta**
- **⅛ teaspoon plus 1 teaspoon pepper, divided**
- **1½ pounds broccoli, florets cut into 1-inch pieces, stalks cut into ½-inch pieces**
- **2 garlic cloves, smashed and peeled**
- **1 pound rigatoni or other short tubular pasta**
- **2 cups fresh basil leaves**
- **1 cup plain Greek yogurt**
- **1 ounce Pecorino Romano cheese, grated (½ cup), plus extra for serving**
- **¼ cup pine nuts, toasted**
- **1 teaspoon grated lemon zest plus 2 tablespoons juice**
- **2 anchovy fillets (optional)**

1. Bring 4 quarts water to boil in large pot. While water comes to boil, heat 1 tablespoon oil in 10-inch skillet over medium heat until shimmering. Add panko and cook, stirring frequently, until golden brown, about 4 minutes. Off heat, stir in ⅛ teaspoon salt and ⅛ teaspoon pepper. Transfer panko to plate to cool.

2. Add broccoli stalks, garlic, and 1 tablespoon salt to boiling water and cook, stirring occasionally, until stalks are tender, about 6 minutes. Using spider skimmer or slotted spoon, transfer stalks and garlic to blender; set aside.

3. Return water to boil. Add broccoli florets and cook until bright green and tender, about 3 minutes. Using spider skimmer, transfer two-thirds of florets to bowl and reserve. Transfer remaining florets to blender with stalks and garlic. Return water to boil, add pasta, and cook, stirring often, until al dente.

4. Meanwhile, add basil, yogurt, Pecorino, pine nuts, lemon zest and juice, anchovies (if using), remaining ½ cup oil, remaining 1 teaspoon salt, and remaining 1 teaspoon pepper to blender. Process until mixture resembles pesto, about 20 seconds, scraping down sides of blender jar. With blender running, slowly add ½ cup water and process until sauce is smooth and thick but fluid, about 20 seconds, adding additional water as needed.

5. Reserve 1 cup cooking water, then drain pasta and return it to pot. Off heat, add sauce and reserved florets and stir gently to combine. Adjust consistency with reserved cooking water as needed. Season with salt to taste and serve immediately, passingpanko and extra Pecorino separately.

TRANSFORM BROCCOLI from dependable standby into something quite luxe in this lush, herbaceous bread crumb–topped pasta. Most of the broccoli is blended into a pesto-like sauce, while some floret pieces are reserved for textural interest.

NOTES

There's no need to peel the broccoli stalks here. Using a conventional blender will produce the smoothest sauce, but an immersion blender can be used if needed. Whole-milk yogurt adds richness, but you can use low-fat yogurt instead.

KITCHEN IMPROV

Short or tubular pasta shapes such as pipette rigate, fusilli, farfalle, orecchiette, ziti, or penne work in place of the rigatoni. Try blanched almonds in place of pine nuts.

tortellini WITH corn AND basil cream sauce

Serves 4 to 6 • Total Time: 30 minutes

- **2 tablespoons unsalted butter**
- **3 ears corn, kernels cut from cobs**
- **1 shallot, chopped**
- **1 red Fresno chile, stemmed and sliced into thin rings**
- **¾ teaspoon table salt, divided, plus salt for cooking pasta**
- **½ teaspoon pepper**
- **1 cup heavy cream**
- **½ cup fresh basil leaves, plus extra for serving**
- **1 ounce Parmesan cheese, grated (½ cup), plus extra for serving**
- **18 ounces fresh or frozen cheese tortellini**

DRESS UP store-bought cheese tortellini with fresh corn and a no-fuss blender basil sauce for a summery pasta dinner. As is usually the case with fresh corn, err on the side of less cooking (rather than more) for the best flavor.

1 Bring 4 quarts water to boil in large pot. While water comes to boil, melt butter in 12-inch skillet over medium heat. Add corn, shallot, Fresno chile, ½ teaspoon salt, and pepper and cook until vegetables are tender, 4 to 6 minutes. Transfer to bowl.

2 Bring cream to simmer in now-empty skillet over medium-high heat. Reduce heat to medium-low and simmer, stirring often, until reduced to ¾ cup, 3 to 5 minutes. Transfer to blender and process with basil, Parmesan, and remaining ¼ teaspoon salt until smooth, about 1 minute, scraping down sides of blender jar as needed.

3 Add tortellini and 1 tablespoon salt to boiling water and cook, stirring often, until al dente. Reserve ½ cup cooking water, then drain pasta and return it to pot. Add corn mixture and sauce and toss to combine. Adjust consistency with reserved cooking water as needed. Season with salt and pepper to taste. Serve, topping individual portions with extra Parmesan and basil.

NOTES

If you don't have a Fresno chile, substitute a jalapeño chile. For a milder dish, remove the chile ribs and seeds. If fresh corn isn't in season, you can substitute 3 cups thawed frozen corn.

KITCHEN IMPROV

You can substitute small cheese ravioli for the tortellini or use a short or tubular pasta such as fusilli, farfalle, orecchiette, ziti, or penne.

crispy skillet gnocchi WITH spicy cumin lamb AND celery

Serves 4 • Total Time: 45 minutes

- 2 teaspoons ground cumin
- 1½ teaspoons Sichuan chili flakes
- 1 teaspoon Sichuan peppercorns, ground
- ½ teaspoon sugar
- 1 tablespoon water
- ⅛ teaspoon baking soda
- 8 ounces ground lamb
- 1 tablespoon soy sauce
- 1 tablespoon Shaoxing wine
- ½ teaspoon cornstarch
- ½ teaspoon table salt
- 1 pound shelf-stable gnocchi
- 6 tablespoons vegetable oil
- 4 garlic cloves, minced
- 1 tablespoon grated fresh ginger
- 4 celery ribs, sliced on bias ¼ inch thick (2 cups)
- 4 teaspoons Chinese black vinegar, plus extra for serving
- ½ cup fresh cilantro leaves, chopped coarse

1 Combine cumin, chili flakes, peppercorns, and sugar in small bowl and set aside. Combine water and baking soda in medium bowl. Add lamb to water mixture and toss to coat. Let sit for 5 minutes. Add soy sauce, Shaoxing wine, cornstarch, and salt to lamb mixture and toss to coat.

2 Separate gnocchi and arrange in single layer in 12-inch nonstick skillet. Drizzle oil evenly over gnocchi. Place skillet over medium-high heat and cook, without moving gnocchi, until well browned on 1 side, 5 to 8 minutes. Stir gnocchi and continue to cook until second sides of most pieces are lightly crisp, about 2 minutes. Using slotted spoon, transfer gnocchi to large plate, leaving oil in skillet.

3 Add lamb to skillet and cook, using wooden spoon to break meat into pieces no larger than ¼ inch, until just cooked through, about 3 minutes. Add garlic and ginger and cook, stirring constantly, until fragrant, about 30 seconds. Stir in cumin mixture and celery and cook until celery is heated through, about 2 minutes. Off heat, stir in vinegar, then gnocchi. Serve, topping individual portions with cilantro and passing extra vinegar separately.

WAKE UP your taste buds with this warmly spiced and smartly prepared meal that uses shelf-stable gnocchi, pan frying it to a pleasingly chewy-crispy texture and combining it with highly seasoned ground lamb and crunchy celery.

NOTES

Use shelf-stable gnocchi. Packages can vary in size; it's okay if your package weighs slightly more than 1 pound. If you can't find Sichuan chili flakes, gochugaru (Korean red pepper flakes) is a good substitute. There is no substitute for Sichuan peppercorns. If Shaoxing wine or Chinese black vinegar is unavailable, substitute dry sherry or balsamic vinegar, respectively.

KITCHEN IMPROV

Try ground beef or ground pork in place of the lamb.

samosa gnocchi chaat

Serves 4 • Total Time: 45 minutes

- 1 pound shelf-stable gnocchi
- 6 tablespoons vegetable oil
- 2 teaspoons cumin seeds
- 1 teaspoon coriander seeds
- 1 teaspoon brown mustard seeds
- ½ teaspoon garam masala
- ¼ teaspoon ground turmeric
- ⅛ teaspoon cayenne pepper
- 1 red onion, chopped fine, divided
- ½ teaspoon plus ⅛ teaspoon table salt, divided
- 2 garlic cloves, minced to paste
- 2 teaspoons grated fresh ginger
- 1 (15-ounce) can chickpeas, rinsed
- 3 ounces (3 cups) baby spinach
- 1 cup frozen peas
- ½ cup chopped fresh cilantro, divided
- 2 teaspoons lemon juice
- 1 cup plain yogurt
- Tamarind, coriander, and/or mango chutney

INDIAN CHAATS, with their glorious tumble of flavors, textures, and colors, are the inspiration here. Skillet-browned gnocchi are crispy-soft; spices and herbs, aromatics, and peas evoke the flavors of samosa filling; and a variety of toppings completes the experience.

1 Separate gnocchi and arrange in single layer in 12-inch nonstick skillet. Drizzle oil evenly over gnocchi. Place skillet over medium-high heat and cook, without moving gnocchi, until well browned on 1 side, 5 to 8 minutes. Stir gnocchi and continue to cook until second sides of most pieces are lightly crisp, about 2 minutes. Using slotted spoon, transfer gnocchi to large plate, leaving oil in skillet.

2 Add cumin seeds, coriander seeds, mustard seeds, garam masala, turmeric, and cayenne to skillet and cook over medium heat until fragrant, about 30 seconds. Add three-quarters of red onion and ½ teaspoon salt and cook until onion is softened, 3 to 5 minutes. Stir in garlic and ginger and cook until fragrant, about 30 seconds.

3 Stir in chickpeas, spinach, and peas and cook until spinach wilts and chickpeas and peas are warmed through, about 3 minutes. Stir in gnocchi, ¼ cup cilantro, and lemon juice.

4 Whisk yogurt and remaining ⅛ teaspoon salt together in bowl. Spread half of yogurt on serving platter, then mound gnocchi mixture on top. Sprinkle with remaining red onion and remaining ¼ cup cilantro. Serve immediately, passing remaining yogurt and chutney separately.

NOTES

Be sure to use shelf-stable gnocchi. Packages can vary in size; it's fine if your package of gnocchi is slightly more than 1 pound. A rasp grater makes quick work of turning the garlic into a paste. In a pinch, you can use yellow mustard seeds in place of the brown mustard seeds or simply omit them.

KITCHEN IMPROV

Sprinkle the finished dish with pomegranate seeds or chaat masala in addition to the onion and cilantro. The store-bought chutneys add bright, sweet finishing flavor, so try to use one or a combination of the three.

gochujang-tahini noodles

Serves 4 • Total Time: 30 minutes

- **5 tablespoons gochujang**
- **3 tablespoons unseasoned rice vinegar**
- **2 tablespoons tahini**
- **2 tablespoons hoisin sauce**
- **2 tablespoons soy sauce**
- **1 tablespoon toasted sesame oil**
- **2 garlic cloves, minced**
- **4 (3-ounce) packages ramen noodles, seasoning packets discarded**
- **4 scallions, sliced thin**
- **1 tablespoon toasted sesame seeds**

TAHINI, GOCHUJANG, rice vinegar, and hoisin combine to make an instant sauce that's zingy, rich, and a little sweet—perfect for coating a tangle of ramen. Enjoy the noodles simply or add as many toppings as you like.

1. Whisk gochujang, vinegar, tahini, hoisin, soy sauce, oil, and garlic together in large bowl.
2. Bring 4 quarts water to boil in large pot. Add noodles and cook, stirring occasionally, until noodles are cooked through but still retain some chew. Drain noodles, rinse under warm water, and drain again. Toss noodles in bowl with sauce to thoroughly combine.
3. Portion noodles into individual bowls, top with scallions and sesame seeds, and serve.

NOTES

If you don't have sesame seeds, you could use crushed peanuts or sunflower seeds.

KITCHEN IMPROV

Any type of wheat noodle will work here; you could use somen, soba, udon, or thin spaghetti. To add more veggies, consider thinly sliced cucumber, snow or sugar snap peas, radishes, carrots, bell pepper, edamame, corn, and/or peas. Bulk up the noodles with any of the proteins on pages 334-335.

lemony shrimp WITH orzo, feta AND olives

Serves 4 • Total Time: 45 minutes

- 1 tablespoon grated lemon zest plus 1 tablespoon juice
- ½ teaspoon table salt
- ½ teaspoon pepper
- 1½ pounds extra-large shrimp (21 to 25 per pound), peeled, deveined, and tails removed
- 1 tablespoon extra-virgin olive oil, plus extra for drizzling
- 1 onion, chopped fine
- 2 garlic cloves, minced
- 2 cups orzo
- 4 cups chicken broth
- 1 cup pitted kalamata olives, chopped coarse
- 4 ounces feta cheese, crumbled (1 cup), divided
- 2 tablespoons chopped fresh parsley

1 Mix lemon zest, salt, and pepper together in medium bowl. Pat shrimp dry with paper towels and toss with lemon zest mixture; set aside.

2 Heat oil in 12-inch nonstick skillet over medium-high heat until shimmering. Add onion and cook until softened, about 5 minutes. Stir in garlic and cook until fragrant, about 30 seconds. Add orzo and cook, stirring frequently, until orzo is coated with oil and lightly browned, about 4 minutes. Add broth, bring to boil, and cook, uncovered, until orzo is al dente, about 6 minutes. Stir in olives, ½ cup feta, and lemon juice. Season with salt and pepper to taste.

3 Reduce heat to medium-low, nestle shrimp into orzo, cover, and cook until shrimp are opaque throughout, about 5 minutes. Sprinkle remaining ½ cup feta and chopped parsley over top, drizzle with extra oil, and serve.

TANGY FETA cheese and shrimp are a classic Greek flavor combo that's hard to beat. This easy skillet recipe turns the pairing into a satisfying dinner with the addition of olives and onion, plus creamy orzo.

NOTES

If the finished orzo is too thick for your tastes, stir in hot water, a few tablespoons at a time, to adjust the consistency.

KITCHEN IMPROV

Jumbo shrimp (16 to 20 per pound) will also work here, although you may need to increase the cooking time in step 3 by a minute or so. Pescatarians can use vegetable broth or a mix of bottled clam juice and water in place of the chicken broth.

vegetarian ramen WITH shiitakes AND soft eggs

Serves 4 • Total Time: 45 minutes

- **4 large eggs**
- **3 tablespoons toasted sesame oil**
- **8 ounces shiitake mushrooms, stemmed and sliced thin**
- **6 scallions, cut into 1-inch pieces**
- **1 (2-inch) piece ginger, peeled and cut into matchsticks**
- **2 tablespoons white miso**
- **8 cups vegetable or chicken broth**
- **4 (3-ounce) packages instant ramen noodles, seasoning packets discarded**
- **2 ounces (2 cups) baby spinach**

PACKAGED RAMEN morphs into a vegetarian feast when you ditch the seasoning packet and add a simple ginger-infused broth and well-chosen garnishes: Sautéed shiitakes, baby spinach (that wilts right in the broth), and jammy eggs make a perfect trio.

1 Bring 1 inch water to rolling boil in large pot over high heat. Place eggs in steamer basket and transfer basket to saucepan. Cover, reduce heat to medium-high, and cook eggs for 6½ minutes. When eggs are almost finished cooking, combine 2 cups ice cubes and 2 cups cold water in bowl. Using tongs or slotted spoon, transfer eggs to ice bath and let sit for 5 minutes. Remove eggs from ice bath and set aside for serving.

2 Bring 4 quarts water to boil in now-empty pot. While water comes to boil, heat oil in Dutch oven over medium-high heat until just smoking. Add mushrooms and scallions and cook until softened and lightly browned, about 5 minutes. Stir in ginger and miso and cook until fragrant, about 30 seconds. Whisk in broth, bring to simmer, and cook until flavors meld, about 10 minutes.

3 Meanwhile, add noodles to boiling water and cook, stirring often, until tender. Drain noodles and distribute evenly among individual bowls.

4 Off heat, stir spinach into broth and let sit until wilted, about 2 minutes. Season with salt to taste. Ladle hot broth into each bowl. Peel and halve soft-cooked eggs and arrange on top of noodles. Serve immediately.

NOTES

You can soft-cook the eggs up to 3 days ahead of time and store them unpeeled in the refrigerator.

KITCHEN IMPROV

Serve the ramen with crispy fried shallots for sprinkling and chili-garlic sauce or sriracha for drizzling on top.

hearty soups and stews

chapter 6

chicken AND leek soup WITH parmesan dumplings

Serves 4 • Total Time: 30 minutes

- **6⅓ cups chicken broth, divided**
- **1 large egg, lightly beaten**
- **1 teaspoon table salt, divided**
- **½ teaspoon baking powder**
- **¼ teaspoon pepper**
- **1 cup all-purpose flour**
- **1 ounce Parmesan cheese, grated (½ cup), plus extra for serving**
- **4 tablespoons unsalted butter**
- **1 pound leeks, white and light green parts only, halved lengthwise, sliced ½ inch thick, and washed thoroughly**
- **3 cups shredded cooked chicken**

THIS STREAMLINED soup finds flavor in unexpected places: Parmesan makes the dumplings taste delicious without any noticeable cheesiness, and softened leeks create a rich base for the soup, turning it into a one-pot meal.

1. Whisk ⅓ cup broth, egg, ½ teaspoon salt, baking powder, and pepper together in medium bowl. Stir in flour and Parmesan until fully combined. Set dumpling dough aside.

2. Melt butter in Dutch oven over medium-high heat. Add leeks and remaining ½ teaspoon salt and cook until softened, 6 to 8 minutes. Stir in remaining 6 cups broth and bring to simmer.

3. Reduce heat to medium. Using 2 spoons, scrape rough tablespoon-size dumplings from dough into soup and cook, without stirring, for 2 minutes. Gently stir to break up dumplings and continue to cook for 2 minutes. Carefully stir in chicken and cook until heated through, about 1 minute. Season with salt and pepper to taste. Serve, passing extra Parmesan separately.

NOTES

Use the recipe for Quick Cooked Chicken (page 334) or shred the meat from one (2½-pound) rotisserie chicken.

KITCHEN IMPROV

You can replace the leeks with 2 thinly sliced onions or use a combo; you'll need about 2 cups. To bulk up the vegetables, stir up to 2 cups frozen vegetables into the soup with the chicken. Top with chopped fresh herbs, a swirl of your favorite pesto or spiced oil, and/or Greek yogurt.

spiced chicken soup WITH squash AND navy beans

Serves 4 • Total Time: 45 minutes

- **1 tablespoon extra-virgin olive oil**
- **2 tablespoons tomato paste**
- **4 garlic cloves, minced**
- **2 teaspoons ground coriander**
- **1 teaspoon ground cardamom**
- **½ teaspoon ground allspice**
- **¼ teaspoon cayenne pepper**
- **3½ cups chicken broth**
- **1 pound butternut squash, peeled, seeded, and cut into 1-inch pieces (3 cups)**
- **1 onion, halved and sliced thin**
- **1¾ teaspoons table salt**
- **12 ounces boneless, skinless chicken thighs, trimmed and cut into ½-inch pieces**
- **1 (15-ounce) can navy beans, undrained**
- **½ cup chopped fresh cilantro**
- **Lemon wedges**

1 Heat oil in Dutch oven over medium-high heat until shimmering. Stir in tomato paste, garlic, coriander, cardamom, allspice, and cayenne and cook until fragrant, about 30 seconds. Stir in broth, squash, onion, and salt, scraping up any browned bits, and bring to simmer. Reduce heat to medium-low and cook, partially covered, for 10 minutes.

2 Stir in chicken and beans and their liquid and cook until chicken is cooked through and squash is tender, about 15 minutes.

3 Use back of spoon to mash portion of squash and beans to thicken soup to desired consistency. Stir in cilantro and season with salt and pepper to taste. Serve with lemon wedges.

NOTES

For the best butternut squash texture, it's important to remove the fibrous flesh just below the skin. Or skip the peeling by purchasing pre-peeled butternut squash halves; you need about 12 ounces to yield 3 cups of flesh.

KITCHEN IMPROV

Other hearty squash like kabocha or acorn can sub for the butternut. Boneless, skinless chicken breasts can replace the thighs. Try alternative creamy beans such as cannellini or pinto. Use other fresh herbs like mint, basil, or parsley. Serve with sour cream or Greek yogurt.

RICHLY SEASONED, this chicken soup gets its depth and subtle heat from baharat, a North African blend featuring coriander, cardamom, and allspice. Butternut squash adds tender texture, canned beans thicken the broth, and cilantro and lemon brighten the finish.

curried chicken soup WITH coconut AND kale

Serves 4 to 6 • Total Time: 40 minutes

- **3 tablespoons extra-virgin olive oil**
- **1 onion, chopped**
- **1 red bell pepper, stemmed, seeded, and chopped**
- **1½ teaspoons table salt**
- **2 tablespoons grated fresh ginger**
- **1 tablespoon curry powder**
- **¼ teaspoon cayenne pepper, plus extra for seasoning**
- **8 ounces kale, stemmed and chopped**
- **1½ pounds boneless, skinless chicken thighs, trimmed and cut into ½-inch pieces**
- **2 cups chicken broth**
- **1 (14-ounce) can coconut milk**
- **1 tablespoon lime juice, plus lime wedges for serving**

1 Heat oil in Dutch oven over medium-high heat until shimmering. Add onion, bell pepper, and salt and cook until softened and lightly browned, 6 to 8 minutes. Stir in ginger, curry powder, and cayenne and cook until fragrant, about 1 minute. Stir in kale, chicken, broth, and coconut milk and bring to boil, scraping up any browned bits.

2 Reduce heat to medium-low and simmer until chicken is cooked through and kale is tender, about 15 minutes. Off heat, stir in lime juice and season with salt and extra cayenne to taste. Serve, passing lime wedges separately.

VEGETABLE-FORWARD creamy curried chicken soup is a stunner in both looks and flavor. Two tablespoons of curry powder tints the coconut milk–enriched broth a brilliant color. Pops of red bell pepper and kale add color, flavor, and nutrients.

NOTES

Serve with store-bought naan or ladle the soup over cooked rice for added heartiness.

KITCHEN IMPROV

Boneless chicken breasts also work well here. Swap Thai curry paste for the curry powder; green, yellow, or red varieties all work. You can use baby kale or baby spinach in place of kale as a lower-prep option; stir the greens into the soup after the chicken is cooked. To dress up the soup, garnish with chopped cilantro or mint, sliced scallions, fried shallots, or toasted unsweetened coconut flakes.

carrot ribbon, chicken AND coconut curry soup

Serves 4 • Total Time: 35 minutes

- **1 pound carrots, peeled**
- **2 tablespoons vegetable oil**
- **2–4 tablespoons Thai yellow curry paste**
- **1 pound 93 percent lean ground chicken**
- **2 cups water**
- **1 cup canned coconut milk**
- **2 tablespoons fish sauce, plus extra for serving**
- **1 tablespoon sugar**
- **6 ounces snow peas, trimmed and sliced ½ inch thick on bias**
- **4 scallions, sliced thin on bias**
- **1 cup fresh Thai basil, torn**
- **1 cup fresh cilantro leaves and tender stems, torn**
- **Lime wedges**
- **Sriracha**

1 Shave carrots lengthwise into thin ribbons with vegetable peeler; set aside. Combine oil and curry paste in Dutch oven and cook over medium heat until fragrant, about 3 minutes, stirring occasionally. Add chicken and cook, breaking up meat into small pieces with wooden spoon, until chicken is no longer pink, 3 to 4 minutes.

2 Add water, coconut milk, fish sauce, sugar, and reserved carrot ribbons. Bring to simmer, then add snow peas and simmer until vegetables are crisp-tender, 3 to 5 minutes.

3 Divide soup evenly among individual serving bowls. Sprinkle with scallions, basil, and cilantro. Serve with lime wedges, sriracha, and extra fish sauce to taste.

NOTES

Be sure to use ground chicken, not ground chicken breast (also labeled 99 percent fat-free). Thai curry paste can range from mild to spicy; taste yours and, if it's very spicy, use the lesser amount.

KITCHEN IMPROV

You can substitute ground turkey, lean ground beef, ground pork, or crumbled extra-firm tofu for the chicken. It's worth seeking out Thai yellow curry paste for its sweet complexity; however, you can substitute red curry paste. Italian basil can be used in place of Thai basil. Top with chopped toasted peanuts and/or fried shallots for extra crunch.

SHAVING CARROTS into ribbons yields colorful vegetable noodles to star in this Southeast Asian–inspired soup that is fragrant with curry paste and herbs. The carrots soak up the flavors of the broth, while ground chicken adds substance and a meaty backbone.

posole verde

Serves 4 • Total Time: 45 minutes

- 1 tablespoon extra-virgin olive oil
- 1 large white onion, chopped fine, divided
- 2 poblano chiles, stemmed, seeded, and chopped
- 2 jalapeño chiles, stemmed, seeded, and minced
- 1 teaspoon table salt, divided
- 1 pound ground pork
- 4 garlic cloves, minced
- 1 teaspoon ground cumin
- 2 (12-ounce) cans whole tomatillos, drained
- 4 cups chicken broth
- 2 (15-ounce) cans white or yellow hominy, rinsed
- 2 tomatoes, cored and cut into ½-inch pieces
- ½ cup fresh cilantro leaves

CANNED TOMATILLOS and hominy keep the simmering time short in this hearty, tangy, flavorful stew. So does using ground pork instead of traditional pork shoulder. Two kinds of chiles—poblano and jalapeño—add complex spiciness.

1 Heat oil in Dutch oven over medium heat until shimmering. Add three-quarters of onion, poblanos, jalapeños, and ½ teaspoon salt and cook until softened and lightly browned, 5 to 7 minutes. Add ground pork and cook, breaking up meat with wooden spoon, until no longer pink, about 3 minutes.

2 Stir in garlic and cumin and cook until fragrant, about 1 minute. Add tomatillos and, using potato masher, crush into bite-size pieces. Stir in broth, hominy, and remaining ½ teaspoon salt. Bring to simmer and cook, stirring occasionally, until flavors meld, about 15 minutes. Season with salt and pepper to taste. Serve, topping individual portions with tomatoes, cilantro, and remaining onion.

NOTES

For a spicier soup, include the jalapeño seeds.

KITCHEN IMPROV

You can substitute ground lamb, ground beef, or 93 percent lean ground turkey or chicken for the pork. Feel free to customize the stew with your favorite toppings, such as sour cream, crumbled queso fresco or feta, sliced radishes, and crumbled tortilla chips.

quick beef AND vegetable soup

Serves 4 • Total Time: 45 minutes

- **1 pound ground beef**
- **1 onion, chopped**
- **1 tablespoon minced fresh oregano or 1 teaspoon dried**
- **1 teaspoon table salt**
- **½ teaspoon pepper**
- **4 cups beef or chicken broth**
- **1 (14.5-ounce) can diced tomatoes**
- **8 ounces Yukon Gold or red potatoes, unpeeled, cut into ½-inch pieces**
- **2 carrots, peeled and cut into ½-inch pieces**
- **6 ounces frozen cut green beans**
- **2 tablespoons chopped fresh parsley**

A SIMPLE HACK—simmering ground beef in broth—lets you enjoy a deeply satisfying bowl of homemade soup that's far superior to any canned version. The meat quickly releases flavor as it cooks, imbuing the soup with true beefiness. From there, the soup is endlessly adaptable.

1 Cook beef, onion, oregano, salt, and pepper in Dutch oven over medium-high heat, breaking up beef with spoon until no longer pink, about 6 minutes. Add broth, tomatoes and their juice, potatoes, and carrots. Bring to boil, reduce heat to low, and simmer, covered, until potatoes are almost tender, 10 to 15 minutes.

2 Add green beans and cook, uncovered, until vegetables are tender and soup has thickened slightly, 10 to 12 minutes. Season with salt and pepper to taste, sprinkle with parsley, and serve.

NOTES

Lean ground beef (either 90 or 85 percent) is ideal here.

KITCHEN IMPROV

Use parsnips, rutabagas, radishes, or celery root for some or all of the root vegetables (you want 1 pound in total). Minced dried mushrooms (added with the broth) will give a savory boost. Add frozen corn or peas instead of (or in addition to) the green beans. Or stir in up to 2 cups precooked grains with the green beans.

easy breads

corn muffins

Serves 4 • Total Time: 45 minutes

- 2/3 cup (3 1/3 ounces) all-purpose flour
- 1/3 cup (1 2/3 ounces) cornmeal
- 1/2 teaspoon baking powder
- 1/2 teaspoon baking soda
- 1/4 teaspoon table salt
- 1/3 cup sour cream
- 1/4 cup (1 3/4 ounces) sugar
- 1 large egg
- 3 tablespoons unsalted butter, melted
- 2 tablespoons whole milk

1 Adjust oven rack to middle position and heat oven to 400 degrees. Spray 4 cups of muffin tin with vegetable oil spray. Whisk flour, cornmeal, baking powder, baking soda, and salt together in bowl. Whisk sour cream, sugar, egg, melted butter, and milk in separate bowl until well combined.

2 Fold sour cream mixture into flour mixture until just combined; do not overmix. Divide batter evenly among prepared muffin cups.

3 Bake until muffins are golden brown and toothpick inserted in center comes out clean, 12 to 17 minutes. Let muffins cool in muffin tin on wire rack for 10 minutes before serving.

MOIST, CORNY-TASTING muffins with a tender crumb are cozy accompaniments to any warm soup bowl The extra-hot oven guarantees a crunchy top.

NOTES

Stone-ground cornmeal is best here; don't use coarse-ground cornmeal.

KITCHEN IMPROV

Add up to 1 tablespoon chopped tender herbs (cilantro, tarragon, or basil) or up to 1 teaspoon hearty herbs (rosemary, thyme, or sage) to the sour cream mixture. You can also fold up to 1/2 cup shredded cheese into the batter before portioning it.

---

drop biscuits

Serves 4 • Total Time: 30 minutes

- 2/3 cup (3 1/3 ounces) all-purpose flour
- 3/4 teaspoon baking powder
- 1/4 teaspoon baking soda
- 1/8 teaspoon sugar
- 1/8 teaspoon table salt
- 1/3 cup buttermilk
- 3 tablespoons unsalted butter, melted, divided

1 Adjust oven rack to middle position and heat oven to 450 degrees. Whisk flour, baking powder, baking soda, sugar, and salt together in bowl. In separate bowl, stir buttermilk and 2 tablespoons melted butter together. Using wooden spoon, stir buttermilk mixture into flour mixture until just incorporated and dough pulls away from sides of bowl.

2 Using greased 1/4-cup dry measure, drop 4 level scoops of dough onto parchment paper–lined rimmed baking sheet. Bake until biscuit tops are golden brown, 12 to 15 minutes.

3 Brush biscuits with remaining 1 tablespoon melted butter, transfer to wire rack, and let cool for 5 minutes. Serve warm or at room temperature.

MIX, SCOOP, drop, and bake. These easiest-ever biscuits are extraordinarily good. The tangy buttermilk encourages a crisp crust and fluffy interior.

NOTES

If needed, sub a combination of 1/3 cup milk and 1 teaspoon lemon juice for the buttermilk; let the mixture sit for 10 minutes before using.

KITCHEN IMPROV

Whisk up to 1 tablespoon minced tender herbs (such as cilantro, tarragon, or basil) or up to 1 teaspoon hearty herbs (like rosemary, thyme, or sage) into the flour mixture before adding the buttermilk.

garlic AND herb breadsticks

Makes 18 breadsticks • Total Time: 35 minutes

- **1 pound pizza dough, room temperature**
- **2 teaspoons dried oregano**
- **1 teaspoon garlic powder**
- **½ teaspoon kosher salt**
- **¼ teaspoon pepper**
- **3 tablespoons unsalted butter, melted**

1. Adjust oven rack to middle position and heat oven to 450 degrees. Divide dough into 2 equal pieces. Roll and stretch 1 piece of dough into 9 by 5-inch rectangle on lightly floured counter. Transfer dough to half of parchment paper–lined rimmed baking sheet, with short sides parallel to long sides of sheet. Repeat with remaining dough piece and place on other half of sheet.
2. Combine oregano, garlic powder, salt, and pepper in bowl. Brush both doughs with half of melted butter, then sprinkle with half of oregano mixture. Flip doughs; repeat with remaining butter and oregano mixture.
3. Using chef's knife or bench scraper, cut doughs crosswise at 1-inch intervals to create nine 5-inch breadsticks from each piece of dough, but do not separate breadsticks. Bake until golden brown, 9 to 12 minutes. Let cool for 5 minutes. Pull breadsticks apart at seams. Serve.

STORE-BOUGHT DOUGH lets you get these buttery breadsticks into the oven in the amount of time it takes the oven to preheat.

NOTES

Make sure the dough is at room temperature or it will be difficult to stretch. If the dough springs back while shaping, let it rest for a few minutes before rolling it again.

KITCHEN IMPROV

Swap in other herb blends or spice seasonings (think za'atar, bagel seasoning, or dukkah) for the oregano mixture. Sprinkle ¼ cup grated Parmesan (or other firm cheese) onto the doughs before cutting them.

---

pan-grilled flatbreads

Makes 4 flatbreads • Total Time: 45 minutes

- **1 tablespoon vegetable oil**
- **1 pound pizza dough, room temperature**
- **2 tablespoons unsalted butter, melted**
- **Flake sea salt**

1. Grease 12-inch cast-iron skillet with oil; heat over medium heat for 5 minutes. Meanwhile, divide dough into quarters. On lightly floured counter, press and roll 1 piece of dough into rough round, about ¼ inch thick. Using fork, poke entire surface of dough.
2. Using paper towels, carefully wipe out skillet, leaving thin film of oil on bottom and sides. Mist top of dough with water. Place dough moistened side down in skillet, then mist top of dough with water. Cover and cook until flatbread is lightly puffed and bottom is spotty brown, 2 to 4 minutes. Flip flatbread, cover, and continue to cook until spotty brown on second side, 2 to 4 minutes. (If large air pockets form, gently poke with fork to deflate.)
3. Transfer flatbread to plate, cover with aluminum foil, and keep warm. Repeat cooking remaining dough pieces. Brush flatbreads with melted butter, sprinkle with sea salt, and serve.

STOVETOP FLATBREADS are tender yet chewy, and these rustic rounds "bake" in a skillet right next to your simmering soup.

NOTES

Let the dough come to room temperature or it will be difficult to stretch. If the dough springs back while shaping, let it rest for a few minutes before rolling it again.

KITCHEN IMPROV

Drizzle the flatbreads with hot honey, chili crisp, or any of your other favorite drizzling sauces. Sprinkle with sliced scallions or chopped fresh herbs such as cilantro, basil, or parsley.

pork meatball soup WITH wonton noodles AND baby bok choy

Serves 4 • Total Time: 35 minutes

- **4 scallions, white parts minced, green parts sliced thin**
- **1 large egg, lightly beaten**
- **3½ teaspoons grated fresh ginger, divided**
- **1 tablespoon soy sauce**
- **1 tablespoon toasted sesame oil**
- **2 teaspoons chili-garlic sauce, plus extra for serving**
- **1 pound ground pork**
- **8 cups chicken broth**
- **6 heads baby bok choy (4 ounces each), halved, washed thoroughly, and cut into 1-inch pieces**
- **8 ounces wonton wrappers, cut into ¾-inch-wide strips**

DECONSTRUCTING WONTON soup makes the process nearly effortless while hitting all the right savory, porky notes. Slice wonton wrappers into wide noodles and stir them into the broth along with crisp baby bok choy and gingery pork meatballs.

1 Combine scallion whites, egg, 1½ teaspoons ginger, soy sauce, sesame oil, and chili-garlic sauce in large bowl. Add pork and mix with your hands until thoroughly combined. Using moistened hands, pinch off and roll mixture into 35 meatballs (about 1 tablespoon each).

2 Meanwhile, bring broth and remaining 2 teaspoons ginger to boil in large Dutch oven over medium-high heat. Add bok choy and return to boil. Stir in wonton wrappers, 1 handful at a time. Carefully add meatballs to pot, cover, and cook until meatballs are cooked through, 3 to 5 minutes. Stir in scallion greens and season with salt to taste. Serve, passing extra chili-garlic sauce separately.

NOTES

The meatball mixture may seem loose at first, but it will firm up once it's cooked.

The meatballs can be shaped and refrigerated up to 2 days in advance. Fully cooked ground pork can retain a slightly pink hue, so don't be alarmed.

Be sure to wash the bok choy once it's halved so that the insides are exposed and any dirt can be easily removed.

KITCHEN IMPROV

You can substitute ground lamb, ground beef, or 93 percent lean ground turkey or chicken for the pork.

spicy tomato soup WITH tortellini AND sausage

Serves 4 • Total Time: 35 minutes

- 1 tablespoon extra-virgin olive oil
- 1 pound hot or sweet Italian sausage, casings removed
- 1 onion, chopped fine
- 3 garlic cloves, minced
- ¼ teaspoon red pepper flakes
- 4 cups chicken broth
- 1 (28-ounce) can crushed tomatoes
- 1 (9-ounce) package fresh or frozen cheese tortellini
- 5 ounces (5 cups) baby kale
- ½ cup heavy cream (optional)
- Grated Parmesan cheese

1 Heat oil in Dutch oven over medium heat until shimmering. Add sausage and onion and cook, breaking up meat with wooden spoon, until sausage is starting to brown and onion is softened, 5 to 7 minutes. Add garlic and pepper flakes and cook until fragrant, about 30 seconds.

2 Stir in broth and tomatoes and bring to simmer, scraping up any browned bits. Cover, reduce heat to low, and simmer gently for 10 minutes, stirring occasionally. Remove lid, stir in tortellini, and simmer, stirring frequently, until tender.

3 Off heat, stir in kale and heavy cream, if using. Season with salt and pepper to taste and serve with Parmesan.

A BACK-POCKET recipe to warm you on a cold, blustery night, this soup requires little more than adding the ingredients to the pot. Italian sausage delivers big flavor fast; cheese tortellini andbaby kale bring heartiness. Make it creamy if you want extra richness.

NOTES

Either pork or chicken Italian sausage works well here.

KITCHEN IMPROV

Swap in small cheese ravioli for the tortellini or baby spinach for the kale. Finish the soup with a dollop of pesto. If there's no stuffed pasta available, a can of white beans would take this in a more stewlike direction.

HIGHLY AROMATIC, this version of tom yum soup is bursting with hot, sour, salty, and sweet flavors. Generous amounts of shrimp and tender rice noodles make it a meal.

thai-style hot AND sour soup WITH shrimp AND noodles

Serves 4 • Total Time: 45 minutes

- 2 lemongrass stalks, trimmed to bottom 8 inches
- 4 scallions, white parts left whole, green parts cut into 1-inch lengths
- 6 makrut lime leaves, torn if large
- 2 Thai chiles, stemmed, 1 left whole, 1 sliced thin
- 1 (2-inch) piece fresh galangal, peeled and sliced into ¼-inch-thick rounds
- 8 cups chicken broth
- 1 tablespoon sugar, plus extra for seasoning
- 4 ounces rice vermicelli
- 8 ounces oyster mushrooms, trimmed and torn into 1-inch pieces
- 3 tablespoons fish sauce, plus extra for seasoning
- 1 pound extra-large shrimp (21 to 25 per pound), peeled, deveined, and tails removed
- 12 ounces cherry tomatoes, halved
- 2 tablespoons lime juice, plus lime wedges for serving
- ½ cup fresh cilantro leaves

1 Place lemongrass, scallion whites, lime leaves, whole Thai chile, and galangal on cutting board and lightly smash with meat pounder or bottom of small skillet until mixture is moist and very fragrant. Transfer lemongrass mixture to Dutch oven. Add broth and sugar, bring to simmer over medium-high heat, and cook for 15 minutes.

2 Meanwhile, place vermicelli in large bowl and cover with boiling water. Let sit until noodles are just tender, 10 to 15 minutes. Drain noodles and rinse under cold running water until cool. Drain noodles very well, then distribute evenly among large soup bowls; set aside.

3 Using slotted spoon, discard solids from broth. Add mushrooms, fish sauce, scallion greens, and sliced Thai chile and simmer for 3 minutes. Off heat, stir in shrimp, cover, and let sit until opaque throughout, about 4 minutes. Stir in tomatoes and lime juice. Season with extra sugar and extra fish sauce to taste.

4 Ladle soup into bowls of noodles, top with cilantro, and serve with lime wedges.

NOTES

Choose vermicelli made from 100 percent rice flour over varieties that include a secondary starch such as cornstarch.

KITCHEN IMPROV

Galangal and makrut lime leaves add a lot to this soup, but you can substitute fresh ginger and three 3-inch strips each of lemon zest and lime zest, respectively. Garnish the soup with extra sliced chiles, chili-garlic sauce or chili jam, crispy shallots, and/or fresh Thai basil leaves. Sliced cremini mushrooms can take the place of the oyster mushrooms. Add several handfuls of baby spinach along with the tomatoes for extra veggies.

creamy butternut AND fennel soup

Serves 4 • Total Time: 45 minutes

- **2 tablespoons extra-virgin olive oil**
- **2 pounds butternut squash, peeled, seeded, and cut into 1-inch pieces (6 cups)**
- **1 large fennel bulb, halved, cored, and sliced 1 inch thick**
- **2 shallots, chopped**
- **2 garlic cloves, minced**
- **1 teaspoon fennel seeds**
- **4 cups vegetable or chicken broth, plus extra as needed**
- **¼ teaspoon table salt**
- **¼ teaspoon pepper**
- **¼ cup heavy cream (optional)**

SILKY SQUASH soup, rich and comforting on its own, becomes more interesting with the addition of both fresh fennel and fennel seeds. Browning the squash with the aromatic fennel, shallots, and garlic builds a savory backbone to balance the squash's sweetness.

1 Heat oil in Dutch oven over medium heat until shimmering. Add squash, fennel, and shallots and cook until vegetables are softened and lightly browned, about 10 minutes. Stir in garlic and fennel seeds and cook until fragrant, about 30 seconds.

2 Stir in broth, salt, and pepper and bring to simmer, scraping up any browned bits. Reduce heat to medium-low, cover, and cook until squash is tender, about 15 minutes.

3 Working in batches, process soup in blender until smooth, 1 to 2 minutes. Return pureed soup to clean pot and bring to brief simmer. Off heat, stir in cream, if using. Adjust consistency with extra broth as needed. Season with salt and pepper to taste and serve.

NOTES

For a chunkier soup, use an immersion blender to blend the soup right in the pot in step 3.

KITCHEN IMPROV

Sprinkle on crumbled soft cheese, such as blue, feta, goat, or queso fresco. Sprinkle on toasted nuts or seeds (especially pepitas or pine nuts), and include a sprinkle of fresh herbs (or use the fennel fronds). Add a meaty component by browning crumbled sausage in the Dutch oven before adding the vegetables; set the crumbles aside for garnishing and use the remaining fat to continue cooking.

chilled cucumber-avocado soup

Serves 4 • Total Time: 25 minutes

- **1 pound English cucumbers, cut into 2-inch pieces, plus extra sliced cucumber for garnishing**
- **1 avocado, halved, pitted, peeled, and cut into 2-inch pieces**
- **2 cups ice water**
- **1 shallot, halved**
- **1 jalapeño chile, stemmed, seeded, and halved**
- **1½ teaspoons table salt**
- **1½ teaspoons sugar**
- **¼ teaspoon pepper**
- **1 cup plain whole-milk yogurt**
- **6 ounces cherry tomatoes, halved**
- **⅔ cup fresh cilantro leaves**
- **½ cup chopped toasted walnuts**
- **2 ounces queso fresco, crumbled (½ cup)**

RIPE AVOCADO, a couple of cucumbers, and ice water blend into a chilled, no-cook soup that's equal parts creamy and refreshing—with shallot, jalapeño, and a pinch of sugar and salt adding just enough edge. Top it with assorted garnishes to create a stunning bowl of soup.

1 Process cucumbers, avocado, ice water, shallot, jalapeño, salt, sugar, and pepper in blender until completely smooth, about 2 minutes, scraping down sides of blender jar as needed. Strain soup through fine-mesh strainer into large bowl, using back of ladle or silicone spatula to press soup through; discard solids.

2 Whisk yogurt into cucumber mixture and season with salt and pepper to taste. Serve, topping individual portions with extra sliced cucumber, tomatoes, cilantro, walnuts, and queso fresco.

NOTES

It's important to use a fully ripened avocado here.
The soup tastes even better after the flavors meld for some time; you can refrigerate it for up to 12 hours.

KITCHEN IMPROV

There's plenty of opportunity to vary the garnishes for this soup. Consider including corn; sliced radishes; chopped hard-cooked egg or shredded cooked chicken; additional fresh herbs or sprouts; other nuts, seeds, or croutons; and drizzles or dollops of flavored oils, pestos, or nut sauces, or extra yogurt.

red lentil soup WITH warm spices

Serves 4 • Total Time: 45 minutes

- **4 tablespoons unsalted butter, divided**
- **1 large onion, chopped fine**
- **1 teaspoon table salt**
- **3/4 teaspoon ground coriander**
- **1/2 teaspoon ground cumin**
- **1/4 teaspoon ground ginger**
- **1/4 teaspoon pepper**
- **1/8 teaspoon ground cinnamon**
- **Pinch cayenne**
- **1 tablespoon tomato paste**
- **1 garlic clove, minced**
- **4 cups chicken or vegetable broth**
- **2 cups water**
- **10½ ounces (1½ cups) red lentils, picked over and rinsed**
- **2 tablespoons lemon juice, plus extra for seasoning**
- **1½ teaspoons dried mint, crumbled**
- **1 teaspoon paprika**
- **1/4 cup chopped fresh cilantro**

RED LENTILS cook quickly into a nubbly-textured soup that needs just a whisk to "puree" it. A North African blend of spices, bloomed in the pot at the start, and a fragrant spiced butter drizzled on before serving complete the transformation of pantry ingredients into an exciting yet comforting soup.

1 Melt 2 tablespoons butter in large saucepan over medium heat. Add onion and salt and cook until softened, about 5 minutes. Stir in coriander, cumin, ginger, pepper, cinnamon, and cayenne and cook until fragrant, about 30 seconds. Stir in tomato paste and garlic and cook for 1 minute. Stir in broth, water, and lentils, scraping up any browned bits, and bring to simmer. Cook, stirring occasionally, until lentils are soft and about half are broken down, about 15 minutes.

2 Whisk soup vigorously until it is coarsely pureed, about 30 seconds. Stir in lemon juice and season with salt and extra lemon juice to taste. Cover to keep warm.

3 Melt remaining 2 tablespoons butter in small skillet. Remove from heat and stir in mint and paprika. Ladle soup into individual bowls and drizzle each portion with 1 teaspoon spiced butter. Sprinkle with cilantro and serve.

NOTES

Don't substitute brown or green lentils for the red lentils.

KITCHEN IMPROV

Try yellow lentils in place of red. Fresh mint or parsley can also be used as a garnish. Serve with yogurt for dolloping on top.

pasta e fagioli

Serves 4 • Total Time: 45 minutes

- **2 tablespoons extra-virgin olive oil, plus extra for drizzling**
- **1 large onion, chopped fine**
- **2 carrots, peeled and chopped fine**
- **1½ ounces pancetta, chopped fine**
- **¾ teaspoon table salt**
- **½ teaspoon pepper**
- **2 tablespoons tomato paste**
- **4 garlic cloves, minced**
- **¼ teaspoon red pepper flakes**
- **4 cups chicken or vegetable broth**
- **2 (15-ounce) cans cannellini beans, undrained**
- **1 cup ditalini**
- **1 ounce Parmesan cheese, grated (½ cup), plus extra for serving**
- **½ cup chopped fresh basil**

ITALIAN PEASANT cooking at its best, this resourceful soup extracts big flavor from every ingredient, including the starchy liquid from the canned beans, which brilliantly seasons and thickens the soup.

1 Heat oil in large saucepan over medium heat until shimmering. Add onion, carrots, pancetta, salt, and pepper and cook until vegetables are softened, 6 to 8 minutes.

2 Stir in tomato paste, garlic, and pepper flakes and cook until fragrant, about 30 seconds. Stir in broth and beans and their liquid, scraping up any browned bits. Bring to simmer and cook, stirring occasionally, until liquid has thickened slightly and flavors meld, about 5 minutes.

3 Increase heat to medium-high and bring to boil. Add pasta and cook, stirring occasionally, until al dente. Off heat, stir in Parmesan and basil. Serve, drizzling individual portions with extra oil and passing extra Parmesan separately.

NOTES

Be sure to not drain the canned beans, since you'll add their liquid to this soup.

KITCHEN IMPROV

Use bacon in place of pancetta. Cannellini beans are traditional, but any mild, creamy bean such as pinto, navy, or great northern will work. Use another small pasta, such as tubettini, elbow macaroni, or small shells, in place of the ditalini. To make this soup vegetarian, omit the pancetta.

quick mediterranean beef stew

Serves 4 • Total Time: 45 minutes

- **1½ pounds sirloin steak tips, trimmed and cut into ¾-inch pieces**
- **1 teaspoon table salt**
- **2 tablespoons extra-virgin olive oil**
- **1 onion, chopped coarse**
- **2 carrots, peeled and chopped coarse**
- **¼ cup tomato paste**
- **1 teaspoon herbes de Provence**
- **2 tablespoons all-purpose flour**
- **½ cup dry red wine**
- **2 cups beef broth**
- **2 (2-inch) strips orange zest**

WEEKNIGHT REIMAGINING of beef stew relies on steak tips. Using this already tender cut of beef eliminates the need for long simmering. Browning the meat and adding red wine, broth, herbes de Provence, and orange peel fills the pot with Mediterranean flavors.

1. Pat beef dry with paper towels and sprinkle with salt. Heat oil in Dutch oven over high heat until just smoking. Add beef and cook, stirring occasionally, until no longer pink, 6 to 8 minutes; transfer to plate.

2. Add onion, carrots, tomato paste, and herbes de Provence to fat left in pot and cook over medium heat, stirring occasionally, until vegetables begin to soften and tomato paste darkens, 6 to 8 minutes. Stir in flour and cook for 1 minute. Stir in wine, scraping up any browned bits and smoothing out any lumps. Stir in broth, orange zest, and beef along with any accumulated juices and bring to simmer.

3. Reduce heat to medium-low, cover, and simmer until beef and vegetables are tender, about 10 minutes. Discard orange zest. Season with salt and pepper to taste and serve.

NOTES

Sirloin steak tips can also be labeled "flap meat" or "bavette steak" and may be sold as whole steaks, strips, or pieces. For best results, try to buy whole steaks or strips and cut them into pieces yourself. If steak tips are unavailable, look for tri-tip or flank steak.

KITCHEN IMPROV

Other root vegetables can be used in place of the carrots; try 8 ounces celery root, parsnips, or turnips. You can swap in dried thyme, rosemary, or a mix of both for the herbes de Provence. If you don't have an orange, lemon zest will work, too. Garnish the stew with chopped kalamata olives, chopped toasted walnuts or almonds, or a swirl of pesto.

picadillo-style beef chili

Serves 4 • Total Time: 45 minutes

- **1 pound 85 percent lean ground beef**
- **1½ teaspoons table salt, divided**
- **1 teaspoon pepper**
- **1 onion, chopped fine**
- **1 jalapeño chile, stemmed, halved, seeded, and sliced thin**
- **1½ tablespoons chili powder**
- **3 garlic cloves, minced**
- **2 (14.5-ounce) cans fire-roasted diced tomatoes, drained**
- **2 cups chicken broth**
- **1 pound Yukon Gold potatoes, peeled and cut into ½-inch pieces**
- **½ cup pimento-stuffed green olives, sliced thin**

FIRE-ROASTED TOMATOES add long-cooked flavor and smoky complexity to this chili inspired by Cuban picadillo. Potatoes and olives—traditional in picadillo—add heartiness and a boost of briny flavor that cuts the beef's richness.

1 Combine ground beef, 1 teaspoon salt, and pepper in Dutch oven and cook over medium-high heat, breaking up meat with wooden spoon, until beginning to brown, about 10 minutes.

2 Stir in onion, jalapeño, chili powder, and garlic and cook until vegetables are softened, about 2 minutes. Stir in tomatoes, broth, potatoes, and remaining ½ teaspoon salt, scraping up any browned bits, and bring to simmer. Reduce heat to medium-low, cover, and cook until potatoes are tender, 15 to 17 minutes. Stir in olives, season with salt and pepper to taste, and serve.

NOTES

Serve with warm flour tortillas or rice, sour cream, and/or hot sauce.

KITCHEN IMPROV

Switch up the protein if you want and use ground lamb, ground pork, or 93 percent lean ground turkey or chicken. Include capers or raisins, traditional in many picadillos, in addition to the olives. You can also garnish with a sprinkle of parsley, toasted almonds, and/or chopped hard-cooked egg.

creamy chickpea AND sweet potato stew

Serves 4 to 6 • Total Time: 45 minutes

- **1 tablespoon vegetable oil**
- **1 onion, chopped fine**
- **1 large sweet potato, peeled and cut into ½-inch pieces**
- **¾ teaspoon table salt**
- **¼ teaspoon red pepper flakes**
- **3 tablespoons tomato paste**
- **1 teaspoon ground coriander**
- **2 (15-ounce) cans chickpeas, undrained**
- **1 (14-ounce) can coconut milk**
- **¾ cup water**
- **⅓ cup natural peanut butter**
- **2 teaspoons grated lime zest plus 2 tablespoons juice**
- **½ cup unsalted dry-roasted peanuts, chopped**
- **½ cup minced fresh cilantro**

FULL-ON FLAVOR is what you'll get from this stew, which is loosely inspired by maafe, the Senegalese peanut stew. As the chickpeas simmer in a broth enriched with coconut milk and peanut butter, they swell to buttery smoothness. Lime zest, cilantro, and peanuts light up each bowl with freshness and crunch.

1 Heat oil in large saucepan over medium heat until shimmering. Add onion, sweet potato, salt, and red pepper flakes and cook, stirring frequently, until onion begins to brown, 6 to 8 minutes. Add tomato paste and coriander and cook, stirring constantly, until tomato paste slightly darkens, 2 minutes.

2 Stir in chickpeas and their liquid, coconut milk, water, and peanut butter, scraping up any browned bits, and bring to simmer. Cover, reduce heat to medium-low, and cook, stirring occasionally, until sweet potato is tender, about 15 minutes.

3 Off heat, stir in lime zest and juice. Season with salt to taste. Serve, passing peanuts and cilantro separately.

NOTES

Both creamy and chunky natural peanut butter work here; avoid sweetened peanut butter.

KITCHEN IMPROV

Add other veggies to the stew: Frozen peas, corn, and/or cut green beans can all be stirred in and allowed to warm through after the sweet potatoes become tender. Serve with rice, fonio, or couscous.

dinner-size salads

chapter 7

chicken AND arugula salad WITH cherries AND feta

Serves 4 • Total Time: 25 minutes

- 3 ounces rustic bread, cut into 1-inch pieces (about 1½ cups)
- ½ cup extra-virgin olive oil, divided
- ¼ teaspoon plus pinch table salt, divided
- 2 tablespoons white wine vinegar
- 2 tablespoons minced fresh parsley
- 1 tablespoon minced shallot
- 1 teaspoon Dijon mustard
- 3 cups shredded cooked chicken
- 5 ounces (5 cups) baby arugula
- 8 ounces fresh sweet cherries, pitted and quartered
- 2 ounces feta cheese, crumbled (½ cup)

1 Pulse bread in food processor until about half of pieces are broken into crumbs measuring between ¼ and ½ inch, about 10 pulses. Combine crumbs, 2 tablespoons oil, and pinch salt in 12-inch skillet and cook over medium heat, stirring often, until crumbs are golden brown, 8 to 10 minutes; transfer to plate.

2 Whisk vinegar, parsley, shallot, mustard, and remaining ¼ teaspoon salt together in large bowl. Whisking constantly, drizzle in remaining 6 tablespoons oil. Add chicken and arugula and toss to combine. Season with salt to taste. Transfer salad to serving platter and sprinkle with cherries, feta cheese, and bread crumbs. Serve.

KITCHEN IMPROV can be easy when salads are the template. Take this one: It's so good as is but lets you use up ingredients on hand through smart swaps.

NOTES

You can use Quick Cooked Chicken (page 334) or shred meat from one 2½-pound rotisserie chicken.

KITCHEN IMPROV

Stick with the prescribed ratio of greens to fruit to cheese (5:8:2 ounces) but vary the components (try mesclun, apricots, and shaved Manchego, for example). Replace the bread crumbs with pita chips or embellish with toasted nuts or sliced olives. Slice leftover steak or pork tenderloin to use instead of chicken.

chicken salad WITH cabbage AND fish sauce

Serves 4 • Total Time: 20 minutes

- 6 tablespoons fish sauce
- ¼ cup sugar
- ¼ cup unseasoned rice vinegar
- 1 Thai chile, minced
- 1 garlic clove, minced
- ¼ teaspoon table salt
- 5 cups thinly sliced green or red cabbage
- 3 cups shredded cooked chicken
- 2 ounces (2 cups) baby arugula, chopped coarse
- 1 red bell pepper, stemmed, seeded, and sliced thin
- 1 Persian cucumber, halved crosswise and sliced thin lengthwise
- 4 radishes, trimmed and sliced thin
- ¾ cup chopped fresh cilantro, mint, and/or Thai basil
- ¼ cup salted dry-roasted peanuts, chopped

Whisk fish sauce, sugar, vinegar, Thai chile, garlic, and salt in large bowl until sugar has dissolved. Add cabbage, chicken, arugula, bell pepper, cucumber, radishes, and herbs and toss thoroughly to combine. Sprinkle salad with peanuts. Serve.

AROMATIC HERBS, loads of fresh vegetables, crunchy peanuts, and a spicy-sweet fish sauce vinaigrette bring huge personality to shredded cooked chicken in this superfast dinner salad inspired by the flavors of Cambodian cuisine.

NOTES

A combination of fresh herbs makes a big difference in this salad so try to include at least two, or ideally all three, herbs. You can use Quick Cooked Chicken (page 334) or shred meat from one 2½-pound rotisserie chicken. For a less spicy salad, use half the Thai chile. If you don't have a Thai chile, use 1 teaspoon sriracha.

KITCHEN IMPROV

Feel free to customize the veggies with what looks good at the market. Try another peppery or bitter green such as mizuna, escarole, radicchio, or endive in place of arugula. To simplify prep, use coleslaw mix in place of the cabbage.

charred broccoli caesar salad WITH chicken

Serves 4 • Total Time: 35 minutes

- ½ cup panko bread crumbs
- 7 tablespoons plus 1 teaspoon extra-virgin olive oil, divided
- 1 ounce Parmesan cheese, grated (½ cup), divided, plus shaved Parmesan for serving
- ½ teaspoon grated lemon zest and 1 tablespoon juice
- 1¾ pounds broccoli
- ½ teaspoon table salt
- ½ teaspoon sugar
- 6 tablespoons mayonnaise
- 3 anchovy fillets, rinsed and minced (optional)
- 2 teaspoons white wine vinegar
- 2 teaspoons Worcestershire sauce
- 2 teaspoons Dijon mustard
- 1 garlic clove, minced to paste
- ½ teaspoon pepper
- 3 cups shredded cooked chicken

DEEPLY CARAMELIZED, gloriously charred wedges of roasted broccoli bring heft and smokiness that take really well to creamy Caesar dressing. Add shredded chicken and panko (crisped in the microwave) for a salad that's satisfying enough for dinner.

1 Adjust oven rack to lowest position, place rimmed baking sheet on lower rack, and heat oven to 500 degrees. Toss panko with 1 teaspoon oil in small bowl until evenly coated. Microwave, stirring frequently, until light golden brown, 2 to 4 minutes; let cool slightly. Stir in 2 tablespoons Parmesan and lemon zest; set aside.

2 Cut broccoli horizontally at juncture of crowns and stalks. Cut crowns into 4 wedges of 3 to 4 inches in diameter or 6 wedges of 4 to 5 inches in diameter. Trim tough outer peel from stalks, then cut into ½-inch-thick planks about 2 to 3 inches long. Toss broccoli with 3 tablespoons oil, salt, and sugar in large bowl. Working quickly, lay broccoli in single layer, flat sides down, on preheated sheet. Roast until stalks and florets are well browned and tender, 9 to 11 minutes.

3 Whisk mayonnaise, anchovies (if using), vinegar, Worcestershire, mustard, garlic, pepper, lemon juice, remaining ¼ cup oil, and remaining 6 tablespoons Parmesan in clean, dry large bowl. Add chicken and broccoli and toss to coat. Serve, sprinkling individual portions with reserved panko mixture and shaved Parmesan.

NOTES

You can use Quick Cooked Chicken (page 334) or shred meat from one 2½-pound rotisserie chicken. We like to include the broccoli stalks, but you can use just crowns. Cider vinegar can be used in place of the white wine vinegar.

KITCHEN IMPROV

Use leftover steak or pork tenderloin instead of chicken. Make a charred green bean Caesar by swapping 1½ pounds trimmed green beans for broccoli; roast as directed, tossing occasionally, until tender and spotty brown. Add halved cherry tomatoes, diced bell pepper, or shredded carrot.

versatile proteins

quick cooked chicken

Serves 4 (Makes 3 cups) • Total Time: 30 minutes

A UNIQUE COOKING method yields superbly moist meat to use wherever you need cooked chicken.

- **3 (6- to 8-ounce) boneless, skinless chicken breasts, trimmed**
- **1/8 teaspoon table salt**
- **1/8 teaspoon pepper**
- **1 teaspoon vegetable oil**

1. Pat chicken dry with paper towels and sprinkle with salt and pepper. Heat oil in 12-inch skillet over medium heat until just smoking. Add chicken and cook until well browned on first side, about 6 minutes. Flip chicken, add 1/4 cup water, and cover skillet. Reduce heat to medium-low and continue to cook until chicken registers 160 degrees, 5 to 7 minutes.

2. Transfer chicken to cutting board and let cool for 10 minutes. Slice, chop, or shred as desired.

NOTES

For even cooking, look for chicken breasts of even thickness; if necessary, pound them to an even thickness. You can refrigerate the cooked chicken for up to 2 days.

KITCHEN IMPROV

You can also use 1½ pounds boneless, skinless thighs; cook them to at least 175 degrees, increasing the covered cooking time to about 5 minutes. Sprinkle the chicken with your favorite spice blend along with the salt and pepper. Swap in white wine for water.

---

sirloin steak tips

Serves 4 • Total Time: 20 minutes

TOP-SHELF STEAKHOUSE flavors at home don't require splurging on a pricey marbled rib-eye steak or a filet. Achieve the same satisfaction with these easy-to-cook (and wallet-friendly) steak tips.

- **1½ pounds sirloin steak tips, trimmed and cut into 3-inch pieces**
- **1 teaspoon table salt**
- **1/2 teaspoon pepper**
- **1 tablespoon vegetable oil**

1. Pat steak tips dry with paper towels and sprinkle with salt and pepper. Heat oil in 12-inch skillet over medium-high heat until just smoking. Add steak tips and cook until browned on all sides and meat registers 120 to 125 degrees (for medium-rare) or 130 to 135 degrees (for medium), 7 to 10 minutes.

2. Transfer steak tips to cutting board and let rest for 5 minutes. Slice steak against grain 1/4 inch thick before serving.

NOTES

Steak tips can also be labeled "flap meat" or "bavette steak" and come as whole steaks, strips, or pieces. Try to buy steaks or strips and cut them yourself. If you can't find steak tips, look for tri-tip or flank steak. You can refrigerate seared steak tips for up to 3 days; slice just before using.

KITCHEN IMPROV

Sprinkle on a spice rub with the salt and pepper before searing. (Avoid rubs containing sugar, which may burn.)

crispy-skinned salmon fillets

Serves 4 • Total Time: 20 minutes

- **4 (6- to 8-ounce) skin-on center-cut salmon fillets, 1 to 1½ inches thick**
- **½ teaspoon table salt**
- **½ teaspoon pepper**

1 Pat salmon dry with paper towels and sprinkle with salt and pepper. Place salmon skin side down in cold 12-inch nonstick skillet and place over medium-high heat. Cook fillets, without moving them, until skin is golden brown and bottom ¼ inch of fillet turns opaque, 6 to 8 minutes.

2 Using 2 spatulas, flip fillets skin side up and continue to cook without moving them until center is still translucent when checked with tip of paring knife and salmon registers 125 degrees (for medium-rare), 6 to 8 minutes; transfer salmon to plate.

PERFECTLY SEARED salmon, with a moist interior, golden exterior, and crispy skin, is easily within reach at home. Don't feel like you need to flake this into a salad or pasta—it's so good on its own!

NOTES

If using wild salmon, reduce cooking times to 4 to 6 minutes per side and cook until the fish registers 120 degrees. The skin protects the fish from drying out while cooking; if you don't want to serve it, you can easily peel it off once the fish is cooked. You can refrigerate the salmon for up to 2 days.

KITCHEN IMPROV

Add a favorite spice rub to the salmon with the salt and pepper in step 1.

---

pan-seared tofu

Serves 4 • Total Time: 20 minutes

- **14 ounces firm or extra-firm tofu, cut into ¾-inch pieces**
- **¼ teaspoon table salt**
- **⅛ teaspoon pepper**
- **1 tablespoon vegetable oil**

1 Spread tofu over paper towel–lined plate and gently press dry with paper towels. Sprinkle with salt and pepper.

2 Heat oil in 12-inch nonstick skillet over medium-high heat until shimmering. Add tofu and cook until lightly browned on all sides, 6 to 8 minutes; transfer to bowl.

SIMPLY SEASONED tofu browned in a skillet is a versatile protein option that can be paired with just about anything.

NOTES

This recipe can be easily doubled; cook the tofu in 2 batches, adding more oil to the skillet as needed. The seared tofu can be refrigerated for up to 2 days.

KITCHEN IMPROV

Add a spice rub to the tofu along with the salt and pepper in step 1.

hummus bowls WITH roasted chicken AND cauliflower

Serves 4 • Total Time: 45 minutes

- **1½ pounds boneless, skinless chicken thighs, trimmed**
- **6 tablespoons extra-virgin olive oil, divided, plus extra for drizzling**
- **1 tablespoon baharat**
- **2 teaspoons table salt, divided**
- **1¼ pounds cauliflower florets, cut into 2-inch pieces**
- **2 cups thinly sliced green or red cabbage**
- **1 tablespoon lemon juice**
- **½ English cucumber, quartered lengthwise and sliced ½ inch thick**
- **2 tomatoes, cored and cut into ½-inch pieces**
- **2 cups hummus**
- **¼ cup chopped fresh mint or parsley**

PROTEIN-PACKED HUMMUS replaces the usual grain base in this tasty bowl. An array of fresh and roasted vegetables, juicy chicken thighs, and the alluring spice blend baharat make this supper especially satisfying. Serve with warm pita.

1 Adjust oven rack 6 inches from broiler element and heat broiler. Line rimmed baking sheet with aluminum foil. Toss chicken with 2 tablespoons oil, baharat, and 1 teaspoon salt in large bowl. Arrange chicken in single layer on half of prepared sheet and broil for 5 minutes. Toss cauliflower with 2 tablespoons oil and ½ teaspoon salt in clean large bowl. Spread cauliflower on empty half of sheet. Broil until cauliflower is well browned and tender and chicken registers at least 175 degrees, 10 to 12 minutes. (Remove chicken from sheet as it finishes cooking.) Let chicken rest for 5 minutes.

2 Meanwhile, combine cabbage, lemon juice, ¼ teaspoon salt, and remaining 2 tablespoons oil in now-empty bowl. Combine cucumber, tomatoes, and remaining ¼ teaspoon salt in second bowl.

3 Cut chicken into bite-size pieces. Spread hummus over bottoms of individual serving bowls. Top with piles of chicken, cauliflower, cabbage, and tomato mixture. Drizzle with extra oil and sprinkle with mint. Serve.

NOTES

Baharat is a warm, savory Middle Eastern spice blend. If you don't have it, combine 1½ teaspoons paprika, ¾ teaspoon pepper, ½ teaspoon ground cumin, and ¼ teaspoon ground cloves.

KITCHEN IMPROV

Feel free to play around with the spices on the chicken. Try broiling brussels sprouts, bell peppers, or mushrooms instead of cauliflower. Not a fan of cabbage? Use baby spinach or arugula dressed with lemon and olive oil instead.

JUST-RIGHT SPICY pasta salad chock-full of roasted vegetables and shredded chicken hits the spot on a steamy summer evening. Jarred pickled jalapeños are less spicy than fresh, and you can use more or fewer of them to adjust the heat level to your liking.

orecchiette salad WITH roasted vegetables, chicken AND jalapeño-lime dressing

Serves 4 to 6 • Total Time: 45 minutes

- **1 pound zucchini, quartered lengthwise and sliced ¼ inch thick**
- **1½ cups frozen corn**
- **2 tablespoons plus ½ cup vegetable oil, divided**
- **1½ teaspoons table salt, divided, plus salt for cooking pasta**
- **8 ounces (2¼ cups) orecchiette**
- **⅓ cup plus ¼ cup jarred sliced jalapeños, drained, divided**
- **4 scallions, white parts sliced thin, green parts cut into 1-inch pieces**
- **¼ cup lime juice (2 limes)**
- **3 cups shredded cooked chicken**
- **¾ cup fresh cilantro leaves, divided**
- **8 radishes, trimmed, halved, and sliced thin**
- **1 large carrot, peeled and shredded**

1. Arrange oven rack 4 inches from broiler element and heat broiler. Toss zucchini and corn with 2 tablespoons oil and ½ teaspoon salt in large bowl. Transfer to rimmed baking sheet and spread into even layer (do not wash bowl). Broil until spotty brown, 8 to 10 minutes, stirring halfway through broiling. Transfer sheet to wire rack to cool.

2. Meanwhile, bring 2 quarts water to boil in large saucepan. Add pasta and 1½ teaspoons salt and cook, stirring occasionally, until pasta is tender throughout, 2 to 3 minutes past al dente. Drain well and rinse with cold water. Drain well and transfer to now-empty bowl.

3. Process ⅓ cup jalapeños, scallion whites, lime juice, and remaining 1 teaspoon salt in blender until coarse paste forms, about 30 seconds. With blender running, drizzle in remaining ½ cup oil and continue to process until dressing is emulsified and smooth, about 1 minute.

4. Chop remaining ¼ cup jalapeños and add to pasta along with chicken, ½ cup cilantro, radishes, carrot, zucchini and corn, and scallion greens. Pour dressing over salad and toss to coat. Transfer to serving bowl. Sprinkle with remaining ¼ cup cilantro and serve.

NOTES

You can use Quick Cooked Chicken (page 334) or shred meat from one 2½-pound rotisserie chicken. This salad is great served cold; in fact, the pasta is intentionally cooked until a little too soft so that it remains tender even when chilled. If making the salad ahead (up to 24 hours), dress the salad and garnish it right before serving.

KITCHEN IMPROV

Feel free to fiddle with the add-ins. Switch up the mix of veggies. Use fresh corn if it's in season—you will need 2 ears. Try another stubby pasta, like penne.

tomato salad WITH steak tips

Serves 4 • Total Time: 30 minutes

- **1½ pounds sirloin steak tips, trimmed and cut into 3-inch pieces**
- **1 teaspoon table salt, divided**
- **½ teaspoon pepper, divided**
- **¼ cup extra-virgin olive oil, divided, plus extra for serving**
- **1 tablespoon minced shallot**
- **1 teaspoon lemon juice**
- **5 ounces (5 cups) little gem lettuce or mesclun**
- **1 cup torn fresh basil, parsley, and/or oregano**
- **1½ pounds mixed ripe tomatoes, cored and sliced ¼ inch thick**
- **2 ounces feta cheese, crumbled (½ cup)**
- **½ cup toasted pepitas or sunflower seeds**

1 Pat steak tips dry with paper towels and sprinkle with ½ teaspoon salt and ¼ teaspoon pepper. Heat 1 tablespoon oil in 12-inch skillet over medium-high heat until just smoking. Add steak tips and cook until browned on all sides and meat registers 120 to 125 degrees (for medium-rare) or 130 to 135 degrees (for medium), 7 to 10 minutes. Transfer steak tips to cutting board and let rest while preparing greens.

2 Whisk shallot, lemon juice, remaining 3 tablespoons oil, remaining ½ teaspoon salt, and remaining ¼ teaspoon pepper together in large bowl. Add lettuce and herbs and toss to combine.

3 Slice steak against grain ¼ inch thick. Arrange tomatoes on large, shallow platter, drizzle with extra oil, and season with salt and pepper to taste. Arrange lettuce mixture over tomatoes and top with steak. Sprinkle with feta and pepitas and serve.

NOTES

Sirloin steak tips can also be labeled "flap meat" or "bavette steak" and may be sold as whole steaks, strips, or pieces. Try to buy steaks or strips and cut them yourself. If steak tips are unavailable, look for tri-tip or flank steak. This salad is best made with ripe, in-season heirloom tomatoes. If those are not available, opt for ripe tomatoes on the vine that are tender to the touch.

KITCHEN IMPROV

Feel free to mix and match baby greens or torn tender lettuce; Bibb or Boston, red oak leaf, arugula, and spinach are all good choices. You can use chopped walnuts, slivered almonds, or pine nuts instead of the seeds.

"SHINGLE SLICED TOMATOES over a platter" is a great way to start so many recipes. Here, a pretty gem lettuce and herb salad is layered over the tomatoes, followed by seared-and-sliced steak, feta, and toasted pepitas for a summery salad that's a stunner.

VARYING TEXTURES—crunchy jicama, soft pinto beans, lightly pickled poblanos—make a refreshing counterpoint to ancho-rubbed seared steak. The complex bitterness of the unsweetened chocolate sprinkle completes this salad's nod to Mexican ingredients.

NOTES

Skirt steaks come from two different muscles, sometimes (not always) labeled as "inside" skirt steak or "outside" skirt steak. Look for the more tender outside cut, which is 3 to 4 inches wide and ½ to 1 inch thick. If you can find only the inside cut (typically 5 to 7 inches wide and ¼ to ½ inch thick), halve the steaks lengthwise before slicing them in step 2.

KITCHEN IMPROV

Flank steak also works well here. Use any mild, creamy bean such as cannellini, navy, or great northern in place of pintos.

pinto bean, ancho AND steak salad WITH pickled poblanos

Serves 4 • Total Time: 45 minutes

- **1 poblano chile, stemmed, seeded, and sliced 1/8 inch thick**
- **1 cup distilled white vinegar**
- **1/3 cup sugar**
- **1 1/4 teaspoons table salt, divided**
- **1 1/2 pounds outside skirt steak, trimmed**
- **2 teaspoons ancho chile powder**
- **3/4 teaspoon pepper, divided**
- **2 tablespoons vegetable oil, divided**
- **2 (15-ounce) cans pinto beans, rinsed**
- **12 ounces jicama, peeled and shredded (1 1/2 cups)**
- **1/2 cup finely chopped red onion**
- **1/4 cup chopped fresh cilantro leaves and stems, plus extra for serving**
- **3 tablespoons lime juice (2 limes)**
- **1 1/2 ounces cotija cheese, crumbled (1/3 cup)**
- **1/2 ounce unsweetened chocolate, chopped fine (optional)**

1 Combine poblano, vinegar, sugar, and 1/4 teaspoon salt in medium bowl. Cover and microwave until steaming, about 2 minutes; set aside.

2 Slice steak with grain into 3-inch-wide pieces. Pat steaks dry with paper towels and sprinkle with chile powder, 1/4 teaspoon pepper, and 1/2 teaspoon salt. Heat 1 tablespoon oil in 12-inch skillet over medium-high heat until just smoking. Add steaks and cook until well browned and meat registers 120 to 125 degrees (for medium-rare) or 130 to 135 degrees (for medium), 2 to 4 minutes per side. Transfer steaks to cutting board and let rest while preparing bean mixture.

3 Drain poblanos. Toss beans, jicama, onion, cilantro, lime juice, remaining 1/2 teaspoon salt, remaining 1/2 teaspoon pepper, and remaining 1 tablespoon oil together in bowl. Spread bean mixture evenly over serving platter. Slice steak thin against grain and arrange over top. Sprinkle with cotija, chocolate (if using), poblanos, and extra cilantro. Serve.

white beans AND chorizo WITH quick marinated tomatoes and onion

Serves 4 • Total Time: 25 minutes

- **3 tablespoons sherry vinegar**
- **3 tablespoons plus 1/4 cup extra-virgin olive oil, divided**
- **1/8 teaspoon plus 1/2 teaspoon table salt, divided**
- **1/4 teaspoon pepper**
- **12 ounces cherry tomatoes, quartered**
- **1/2 red onion, sliced thin**
- **6 ounces Spanish-style chorizo sausage, cut into 1/2-inch pieces**
- **2 (15-ounce) cans cannellini beans, rinsed**
- **3 garlic cloves, minced**
- **1/4 teaspoon smoked paprika**
- **1/4 cup water**
- **1 cup coarsely chopped fresh parsley**

CREAMY WHITE BEANS are at the forefront of this simple but inventive meal. Marinating the vegetables while the chorizo cooks brings out their sweetness, and warming the beans in the chorizo oil imbues the dish with flavor. Serve with crusty bread.

1. Whisk vinegar, 1 tablespoon oil, 1/8 teaspoon salt, and pepper together in medium bowl. Add tomatoes and onion and toss to coat; set aside to marinate.

2. Cook chorizo and 2 tablespoons oil in 12-inch skillet over medium-high heat until evenly browned and crisp, 4 to 6 minutes, stirring often. Using slotted spoon, transfer chorizo to paper towel–lined plate.

3. Add beans, garlic, paprika, and remaining 1/2 teaspoon salt to fat left in skillet, reduce heat to medium, and cook until beans are warmed through, 2 to 4 minutes. Off heat, add water, scraping up any browned bits. Stir in chorizo, tomato mixture, parsley, and remaining 1/4 cup extra-virgin olive oil. Serve.

NOTES

Look for Spanish-style chorizo, which has been cured. Nutty-tasting sherry vinegar complements the chorizo well, but if you don't have it, red wine vinegar works.

KITCHEN IMPROV

This recipe is easy to customize. Trade chorizo for andouille. Use a different bean, like pinto or great northern. Add fresh corn to brown with the chorizo. Toast slabs of bread and drizzle liberally with good olive oil to serve alongside.

bún chả

Serves 4 • Total Time: 45 minutes

- 8 ounces rice vermicelli
- 1 small Thai chile, stemmed and minced
- 3 tablespoons plus 1½ teaspoons sugar, divided
- 1 garlic clove, minced
- 6 tablespoons fish sauce, divided
- ¼ cup lime juice (2 limes)
- 1 large shallot, minced
- ½ teaspoon baking soda
- ½ teaspoon pepper
- 1 pound ground pork
- 2 teaspoons vegetable oil
- 1 head Boston lettuce (8 ounces), torn into bite-size pieces
- 1 English cucumber, peeled, quartered lengthwise, seeded, and sliced thin on bias
- 1 cup fresh cilantro leaves
- 1 cup fresh mint leaves, torn if large

1 Place vermicelli in large bowl and cover with boiling water. Let sit until noodles are just tender, about 10 minutes. Drain noodles and rinse under cold running water until cool. Drain noodles very well, then spread in even layer on rimmed baking sheet and set aside.

2 Meanwhile, using mortar and pestle (or on cutting board using flat side of chef's knife), mash Thai chile, 1 tablespoon sugar, and garlic to fine paste; transfer to medium bowl. Whisk in ⅔ cup hot water, 5 tablespoons fish sauce, lime juice, and 2 tablespoons sugar until sugar has dissolved; set aside.

3 Combine shallot, baking soda, pepper, remaining 1½ teaspoons sugar, and remaining 1 tablespoon fish sauce in medium bowl. Add pork and mix with your hands until thoroughly combined. Using your moistened hands, shape pork mixture into 12 patties, each about 2½ inches wide and ½ inch thick.

4 Heat 12-inch cast-iron skillet over medium heat for 3 minutes. Add oil, increase heat to medium-high, and heat until oil is just smoking. Transfer patties to skillet and cook until well browned on both sides, about 3 minutes per side. Transfer patties to bowl with sauce and gently toss to coat. Let sit for 5 minutes.

5 Transfer patties to serving plate, reserving sauce. Arrange lettuce, cucumber, cilantro, and mint separately on large platter. Serve, passing noodles, salad, patties, and sauce separately.

VIBRANT VIETNAMESE bún chả features seasoned pork patties, crisp vegetables, springy rice noodles, and a zesty sauce. Set out the components separately and let everyone compose their own salads.

NOTES

If you don't have a cast-iron skillet, you can use a stainless-steel skillet; add the oil to the skillet and heat over medium-high heat until just smoking before adding the patties. For a less spicy sauce, use half of a chile. If you don't have a Thai chile, substitute ¾ teaspoon sriracha.

KITCHEN IMPROV

You can use 93 percent lean ground turkey or ground chicken instead of pork. Bulk up the salad veggies by including bean sprouts, shredded carrots, and/or halved cherry tomatoes.

napa cabbage AND noodle salad WITH shrimp AND citrus

Serves 4 • Total Time: 30 minutes

- 1½ pounds jumbo shrimp (16 to 20 per pound), peeled and deveined
- 3 tablespoons fish sauce, divided
- 8 ounces rice vermicelli
- ⅓ cup canned coconut milk
- 2 tablespoons sriracha
- 1 teaspoon grated lime zest plus 3 tablespoons juice (2 limes)
- 1 tablespoon sugar
- ½ small head napa cabbage, cored and sliced thin (4 cups)
- 1 tablespoon vegetable oil
- 3 clementines, peeled and pulled apart into individual segments
- 2 scallions, sliced thin on bias
- 2 tablespoons chopped fresh mint
- 2 tablespoons chopped fresh basil
- ¼ cup chopped salted dry-roasted peanuts

1 Combine shrimp and 1 tablespoon fish sauce in bowl; set aside. Place vermicelli in large bowl and cover with boiling water. Let sit until noodles are just tender, about 10 minutes. Drain noodles, rinse under cold running water until cool, then drain again.

2 Whisk coconut milk, sriracha, lime zest and juice, sugar, and remaining 2 tablespoons fish sauce together in second large bowl. Add napa cabbage and noodles and toss to combine. Divide among 4 serving bowls.

3 Heat oil in 12-inch nonstick skillet over medium-high heat until shimmering. Add shrimp and cook until opaque, about 2 minutes. Divide shrimp, clementines, scallions, mint, basil, and peanuts evenly over salads. Serve.

SHREDDED NAPA CABBAGE and cooled rice noodles bring crunch and chew to this refreshing dinner salad. Let the shrimp marinate in fish sauce while you prepare the salad; the condiment's salt and glutamate provide deep seasoning.

NOTES

Give the can of coconut milk a good shake before opening; this will make it easier to measure.

KITCHEN IMPROV

Clementines are nice here because they're easy to peel, but you can also use 1 cup of chopped orange or grapefruit segments.

hearty green salad WITH hot-smoked salmon

Serves 4 • Total Time: 45 minutes

- 1 small red onion, sliced thin
- 1/2 cup white wine vinegar
- 2 tablespoons sugar
- 2 teaspoons table salt, divided, plus salt for cooking asparagus
- 12 ounces asparagus, trimmed and cut into 2-inch lengths
- 1/2 cup plain Greek yogurt
- 5 tablespoons extra-virgin olive oil, divided
- 2 tablespoon capers, rinsed and chopped
- 1/2 teaspoon pepper
- 1 teaspoon Dijon mustard
- 2 romaine lettuce hearts (12 ounces), torn into bite-size pieces
- 4 ounces (4 cups) baby arugula
- 1 English cucumber, quartered lengthwise, seeded, and sliced on bias 1/4 inch thick
- 12 ounces cherry tomatoes, halved
- 8 ounces hot-smoked salmon, skin removed, broken into 1-inch flakes (1/2 cup)
- 4 hard-cooked large eggs, peeled and quartered lengthwise
- 1/4 cup chopped fresh dill

1 Combine onion, vinegar, sugar, and 1½ teaspoons salt in medium bowl. Cover and microwave until steaming, about 2 minutes. Let sit, stirring occasionally, until onion is pink and slightly softened, about 15 minutes. Using slotted spoon, transfer onion to plate, leaving liquid in bowl.

2 Meanwhile, combine asparagus, 1/4 cup water, and 1/2 teaspoon salt in second medium bowl. Cover and microwave until crisp-tender, about 2 minutes. Using slotted spoon, transfer asparagus to plate; discard water.

3 In now-empty bowl, whisk 1/4 cup onion pickling liquid, yogurt, 2 tablespoons oil, capers, and pepper. Add mustard, remaining 1/2 teaspoon salt, and remaining 3 tablespoons oil to remaining pickling liquid and whisk to combine.

4 Combine lettuce and arugula in large bowl. Add mustard mixture and toss to coat. Distribute greens evenly among shallow serving bowls. Sprinkle each salad with onion. Arrange cucumber, tomatoes, and asparagus in piles atop greens. Drizzle with yogurt dressing and top with salmon and eggs. Sprinkle with dill and serve.

NEARLY NO-COOK meals are welcome on scorching summer evenings. With hard-cooked eggs stashed in your fridge, this protein-packed green salad is just the ticket. The mustardy yogurt dressing is zested up with the brine from quick-pickling the onions.

NOTES

Fillets of hot-smoked salmon are fully cooked and can usually be found alongside cold-smoked salmon in your supermarket. To save time, start the pickled onion before you gather and prep the other ingredients. You can also make the pickled onion up to a week ahead; store it in its pickling liquid in the refrigerator.

KITCHEN IMPROV

Try other lettuces such as red oak leaf or iceberg in place of the romaine; swap in baby kale or spinach for the arugula. Use hot-smoked mackerel or trout instead of salmon.

oil-poached tuna AND potato salad

Serves 4 • Total Time: 35 minutes

- 1 pound skinless tuna steaks, 1 inch thick
- 1½ teaspoons table salt, divided, plus salt for cooking potatoes
- 1 teaspoon pepper, divided
- ½ red onion, sliced thin
- ½ teaspoon grated lemon zest plus ¼ cup juice (2 lemons)
- 1 pound small red or Yukon Gold potatoes, unpeeled, quartered
- ¾ cup extra-virgin olive oil
- 1 head frisée (6 ounces), cut into 1-inch pieces
- 1 orange, peeled, quartered, and sliced
- ⅓ cup chopped fresh parsley
- ¼ cup pitted oil-cured black olives, chopped coarse

THE FLAVORFUL TUNA poaching oil becomes the base of the dressing for this luxurious potato salad. Cooking tuna gently in olive oil imbues it with extra richness and keeps its texture moist and ultratender.

1 Pat tuna dry with paper towels and sprinkle with 1 teaspoon salt and ¾ teaspoon pepper. Combine onion and lemon juice in large bowl; set aside. Bring 2 quarts water to boil in large saucepan over medium-high heat. Add potatoes and 2 tablespoons salt and cook until tender, 8 to 10 minutes. Drain potatoes, then spread out on large plate to cool.

2 Meanwhile, heat oil in medium saucepan over medium-low heat until shimmering. Add tuna and cook, covered, until reddish pink at center when checked with tip of paring knife and registering 120 to 125 degrees (for medium-rare), 8 to 10 minutes, flipping tuna halfway through cooking. (Adjust heat as necessary to maintain small bubbles around edges of tuna.) Transfer tuna to plate and flake into large pieces with fork.

3 Mix ¼ cup oil from saucepan, lemon zest, remaining ½ teaspoon salt, and remaining ¼ teaspoon pepper into onion mixture. Add potatoes, frisée, orange, parsley, and olives and toss to combine. Season with salt and pepper to taste. Transfer salad to platter and arrange tuna on top. Serve.

NOTES

Be sure to thoroughly rinse the frisée to remove any grit. For tuna cooked to medium, observe the timing for medium-rare, then tent the steaks with aluminum foil for 5 minutes before flaking into pieces.

KITCHEN IMPROV

This oil poaching technique also works well with salmon. The texture of frisée is really nice here, but another mildly bitter green, such as escarole or chicory, will work. You can replace the parsley with basil and use green olives instead of black.

seared scallops WITH citrus AND avocado salad

Serves 4 • Total Time: 30 minutes

- **2 oranges**
- **1 grapefruit**
- **1½ pounds large sea scallops, tendons removed**
- **6 tablespoons extra-virgin olive oil, divided**
- **1 teaspoon table salt, divided**
- **1 shallot, sliced thin**
- **1 tablespoon white wine vinegar**
- **2 teaspoons Dijon mustard**
- **2 teaspoons minced fresh tarragon**
- **4 ounces (4 cups) baby arugula**
- **2 avocados, halved, pitted, and sliced ¼ inch thick**

1 Grate ½ teaspoon zest from 1 orange; set aside. Cut away peel and pith from oranges and grapefruit. Holding fruit over bowl, use paring knife to slice between membranes to release segments; set aside.

2 Pat scallops dry with paper towels and sprinkle all over with ¾ teaspoon salt. Heat 1 tablespoon oil in 12-inch nonstick skillet over high heat until just smoking, about 2 minutes. Add half of scallops, flat side down, in single layer around circumference of skillet; cook until browned, about 2 minutes per side. Transfer scallops to plate and tent with foil. Repeat with 1 tablespoon oil and remaining scallops.

3 Whisk shallot, vinegar, mustard, tarragon, orange zest, remaining ¼ cup oil, and remaining ¼ teaspoon salt together in large bowl. Add arugula and toss to coat. Add avocados, oranges, and grapefruit and toss gently to combine. Serve scallops over individual portions of salad.

NOTES

If you want to put a restaurant-worthy sear on scallops (and you do!), shopping is just as important as a hot pan. You want ivory or pinkish "dry" scallops, which have better flavor and are much easier to sear than bright white "wet" scallops, which have been treated with additives that make them shed more liquid when they cook.

KITCHEN IMPROV

Try other varieties of citrus; use a different vinegar (champagne or sherry is nice), or a different herb, such as basil or parsley. Use other tender greens, like baby spinach, frisée, or Bibb or Boston lettuce. You could even use extra-large shrimp instead of scallops: Cook them until opaque throughout, about 2 minutes per side.

BRIGHT CITRUS, tender scallops, and creamy avocado create contrasting textures and colors in this memorable salad. Getting a good sear on the scallops makes all the difference, so make sure your pan is hot and pat those scallops dry before cooking.

farro salad WITH peaches AND pickled jalapeños

Serves 4 • Total Time: 45 minutes

- **1 cup whole farro**
- **½ teaspoon table salt, divided, plus salt for cooking farro**
- **1 large jalapeño chile, stemmed, halved, seeded, and sliced thin**
- **1 large shallot, sliced thin**
- **⅓ cup white wine vinegar**
- **2 teaspoons honey, divided**
- **⅓ cup extra-virgin olive oil**
- **1 teaspoon grated lime zest plus 1 tablespoon juice**
- **½ teaspoon ground coriander**
- **¼ teaspoon pepper**
- **1¼ pounds ripe but firm peaches, halved, pitted, and cut into ½-inch-thick wedges, wedges halved crosswise**
- **5 ounces fresh mozzarella, torn (1 cup)**
- **½ cup torn fresh mint**

1. Bring 2 quarts water to boil in large saucepan. Add farro and 1 tablespoon salt, return to boil, and cook until farro is tender with slight chew, 15 to 30 minutes. Drain farro, rinse under cold water, then drain well; set aside.
2. Meanwhile, combine jalapeño, shallot, vinegar, 1 teaspoon honey, and ¼ teaspoon salt in medium bowl. Cover and microwave until steaming, about 2 minutes. Let sit, stirring occasionally, until vegetables have softened slightly, about 15 minutes. Drain pickled vegetables, reserving 2 tablespoons pickling liquid.
3. Whisk oil, reserved pickling liquid, lime zest and juice, coriander, pepper, remaining ¼ teaspoon salt, and remaining 1 teaspoon honey together in large bowl. Add farro, peaches, mozzarella, mint, and pickled vegetables and toss to coat. Season with salt and pepper to taste. Serve.

PEACHES AND FRESH mozzarella shine together and complement the pleasant chew of nutty farro. Quick-pickled jalapeños—and some pickling liquid—add brightness and slight heat to a salad that's sweet, tangy, creamy, chewy, soft, and spicy.

NOTES

Make-ahead elements add to this salad's appeal: The farro can be refrigerated for 5 days and the pickles for 2 days. Whole farro offers the best flavor and texture. Pearl farro can be used if you're pressed for time; start checking for doneness after 10 minutes. Don't use quick-cooking or presteamed farro.

KITCHEN IMPROV

Other whole grains can be used in place of the farro; note that cooking times may change. Bulk up the salad with a few cups of baby arugula or kale. Use a combination of herbs: Basil, cilantro, and tarragon all work well.

three-pea salad WITH burrata AND spicy shallot–pine nut crisp

Serves 4 • Total Time: 45 minutes

- **½ cup plus 2 tablespoons extra-virgin olive oil, divided**
- **1 small shallot, sliced thin**
- **2 tablespoons chopped pine nuts**
- **1½ teaspoons dried oregano**
- **1½ teaspoons fennel seeds**
- **1 teaspoon kosher salt, plus salt for cooking peas**
- **1–2 teaspoons red pepper flakes**
- **8 ounces country-style bread, torn into 1-inch pieces (6 cups)**
- **1 pound sugar snap peas, strings removed**
- **1 pound snow peas, strings removed**
- **1½ cups frozen peas**
- **3 tablespoons white wine vinegar**
- **2 teaspoons Dijon mustard**
- **8 ounces burrata cheese, room temperature**

1. Bring 2 quarts water to boil in large saucepan. While water comes to boil, cook ½ cup oil and shallot in 12-inch nonstick skillet over medium-high heat, stirring frequently, until shallots are deep golden brown, about 5 minutes. Off heat, use slotted spoon to transfer shallots to heatproof medium bowl. Let oil cool slightly.

2. Add pine nuts, oregano, fennel seeds, salt, and pepper flakes to bowl with shallots. Carefully pour oil into bowl (mixture may bubble slightly) and stir to combine; set aside.

3. Toss bread with 2 tablespoons water, squeezing gently so bread absorbs water. Heat remaining 2 tablespoons oil in now-empty skillet over medium heat until shimmering. Add bread and cook, stirring frequently, until browned and crisp, 6 to 8 minutes; set aside.

4. Fill large bowl halfway with ice and water. Nestle colander into ice bath. Line large plate with paper towels. Add snap peas and 1 tablespoon salt to boiling water and cook for 1 minute. Add snow peas and frozen peas and cook until snap peas are bright green and tender, about 1 minute. Using spider skimmer or slotted spoon, transfer peas to prepared colander. Once peas are chilled, lift colander from ice bath and transfer peas to prepared plate; pat dry with extra paper towels.

5. Whisk vinegar, mustard, and 2 tablespoons shallot–pine nut crisp in clean, dry large bowl. Add peas and toss to coat. Season with salt and pepper to taste. Transfer peas to serving platter, top with bread and burrata, and drizzle with remaining shallot–pine nut crisp. Serve, breaking up burrata with spoon and allowing creamy liquid to meld with dressing.

VIBRANT THREE-PEA salad—sugar snap peas, snow peas and frozen English peas—gets a luscious upgrade with creamy burrata and a fiery shallot-pine nut crisp. Fresh, crunchy, and rich, it balances coolness and heat in every bite.

NOTES

You can refrigerate the shallot-pine nut crisp for up to 1 week; bring it to room temperature before using. You can refrigerate the blanched peas for up to 24 hours.

KITCHEN IMPROV

The combination of sugar snap peas and snow peas makes for a more interesting salad, but you can use all one variety. Alternatively, you can substitute 5 ounces baby arugula for either the sugar snap peas or the snow peas. Dollops of creamy ricotta or torn fresh mozzarella are nice alternatives to the burrata.

crispy coconut rice AND pigeon pea salad WITH tropical fruit

Serves 4 • Total Time: 45 minutes

- 1 cup long-grain white rice, rinsed
- 1 cup water
- 2/3 cup canned coconut milk
- 1 teaspoon table salt, divided
- 3 tablespoons vegetable oil
- 3 tablespoons lime juice
- 1 tablespoon packed brown sugar
- 1 tablespoon soy sauce
- 1 teaspoon ground allspice
- 2 cups thinly sliced red or green cabbage
- 2 cups ½-inch papaya pieces
- 2 cups ½-inch mango pieces
- 1 (15-ounce) can pigeon peas, rinsed
- 1 cup fresh cilantro leaves
- ½ red onion, chopped fine
- 1 serrano chile, stemmed and sliced thin
- ½ cup unsweetened flaked coconut (optional)

IN THE DOMINICAN REPUBLIC, as in many cultures, the most cherished part of a pot of rice is the crispy layer that sticks to the bottom. This salad features a coconut-scented skillet full of that crunchy, chewy rice. Add pigeon peas (a Caribbean staple), chunks of fruit, and colorful red cabbage, and you get a textural symphony of tropical flavors.

1. Bring rice, water, coconut milk, and ½ teaspoon salt to boil in 12-inch nonstick skillet over high heat. Reduce heat to low, cover, and simmer until all liquid has been absorbed, 18 to 20 minutes, adjusting heat as needed to maintain bare simmer.

2. Uncover and drizzle oil around edge of skillet. Increase heat to medium-high and cook, undisturbed, until rice is lightly browned and crisp on bottom and makes continuous popping sounds, about 4 minutes. With large spatula, flip rice in sections and compress in skillet, trying to keep clumps intact. Cook until lightly brown and crisp on second side, about 4 minutes. Transfer rice to large plate and cool for 10 minutes.

3. Whisk lime juice, sugar, soy sauce, allspice, and remaining ½ teaspoon salt together in large bowl. Add cabbage, papaya, mango, pigeon peas, cilantro, onion, serrano, and rice and gently toss to combine. Sprinkle with toasted coconut, if using, and serve.

NOTES

Give the can of coconut milk agood shake before opening; this will make it easier to measure. To tone down the spiciness, remove the seeds from the serrano chile, or omit it altogether.

KITCHEN IMPROV

Use coleslaw mix in place of the cabbage. If you can't find ripe papaya, use pineapple chunks, cut cantaloupe, or even halved cherry tomatoes.

tortellini salad WITH broccoli, cannellini beans AND castelvetrano olives

Serves 4 to 6 • Total Time: 45 minutes

- **12 ounces fresh or frozen cheese tortellini**
- **3/4 teaspoon table salt, plus salt for cooking pasta**
- **1 pound broccoli, stems sliced 1/4 inch thick, florets cut into bite-size pieces**
- **1 (15-ounce) can cannellini beans, drained**
- **1 ounce Parmesan cheese, grated (1/2 cup)**
- **2 tablespoons panko bread crumbs**
- **1/4 teaspoon pepper**
- **1/2 cup jarred sliced banana peppers, divided, plus 1/4 cup brine**
- **1/2 cup pitted Castelvetrano olives, halved, divided**
- **2 garlic cloves, chopped**
- **1/2 cup extra-virgin olive oil**
- **10 ounces cherry tomatoes, halved**

1 Line rimmed baking sheet with dish towel. Bring 2 quarts water to boil in large saucepan. Add pasta and 1½ teaspoons salt and cook until tender, about 5 minutes. Add broccoli and beans to saucepan with pasta and cook until broccoli is crisp-tender, 1 to 2 minutes. Drain well and transfer to prepared sheet.

2 Combine Parmesan, panko, and pepper in small bowl and toss until well mixed. Spray large plate lightly with vegetable oil spray. Transfer Parmesan mixture to plate and spread into 8-inch round. Microwave for 2 minutes. Continue to microwave in 30-second increments until mixture is golden brown. Run thin metal spatula under cheese crisp and turn over (it's OK if cheese breaks). Microwave for 30 seconds. Set aside to cool (cheese will continue to crisp as it cools).

3 Combine 1/4 cup banana peppers, brine, 1/4 cup olives, garlic, and salt in blender and process until coarse paste forms, about 30 seconds. With blender running, drizzle in oil and continue to process until dressing is emulsified and smooth, about 1 minute.

4 Combine pasta, broccoli, beans, tomatoes, remaining 1/4 cup banana peppers, and remaining 1/4 cup olives in large bowl. Add dressing and toss to coat. Transfer to serving bowl. Crumble cheese crisp over salad and serve.

ZESTY OLIVE and pickled pepper dressing makes this veggie-packed pasta salad sparkle. Once the cooked pasta, broccoli, and beans have cooled, refrigerate them while preparing the rest of the salad for a cool meal to enjoy on a hot night. Parmesan crisps, reminiscent of frico, are a snap to prepare in the microwave.

NOTES

Intentionally cooking the tortellini a little past al dente ensures that it remains tender, even when served cold. If making the salad ahead (up to 24 hours), dress and garnish it with the cheese crisps right before serving.

KITCHEN IMPROV

Use sliced pickled cherry peppers or pepperoncini instead of banana peppers. Any pitted green olive will work in place of the mild, meaty Castelvetranos.

sandwiches and other handhelds

chapter 8

avocado chicken salad sandwiches WITH jicama AND banana peppers

Serves 4 • Total Time: 20 minutes

- **1½ ripe avocados, halved and pitted**
- **¼ cup jarred banana pepper rings, chopped, plus 1½ tablespoons brine**
- **3 tablespoons buttermilk**
- **3 tablespoons sour cream**
- **1 teaspoon table salt**
- **½ teaspoon pepper**
- **½ teaspoon garlic powder**
- **½ teaspoon onion powder**
- **3 cups cooked chicken, cut into ½-inch pieces**
- **5 ounces jicama, peeled and cut into ½-inch pieces (1 cup)**
- **¼ cup finely chopped red onion**
- **1 tablespoon chopped fresh chives**
- **1 tablespoon chopped fresh dill**
- **8 slices hearty sandwich bread, toasted**

1 Process avocados, pepper brine, buttermilk, sour cream, salt, pepper, garlic powder, and onion powder in food processor until smooth, about 30 seconds, scraping down sides of bowl as needed; transfer dressing to large bowl.

2 Add chicken to dressing and stir until all pieces are evenly coated. Add jicama, red onion, chives, dill, and banana peppers and stir to combine. Season with salt and pepper to taste.

3 Spread chicken salad evenly over 4 bread slices and top with remaining 4 bread slices. Serve.

CREAMY AVOCADO with an assist from sour cream and buttermilk makes a silky dressing with more personality than mayo-based versions. Jarred banana peppers add kick to the salad, and a splashof their brine gives the dressing zip.

NOTES

You can use the recipe for Quick Cooked Chicken (page 334) or cube meat from a 2½-pound rotisserie chicken. The chicken salad can be refrigerated for up to 24 hours.

KITCHEN IMPROV

Change up the veggies: Use radishes or celery rather than jicama; sub pepperoncini, cornichons, or green olives for the banana peppers; or swap cilantro or parsley for the chives and dill. Serve the chicken salad on a bed of greens or as an open-face tartine on toasted bread.

spicy kimchi fried chicken sandwiches

Serves 4 • Total Time: 30 minutes

- **1 large egg**
- **1¼ cups panko bread crumbs**
- **4 (3- to 5-ounce) boneless, skinless chicken thighs, trimmed**
- **½ teaspoon table salt**
- **½ teaspoon garlic powder**
- **½ cup vegetable oil**
- **1 cup cabbage kimchi, drained and chopped coarse, with 2 tablespoons juice reserved**
- **2 tablespoons unsalted butter, melted**
- **1 teaspoon unseasoned rice vinegar**
- **¼ teaspoon cayenne pepper**
- **4 hamburger buns, toasted**
- **2 cups shredded iceberg lettuce**
- **¼ cup mayonnaise**

THIS EPIC chicken sandwich delivers crunch, bold spice, and tang without the fuss of deep frying. Using boneless chicken thighs gives the sandwiches a meatiness that's balanced by a brushed-on sauce of kimchi juice, butter, and vinegar and a crisp topping of kimchi and iceberg lettuce.

1 Lightly beat egg in shallow dish. Place panko in second shallow dish. Pat chicken dry with paper towels and sprinkle with salt and garlic powder. Working with 1 piece at a time, dip in egg, allowing excess to drip off, then coat with panko mixture, pressing gently to adhere; transfer to plate.

2 Line second plate with double layer of paper towels. Heat oil in 12-inch skillet over medium-high heat until shimmering. Place chicken in skillet and cook until deep golden brown and chicken registers at least 160 degrees, about 4 minutes per side; transfer to prepared plate.

3 Combine reserved kimchi juice, melted butter, vinegar, and cayenne in bowl. Using pastry brush, coat top of chicken with half of kimchi sauce. Transfer 1 chicken piece sauce side down to each bun bottom. Brush remaining kimchi sauce over chicken. Top each chicken piece with ¼ cup chopped kimchi, then ½ cup lettuce. Spread bun tops evenly with mayonnaise. Invert bun top onto each sandwich and serve.

NOTES

If you prefer less spice, reduce or omit the cayenne.

KITCHEN IMPROV

You can also make these sandwiches with chicken breast cutlets. Halve two 8-ounce boneless, skinless chicken breasts crosswise and pound between two sheets of plastic wrap to a uniform ½-inch thickness. Depending on the size of your skillet, you may need to fry the cutlets in batches. Shaved cucumbers or carrots are a nice alternative to shredded lettuce.

chicken AND plantain lettuce wraps WITH mafé sauce

Serves 4 • Total Time: 45 minutes

- **1½ pounds boneless, skinless chicken thighs, trimmed**
- **3 tablespoons vegetable oil, divided**
- **1¾ teaspoons table salt, divided**
- **1 teaspoon pepper, divided**
- **2 large ripe plantains, peeled, halved lengthwise, and sliced on bias ½ inch thick**
- **1 tablespoon tomato paste**
- **1 garlic clove, minced to a paste**
- **½ teaspoon grated fresh ginger**
- **½ teaspoon red pepper flakes**
- **½ cup hot water**
- **⅓ cup creamy no-sugar-added natural peanut butter**
- **1½ teaspoons fish sauce**
- **2 tomatoes, cored and cut into ¼-inch pieces**
- **3 scallions, sliced thin**
- **1 tablespoon lime juice, plus lime wedges for serving**
- **1 head (8 ounces) green leaf lettuce, leaves separated**
- **½ cup chopped unsalted, dry-roasted peanuts**

1 Adjust oven rack 6 inches from broiler element and heat broiler. Line rimmed baking sheet with aluminum foil. Pat chicken dry with paper towels, then toss with 1 tablespoon oil, 1 teaspoon salt, and ½ teaspoon pepper on prepared sheet. Arrange chicken in even layer over half of sheet and broil for 8 minutes.

2 Toss plantains with 1 tablespoon oil, ½ teaspoon salt, and remaining ½ teaspoon pepper in bowl. Spread plantains evenly over empty half of sheet. Broil until plantains are well browned and chicken registers at least 175 degrees, about 7 minutes. Transfer plantains to serving platter and let chicken rest on cutting board while preparing sauce.

3 Combine remaining 1 tablespoon oil, tomato paste, garlic, ginger, and pepper flakes in medium bowl. Microwave until fragrant and bubbly, about 1 minute. Whisk in hot water, peanut butter, and fish sauce until smooth. Combine tomatoes, scallions, lime juice, and remaining ¼ teaspoon salt in separate bowl.

4 Slice chicken into ½-inch strips and transfer to platter with plantains. Serve chicken and plantains in lettuce leaves, passing mafé sauce, tomato-scallion mixture, peanuts, and lime wedges separately.

BONELESS CHICKEN thighs and plantains get a nice char under the broiler while you whisk together a savory Senegalese-style peanut sauce. Green leaf lettuce leaves add a fresh and slightly crunchy contrast.

NOTES

Look for plantains that are almost completely black and yield to firm pressure, like a ripe avocado. Mafé sauce, unlike Thai peanut sauce, is not meant to be sweet, so be sure to use no-sugar-added peanut butter. A rasp grater makes quick work of grating ginger and mincing garlic to a paste.

KITCHEN IMPROV

For more crunch, use romaine or napa cabbage leaves for your wrappers. Want more veg? Toss in 8 ounces okra with the plantains or add 8 ounces asparagus, cut into 3-inch lengths.

SIMMERING CHICKEN thighs with chipotle chiles and fire-roasted tomatoes delivers a taco filling with a smoky-earthy depth of flavor. Letting the thighs cook to 195 degrees breaks down lots of collagen, turning the meat super-tender and enriching the sauce.

chicken tinga tacos

Serves 4 • Total Time: 45 minutes

- **1½ pounds boneless, skinless chicken thighs, trimmed**
- **½ teaspoon table salt**
- **3 tablespoons vegetable oil, divided**
- **1 onion, halved and sliced thin**
- **3 garlic cloves, minced**
- **1 teaspoon ground cumin**
- **¼ teaspoon ground cinnamon**
- **1 (14.5-ounce) can fire-roasted diced tomatoes**
- **½ cup chicken broth**
- **2 tablespoons minced canned chipotle chile in adobo sauce plus 2 teaspoons adobo sauce**
- **½ teaspoon brown sugar**
- **1 teaspoon grated lime zest plus 2 tablespoons juice, plus lime wedges for serving**
- **8–12 (6-inch) corn or flour tortillas, warmed**

1 Pat chicken dry with paper towels and sprinkle with salt. Heat 1 tablespoon oil in Dutch oven over medium-high heat until just smoking. Add chicken and cook until browned on first side, about 3 minutes; transfer to plate.

2 Add onion and remaining 2 tablespoons oil to now-empty pot and cook over medium heat until softened, about 5 minutes. Add garlic, cumin, and cinnamon and cook until fragrant, about 1 minute. Stir in tomatoes and their juice, broth, chipotle and adobo sauce, and sugar and bring to boil, scraping up any browned bits.

3 Return chicken and any accumulated juices to pot, reduce heat to medium-low, cover, and simmer until chicken registers 195 degrees, about 12 minutes, flipping chicken after 5 minutes. Transfer chicken to cutting board, let cool slightly, then shred into bite-size pieces using 2 forks.

4 Transfer contents of pot to blender and process until smooth. Combine chicken, sauce, and lime zest and juice in now-empty pot and season with salt and pepper to taste. Serve with tortillas and lime wedges.

NOTES

Fire-roasted diced tomatoes echo the smoky flavor of the chipotles, but regular diced tomatoes are fine here, too.

KITCHEN IMPROV

You can substitute boneless, skinless chicken breasts for the thighs: Cook the breasts to 160 degrees, about 10 minutes. Serve with your favorite taco fillings, like diced avocado, crumbled cotija or queso fresco, Mexican crema, and fresh cilantro leaves. This braised chicken is equally delicious as a topping for tostadas or in a taco bowl.

when reuben met rachel turkey burgers

Serves 4 • Total Time: 35 minutes

- ½ **cup mayonnaise, divided**
- 2 **tablespoons ketchup**
- 2 **tablespoons sweet pickle relish**
- 1 **tablespoon prepared horseradish**
- ½ **cup panko bread crumbs**
- ½ **teaspoon table salt**
- ¼ **teaspoon pepper**
- 1 **pound 93 percent lean ground turkey**
- 1 **tablespoon vegetable oil**
- 4 **slices deli Swiss cheese (4 ounces)**
- 1 **cup sauerkraut, drained**
- 4 **hamburger buns, toasted**

THIS JUICY burger borrows elements from two classic deli sandwiches: Sauerkraut nods to the Reuben, turkey to the Rachel, and Swiss cheese and a tangy homemade Thousand Island dressing brings them together. Serve with chips and a dill pickle, of course.

1 Combine ¼ cup mayonnaise, ketchup, relish, and horseradish in bowl; set aside. Combine remaining ¼ cup mayonnaise, panko, salt, and pepper in large bowl. Add turkey and mix with your hands until thoroughly combined. Divide turkey mixture into 4 equal portions, then shape each portion into ¾-inch-thick patty, about 4 inches in diameter.

2 Heat oil in 12-inch nonstick skillet over medium heat until shimmering. Add patties, reduce heat to medium-low, and cook until well browned and meat registers 160 degrees, about 5 minutes per side.

3 Top each burger with 1 slice cheese and ¼ cup sauerkraut. Remove skillet from heat, cover, and let sit until cheese is melted and sauerkraut is heated through, about 2 minutes. Spread sauce over bun bottoms then top with burgers and bun tops. Serve.

NOTES

Be sure to use ground turkey, not ground turkey breast (also labeled 99 percent fat-free). When mixing and shaping the patties, do not overwork the meat or the burgers may become dense.

KITCHEN IMPROV

If you don't have ground turkey, you can substitute ground chicken or ground pork. For an even greater deli vibe, mix ½ teaspoon caraway seeds with the sauerkraut and serve the burgers on poppy seed or onion kaiser rolls. Want to go full Rachel? Skip the sauerkraut and top the burgers with prepared coleslaw just before serving.

WELL-SEASONED, easy-to-make pork meatballs paired with crunchy vegetables make these Vietnamese-inspired sandwiches irresistible. Letting the vegetable mixture sit while making the meatballs pickles them slightly.

pork meatball banh mi

Serves 4 • Total Time: 30 minutes

- **3 carrots, peeled and cut into 2-inch matchsticks**
- **½ English cucumber, cut into 2-inch matchsticks**
- **½ cup chopped fresh cilantro, divided**
- **4 scallions, white and green parts separated and sliced thin**
- **2 tablespoons seasoned rice vinegar**
- **5 teaspoons fish sauce, divided**
- **¾ teaspoon pepper, divided**
- **½ teaspoon table salt, divided**
- **1½ pounds ground pork**
- **⅓ cup mayonnaise**
- **2 (12-inch) baguettes, ends trimmed, halved crosswise, and split lengthwise**

1 Combine carrots, cucumber, ¼ cup cilantro, scallion greens, vinegar, 2 teaspoons fish sauce, ¼ teaspoon pepper, and ¼ teaspoon salt in bowl; set aside, tossing occasionally.

2 Using your hands, thoroughly combine pork, scallion whites, remaining ¼ cup cilantro, remaining 1 tablespoon fish sauce, remaining ½ teaspoon pepper, and remaining ¼ teaspoon salt in separate bowl. Pinch off and roll pork mixture into 16 meatballs (about 2 tablespoons each). Arrange meatballs in 12-inch nonstick skillet and cook over medium-high heat until browned on all sides, about 10 minutes. Cover and continue to cook until meatballs register 160 degrees, about 4 minutes.

3 Spread mayonnaise evenly on cut sides of each baguette. Divide vegetable mixture and meatballs evenly among sandwiches. Serve.

NOTES

If you don't have seasoned rice vinegar, use unseasoned combined with 1 teaspoon sugar and a pinch of salt.

To make this sandwich spicier, top with thinly sliced jalapeño.

KITCHEN IMPROV

Ground pork is perfect here, but ground beef, lamb, or 93 percent lean turkey or chicken also works. Include other crisp vegetables such as fennel, celery, daikon, or jicama; just keep the total to roughly 3 cups. While a crusty baguette is classic, rustic sub or ciabatta rolls are suitable alternatives.

Or skip the bread, add more cucumber and greens, and serve as a salad or atop a rice bowl (add a squirt of sriracha to the mayo and dollop on top).

philly-style sausage AND broccoli rabe subs WITH portobellos

Serves 4 • Total Time: 45 minutes

- **4 (8-inch) Italian sub rolls**
- **3 tablespoons extra-virgin oil, divided**
- **3 garlic cloves, sliced thin**
- **1 pound broccoli rabe, trimmed and cut into ½-inch pieces**
- **¼ teaspoon plus ⅛ teaspoon table salt, divided**
- **8 ounces hot or sweet Italian sausage, casings removed**
- **1 pound portobello mushroom caps, stemmed and sliced ¼ inch thick**
- **1 teaspoon fennel seeds, cracked**
- **1 teaspoon minced fresh rosemary**
- **1 teaspoon soy sauce**
- **4 ounces fontina cheese, shredded (1 cup)**
- **2 tablespoons sliced jarred hot cherry peppers (optional)**

1 Adjust oven rack to middle position and heat oven to 450 degrees. If needed, slice rolls to make them easier to open (without slicing all the way through). Use spoon to scrape inside of rolls and remove all but ¼ inch of interior crumb; discard removed crumb. Set rolls aside.

2 Cook 1 tablespoon oil and garlic in 12-inch nonstick skillet over medium heat until garlic is light golden, 3 to 5 minutes. Add broccoli rabe and ¼ teaspoon salt and cook, stirring occasionally, until tender, 4 to 6 minutes. Transfer to bowl and cover to keep warm.

3 Heat 1 teaspoon oil in now-empty skillet over medium-high heat until just smoking. Add sausage and cook, breaking up meat into small pieces with wooden spoon, until lightly browned, about 5 minutes. Transfer to separate bowl.

4 Add 1 tablespoon oil to fat left in skillet and heat over medium-high heat until shimmering. Add mushrooms and remaining ⅛ teaspoon salt. Cover and cook, stirring occasionally, until mushrooms have released their liquid, 3 to 5 minutes. Uncover and continue to cook, stirring occasionally, until well browned, 5 to 7 minutes. Reduce heat to low. Clear center of skillet and add remaining 2 teaspoons oil, fennel seeds, and rosemary. Stir in soy sauce and cooked sausage, then stir in cheese until melted. Remove from heat and cover to keep warm.

5 Arrange reserved rolls on rimmed baking sheet and bake until lightly toasted, about 3 minutes. Divide mushroom-sausage mixture and broccoli rabe evenly among rolls. Top with cherry peppers, if using, and serve.

A WEEKNIGHT-FRIENDLY homage to the iconic meaty-cheesy, satisfyingly messy subs of Philadelphia, this sandwich ups the amount of veggies while hitting all the right notes: intensely flavored pork, garlicky sautéed greens and mushrooms, melty cheese, and piquant cherry peppers, all piled into Italian sub rolls.

NOTES

If portobello mushroom caps are unavailable, substitute cremini or button mushrooms.

KITCHEN IMPROV

If you're not a fan of broccoli rabe, you can use broccolini instead. Raw chicken or turkey sausages will work here, too. Sharp provolone also tastes great in these sandwiches instead of fontina.

korean sizzling beef lettuce wraps

Serves 4 • Total Time: 30 minutes

- **1 English cucumber, halved and sliced thin**
- **1/4 cup seasoned rice vinegar**
- **1/4 cup mayonnaise**
- **2 tablespoons sriracha**
- **3 tablespoons soy sauce**
- **2 tablespoons packed brown sugar**
- **4 garlic cloves, minced**
- **1 tablespoon toasted sesame oil**
- **1 1/2 pounds 85 percent lean ground beef**
- **1 head Bibb lettuce (8 ounces), leaves separated**

THERE'S SOMETHING so fun about eating with your hands. These beefy lettuce wraps with Korean flavors are ridiculously simple and utterly satisfying.

1 Combine cucumber and vinegar in bowl; set aside. Combine mayonnaise and sriracha in second bowl; set aside. Combine soy sauce, sugar, garlic, and oil in third bowl.

2 Cook beef in 12-inch nonstick skillet over high heat, breaking up meat into small pieces with wooden spoon, until any juices have evaporated and beef begins to fry in its own fat, 8 to 10 minutes. Add soy sauce mixture and cook until nearly evaporated, about 2 minutes.

3 Serve beef mixture, pickled cucumber, and sriracha mayonnaise with lettuce leaves.

NOTES

If you don't have seasoned rice vinegar, use unseasoned combined with 1 teaspoon sugar and a pinch of salt.

KITCHEN IMPROV

You can use ground pork or 93 percent lean ground chicken or turkey here, too. If using chicken or turkey, heat 1 tablespoon vegetable oil in the skillet before adding the meat and cook until no longer pink (some moisture will remain in the skillet). You can also serve the beef mixture with steamed rice and kimchi. Other kinds of butterhead lettuce work, or try iceberg or oak leaf lettuce. For an unexpected side, slice up oranges or mangos, drizzle with olive oil, and sprinkle with chili powder and coarse salt.

cast-iron pork fajitas

Serves 4 to 6 • Total Time: 45 minutes

- 1¼ teaspoons table salt, divided
- 1½ teaspoons pepper, divided
- 1 teaspoon ground cumin
- 1 teaspoon chili powder
- 1 teaspoon garlic powder
- 1 teaspoon dried oregano
- ⅛ teaspoon ground allspice
- 2 (12- to 16-ounce) pork tenderloins, trimmed
- 3 tablespoons vegetable oil, divided
- 2 red, orange, and/or green bell peppers, stemmed, seeded, and cut into ¼-inch-wide strips
- 1 onion, halved and sliced ¼ inch thick
- 2 garlic cloves, minced
- ¼ cup chopped fresh cilantro
- 1 tablespoon lime juice, plus lime wedges for serving
- 8–12 (6-inch) flour tortillas, warmed

1 Combine 1 teaspoon salt, 1 teaspoon pepper, cumin, chili powder, garlic powder, oregano, and allspice in bowl. Cut tenderloins in half crosswise. Working with 1 piece at a time, cover pork with plastic wrap and, using meat pounder, pound to even ¾-inch thickness. Pat pork dry with paper towels and sprinkle with spice mixture.

2 Heat 12-inch cast-iron skillet over medium heat for 3 minutes. Add 2 tablespoons oil to skillet and swirl to coat. Place pork in skillet and cook until meat is well browned on both sides and registers 135 to 140 degrees, 5 to 7 minutes per side. Transfer to cutting board, tent with aluminum foil, and let rest while preparing pepper mixture.

3 Add remaining 1 tablespoon oil and bell peppers to now-empty skillet and cook for 3 minutes. Stir in onion, remaining ¼ teaspoon salt, and remaining ½ teaspoon pepper and cook until vegetables are just softened, 3 to 5 minutes. Stir in garlic and cook until fragrant, about 30 seconds. Off heat, stir in cilantro and lime juice.

4 Slice pork thin crosswise. Stir any accumulated pork juices from cutting board into vegetables. Push vegetables to 1 side of skillet and place pork on empty side. Serve pork and vegetables with tortillas and lime wedges.

NOTES

If you don't have a cast-iron pan, use a nonstick skillet instead; in step 2, add 2 tablespoons oil to the skillet, swirl to coat, and heat until the oil is just smoking.

KITCHEN IMPROV

Setting out plenty of toppings adds to the fun as everyone can customize their own meal. Try pico de gallo, sliced avocado or guacamole, sour cream, and/or your favorite hot sauce. To make chicken fajitas, substitute four (6- to 8-ounces) boneless, skinless chicken breasts for the pork. Pound the breasts as directed and cook to 160 degrees, adjusting the cooking time in step 2 as needed.

A CAST-IRON skillet offers several advantages in cooking, but with fajitas the pan's heat retention is especially useful. Bringing the skillet to the table keeps the meat and veggies warm throughout the meal, so your last overstuffed tortilla is as good as the first one.

smoked mackerel tartines WITH dill pickled radishes

Serves 4 • Total Time: 30 minutes

- **3½ teaspoons lemon juice, divided**
- **½ teaspoon sugar**
- **⅛ teaspoon table salt**
- **4 radishes, trimmed, halved, and sliced ¼ inch thick**
- **1 teaspoon chopped fresh dill, plus 2 tablespoons dill fronds**
- **4 ounces cream cheese, softened**
- **¼ cup minced shallot**
- **2 teaspoons Worcestershire sauce**
- **½ teaspoon hot sauce**
- **4 slices country bread, 6 inches wide and ¾ inch thick**
- **2 tablespoons salted butter, softened**
- **2 (4- to 5-ounce) tins oil-packed smoked mackerel, drained, with oil reserved**
- **½ teaspoon coarsely ground pepper**

1 Combine 1½ teaspoons lemon juice, sugar, and salt in medium bowl and microwave until mixture is steaming and sugar and salt are dissolved, 10 to 20 seconds. Add radishes and chopped dill and stir to coat; set aside. In small bowl, stir cream cheese, shallot, Worcestershire, hot sauce, and remaining 2 teaspoons lemon juice until well combined.

2 Heat 12-inch skillet over medium heat until hot, about 2 minutes. While skillet heats, transfer radishes to paper towel–lined plate to drain. Spread 1 side of each bread slice with 1½ teaspoons butter. Working in 2 batches, cook bread butter side down in skillet until evenly browned, 3 to 5 minutes.

3 Transfer bread browned side down to cutting board. Spread each piece evenly with cream cheese mixture. Break mackerel into flakes and arrange over cream cheese mixture. Drizzle each tartine with 1 teaspoon reserved oil and sprinkle with pepper. Arrange radishes and dill fronds on top and serve.

TINNED FISH can be a busy cook's best friend for quick pantry meals. Smoked mackerel shines in these simple tartines, which are a great way to use up the last slices of country bread that are just starting to stale. Add a simple salad, and dinner is ready.

NOTES

Look for tins labeled "mackerel fillets" or "mackerel," which typically contain boneless, skinless fillets, versus tins labeled "small mackerel," which often contain small fish with the skin and bones intact.

KITCHEN IMPROV

Substitute smoked trout or good-quality oil-packed tuna if you like. If you don't have dill, any fresh herb will do.

crispy fish cake sandwiches

Serves 4 • Total Time: 40 minutes

- **3 cups shredded green cabbage**
- **½ red onion, sliced thin, rinsed thoroughly, and patted dry**
- **½ red, orange, or yellow bell pepper, cut into thin strips**
- **2 tablespoons lime juice**
- **¾ teaspoon plus ⅛ teaspoon table salt, divided**
- **¾ cup fresh parsley leaves**
- **¾ cup fresh cilantro leaves**
- **1 garlic clove, minced**
- **¾ teaspoon red pepper flakes**
- **¾ cup mayonnaise**
- **1 tablespoon red wine vinegar**
- **1 pound skinless cod fillets, cut into 1-inch pieces**
- **1½ cups panko bread crumbs, divided**
- **¼ cup vegetable oil**
- **4 hamburger buns, toasted**

1. Combine cabbage, onion, bell pepper, lime juice, and ½ teaspoon salt in bowl; set aside.
2. Pulse parsley, cilantro, garlic, pepper flakes, and ⅛ teaspoon salt in food processor until coarsely chopped, about 5 pulses. Add mayonnaise and vinegar and pulse until mixture is combined but not smooth, about 5 pulses, scraping down sides of bowl as needed. Transfer sauce to bowl; do not clean food processor.
3. Add cod to food processor and pulse until coarsely chopped into ¼-inch pieces, about 5 pulses; transfer to large bowl. Gently fold in 6 tablespoons sauce, ¾ cup panko, and remaining ¼ teaspoon salt. Spread remaining ¾ cup panko in shallow dish. Using your lightly moistened hands, divide cod mixture into 4 equal portions, then gently shape each portion into 1-inch-thick cake, about 3½ inches in diameter. Working with 1 cake at a time, dredge in panko, pressing lightly to adhere; transfer to plate.
4. Heat oil in 12-inch nonstick skillet over medium heat until shimmering. Cook cakes until golden brown, 5 to 7 minutes per side, reducing heat as needed if panko is browning too quickly. Transfer cakes to paper towel–lined plate and let drain, about 30 seconds per side. Spread remaining sauce evenly over bun tops. Transfer cod cakes to bun bottoms, top with slaw and bun tops, and serve.

NOTES

If buying skin-on fillets, purchase 1¼ pounds of fish and ask your fishmonger to skin it for you or do it yourself using a sharp knife. When processing the cod, it's OK to have some pieces that are larger than ¼ inch. It is important to avoid overprocessing the fish.

KITCHEN IMPROV

Haddock, hake, or pollock are all good substitutes for cod. A combination of herbs is nice, but you can also use 1½ cups of either parsley or cilantro. Coleslaw mix can be used in place of the cabbage. If you're not interested in a sandwich, the crispy patties, slaw, and sauce also make for a great combination served over hearty grains or baby greens.

FLAKY COD and herby mayo are your shortcut to crisp, golden fish cakes. Tuck the pan-fried fish cakes into a toasted bun and finish with a bright, crunchy slaw for snap in every bite.

honey-sriracha shrimp lettuce wraps

Serves 4 • Total Time: 30 minutes

- **1 carrot, peeled and cut into 2-inch matchsticks**
- **2 tablespoons seasoned rice vinegar**
- **¼ cup mayonnaise**
- **¼ cup sriracha, divided**
- **1 tablespoon honey**
- **1 tablespoon soy sauce**
- **1½ pounds extra-large shrimp (21 to 25 per pound), peeled, deveined, and tails removed, cut into ½-inch pieces**
- **¼ teaspoon table salt**
- **2 tablespoons vegetable oil**
- **4 scallions, white parts minced, green parts sliced thin on bias**
- **1 head Bibb lettuce (8 ounces), leaves separated**

LETTUCE WRAPS benefit from exciting condiments. Pickled carrot and sriracha mayo—each made with just two ingredients—add complexity to a savory-sweet shrimp stir-fry that gets tucked into Bibb lettuce. Requiring very little cooking, the wraps are ideal for a hot day or whenever you want a light, fresh dinner.

1 Combine carrot and vinegar in bowl; set aside, tossing occasionally. Combine mayonnaise and 2 tablespoons sriracha in second bowl. Whisk honey, soy sauce, and remaining 2 tablespoons sriracha together in third bowl.

2 Pat shrimp dry with paper towels and sprinkle with salt. Heat oil in 12-inch nonstick skillet over medium-high heat until just smoking. Add shrimp and scallion whites and cook, tossing occasionally, until shrimp are spotty brown and opaque throughout, about 3 minutes. Add honey mixture and cook until sauce is thickened and clings to shrimp, about 1 minute. Serve shrimp with lettuce, pickled carrot, sriracha mayonnaise, and scallion greens.

NOTES

If you don't have seasoned rice vinegar, use unseasoned combined with 1 teaspoon sugar and a pinch of salt.

KITCHEN IMPROV

Feel free to expand on the toppings with torn fresh cilantro or basil leaves, chopped toasted peanuts, and/or store-bought crispy fried shallots. Tender cup-shaped Bibb lettuce is ideal here, but you can also use romaine, green leaf, or red leaf lettuce.

blackened salmon tacos WITH slaw, avocado AND grapefruit

Serves 4 • Total Time: 35 minutes

- **2 cups thinly sliced red cabbage**
- **1/4 cup chopped fresh cilantro**
- **1/4 cup Mexican crema, plus extra for serving**
- **1 tablespoon lime juice**
- **1 teaspoon table salt, divided**
- **3/4 teaspoon pepper, divided**
- **2 grapefruits**
- **2 teaspoons paprika**
- **1 teaspoon garlic powder**
- **1/2 teaspoon ground coriander**
- **1/4 teaspoon ground fennel**
- **1/8 teaspoon cayenne pepper**
- **3 (8-ounce) skin-on center-cut salmon fillets, 1 1/2 inches thick**
- **8–12 (6-inch) corn or flour tortillas, warmed**
- **1 avocado, halved, pitted, and sliced thin**

1 Adjust oven racks to upper-middle and lower-middle positions and heat broiler. Combine cabbage, cilantro, crema, lime juice, 1/2 teaspoon salt, and 1/4 teaspoon pepper in bowl; set aside for serving. Cut away peel and pith from grapefruits. Holding fruit over bowl, use paring knife to slice between membranes to release segments; set aside for serving.

2 Combine paprika, garlic powder, coriander, fennel, cayenne, remaining 1/2 teaspoon salt, and remaining 1/2 teaspoon pepper in bowl. Pat salmon dry with paper towels and sprinkle flesh sides with spice mixture. Arrange salmon skin side down on aluminum foil–lined rimmed baking sheet and broil on upper rack until well browned, about 6 minutes.

3 Transfer sheet to lower rack and continue to cook until salmon registers 125 degrees (for medium-rare), 6 to 8 minutes. Using 2 forks, gently flake salmon apart on sheet into 2-inch pieces; discard skin. Serve salmon with tortillas, passing slaw, avocado, grapefruit segments, and extra crema separately.

NOTES

If you can't find Mexican crema, substitute 1/4 cup sour cream mixed with 1 tablespoon water. If cooking wild salmon, cook fillets to 120 degrees (for medium-rare) and start checking for doneness after 5 minutes in step 3.

KITCHEN IMPROV

Coleslaw mix can be used in place of the red cabbage, and 3 oranges—Cara Caras are especially nice—can be used in place of the grapefruit.

We make our own blackening spice blend here, but you can substitute 1 1/2 tablespoons of your favorite store-bought version (think Cajun, Creole, or barbecue) for the spices and salt used in step 2.

SALMON BRINGS its own natural richness to fish tacos without any need for battering or frying. Instead, a sprinkle of blackening spice amps up its flavor, while broiling creates crisp edges. Creamy avocado, bright citrus, and red cabbage slaw add color and contrast.

THESE NO-COOK vegetable wraps are a refreshingly cool way to serve up dinner on a hot summer night. The flavor explosion from the easy feta spread transforms a big pile of raw vegetables into a deliciously satisfying wrap.

raw vegetable wraps WITH feta AND dill

Serves 4 • Total Time: 25 minutes

- 2 tomatoes, cored and sliced thin
- 3/4 teaspoon kosher salt, divided
- 3/4 teaspoon pepper, divided
- 8 ounces marinated feta cheese (2 cups), plus 1/4 cup marinated feta oil
- 1/4 cup chopped fresh dill
- 2 tablespoons oil-packed sun-dried tomatoes, chopped
- 4 (12-inch) flour tortillas, warmed
- 6 ounces (3 cups) alfalfa sprouts
- 2 carrots, peeled and shaved into ribbons
- 2 Persian cucumbers, sliced thin on bias
- 1 cup jarred roasted red pepper, rinsed, patted dry, and sliced thin
- 2 cups thinly sliced red cabbage
- 2 avocados, halved, pitted, and sliced thin

1 Arrange tomato slices on paper towel–lined plate and sprinkle with 1/2 teaspoon salt and 1/2 teaspoon pepper. Using fork, mash feta and feta oil, dill, sun-dried tomatoes, and remaining 1/4 teaspoon pepper in bowl until well combined.

2 Divide feta mixture evenly among tortillas and spread into even layer, leaving 3-inch border around edge. Working with one wrap at a time, sprinkle one-quarter of sprouts in 3-inch-wide strip just below center of wrap, then top with tomatoes, carrot ribbons, cucumbers, red peppers, cabbage, and avocados; sprinkle with pinch salt. Fold bottom of tortilla over vegetables, then fold sides in over top. Roll bundle tightly away from you, tucking in sides as you roll. Cut wraps in half and serve.

NOTES

A vegetable peeler makes quick work of shaving the carrots into ribbons. Look for extra-large 12-inch tortillas for these wraps; if you can only find 10-inch tortillas, divide the ingredients among 6 tortillas. Quickly warming the tortillas in a skillet makes them more pliable and easier to roll into wraps. The feta spread can be refrigerated for up to 1 week.

KITCHEN IMPROV

Coleslaw mix can be used in place of the red cabbage. You can also substitute 1/2 English cucumber, halved lengthwise, for the Persian cucumbers and arugula for the alfalfa sprouts. If you can't find marinated feta, substitute 8 ounces traditional feta, crumbled, and 1/4 cup extra-virgin olive oil. Either way, the feta spread is so good you might find yourself making more of it to put on just about everything.

chickpea salad sandwiches WITH quick pickles

Serves 4 • Total Time: 20 minutes

- **½ English cucumber, sliced thin**
- **½ small red onion, sliced thin**
- **¼ cup cider vinegar**
- **½ teaspoon table salt for brining**
- **2 (15-ounce) cans chickpeas, rinsed, divided**
- **½ cup mayonnaise**
- **1 tablespoon lemon juice**
- **½ teaspoon table salt**
- **2 tablespoons chopped fresh dill**
- **8 slices pumpernickel sandwich bread**
- **6 hard-cooked eggs, sliced thin**
- **4 leaves Bibb lettuce**

1 Combine cucumber, onion, vinegar, and ½ teaspoon salt in bowl; set aside, tossing occasionally.

2 Process ¾ cup chickpeas, mayonnaise, lemon juice, and salt in food processor until smooth, about 30 seconds, scraping down sides of bowl as needed. Add dill and remaining chickpeas to food processor and pulse until coarsely chopped with some larger pieces remaining, about 4 pulses. Season with salt to taste.

3 Drain cucumber mixture. Spread chickpea salad evenly over 4 bread slices. Layer eggs, cucumber mixture, and then lettuce over salad. Top with remaining 4 bread slices. Serve.

CHICKPEAS WORK remarkably well as a plant-focused spin on a deli standby. Buzzing some chickpeas till smooth and pulsing others till chunky in the food processor gives the sandwiches nice textural contrast, while quick-pickled cucumber and onion adds satisfying tang.

NOTES

The pickled cucumbers and chickpea salad can be assembled and refrigerated up to 24 hours in advance.

KITCHEN IMPROV

Any hearty sandwich bread can be used in place of the pumpernickel. The dill is perfect here, but feel free to use another herb, or use another delicate lettuce in place of Bibb. Toast the bread and add tomato slices for extra heft, add sprouts, or replace the eggs with sliced avocado—you get the idea.

tofu katsu sandwiches

Serves 4 • Total Time: 35 minutes

- 1/4 cup ketchup
- 2 tablespoons plus 2 teaspoons soy sauce, divided
- 4 teaspoons Worcestershire sauce
- 1 teaspoon garlic powder
- 3/4 teaspoon sugar, divided
- 2 large eggs
- 1 tablespoon all-purpose flour
- 1 1/2 cups panko bread crumbs
- 14 ounces extra-firm tofu, cut crosswise into 8 slabs
- 1/2 cup vegetable oil
- 1 1/4 teaspoons unseasoned rice vinegar
- 3/4 teaspoon toasted sesame oil
- 1 1/2 cups shredded red or green cabbage
- 8 slices soft white sandwich bread

1. Whisk ketchup, 2 teaspoons soy sauce, Worcestershire, garlic powder, and 1/2 teaspoon sugar together in bowl; set sauce aside.
2. Set wire rack in rimmed baking sheet and line half of rack with triple layer of paper towels. Whisk eggs, flour, and remaining 2 tablespoons soy sauce together in shallow dish. Place panko in large zipper-lock bag and lightly crush with rolling pin; transfer to second shallow dish. Pat tofu dry with paper towels. Working with 1 tofu slab at a time, dredge in egg mixture, allowing excess to drip off, then coat all sides with panko, pressing gently to adhere. Transfer to unlined side of wire rack.
3. Heat vegetable oil in 12-inch nonstick skillet over medium-high heat until shimmering. Add half of tofu and cook until deep golden brown, 2 to 3 minutes per side. Transfer to lined side of wire rack and repeat with remaining tofu.
4. Combine vinegar, sesame oil, and remaining 1/4 teaspoon sugar in bowl. Add cabbage and toss to coat. Season with salt and pepper to taste. Arrange cabbage and tofu on 4 bread slices. Drizzle with sauce and top with remaining 4 bread slices. Serve.

TOFU "CUTLETS" with a crispy panko crust, lightly dressed cabbage salad, and homemade tonkatsu sauce, all served on squishy white bread, make for sandwiches packed with multidimensional textures and flavors.

NOTES

If you can find it, use milk bread, which is typical of katsu sandwiches; the fluffy slices contrast delightfully with the crisp tofu.

KITCHEN IMPROV

You can substitute coleslaw mix for the shredded cabbage and bottled tonkatsu sauce for the homemade sauce, if you prefer.

chipotle mushroom AND cauliflower tacos

Serves 4 • Total Time: 45 minutes

- **1¼ pounds cremini mushrooms, trimmed and quartered**
- **1¼ pounds cauliflower florets, cut into 1-inch pieces**
- **¼ cup vegetable oil**
- **2 teaspoons table salt, divided**
- **¼ cup minced canned chipotle chile in adobo sauce, divided**
- **½ red onion, sliced thin**
- **½ cup distilled white vinegar**
- **2 tablespoons sugar**
- **⅔ cup Mexican crema**
- **3 cups thinly sliced red cabbage**
- **8–12 (6-inch) corn or flour tortillas, warmed**

WARM, SMOKY roasted mushrooms and cauliflower, cool crema, and crunchy cabbage combine for an irresistible vegetarian taco.

1 Adjust oven rack to lowest position and heat oven to 500 degrees. Toss mushrooms, cauliflower, oil, and 1½ teaspoons salt together on rimmed baking sheet. Roast until liquid has mostly evaporated, 23 to 25 minutes. Stir 3 tablespoons chipotle into mushroom mixture and continue to roast until lightly browned, 3 to 5 minutes.

2 Meanwhile, combine onion, vinegar, sugar, and remaining ½ teaspoon salt in large bowl. Microwave, covered, until hot, about 2 minutes. Combine crema and remaining 1 tablespoon chipotle in small bowl.

3 Stir cabbage into onion mixture. Serve mushroom-cauliflower mixture with tortillas, cabbage mixture, and chipotle crema.

NOTES

Dial back the chipotles in step 1 if you want less spice. If you can't find Mexican crema, substitute ½ cup sour cream mixed with 2 tablespoons water.

KITCHEN IMPROV

Coleslaw mix can be used in place of the red cabbage. Serve with fresh cilantro leaves, crumbled cotija or queso fresco, and lime wedges. The roasted mushroom-cauliflower mixture and toppings are also delicious served as a bowl over rice pilaf or a hearty grain.

nutritional information for our recipes

We calculate the nutritional values of our recipes per serving; if there is a range in the serving size, we used the highest number of servings to calculate the nutritional values. We entered all the ingredients, using weights for important ingredients such as meat, cheese, and most vegetables. We also used our preferred brands in these analyses. We did not include additional salt or pepper for food that's "seasoned to taste."

	Cal	Total Fat (g)	Sat Fat (g)	Chol (mg)	Sodium (mg)	Carbs (g)	Fiber (g)	Total Sugar (g)	Protein (g)
chapter 1. never boring chicken									
Crispy Za'atar Chicken Cutlets with Sweet Potato Wedges	630	33	5	130	760	48	6	10	32
Skillet Chicken Breasts with Burst Cherry Tomato Sauce	430	25	7	140	910	6	1	3	40
Crispy Ranch Chicken and Broccoli	650	43	15	180	1540	22	4	3	44
Barbecue-Rubbed Chicken Thighs with Deviled Egg Potato Salad	630	31	6	375	1460	29	4	3	56
Sticky Gochujang Chicken Thighs with Carrot-Kimchi Salad	620	28	10	215	1360	26	4	16	44
Roasted Chicken Thighs with Asparagus, Arugula, and Walnut Salad	660	50	10	215	1190	9	3	4	43
Honey-Glazed Chicken Drumsticks with Charred Corn and Pineapple Salad	380	13	3	125	1170	41	2	19	26
Skillet-Roasted Chicken with Garlicky Spinach and Beans	320	11	2.5	95	840	12	4	1	38
Thai Curry Chicken with Sweet Potatoes and Green Beans	480	33	17	145	1020	19	3	6	28
Coriander-Cumin Chicken with Potatoes and Carrots	770	49	10	230	1080	39	7	7	43
Sheet-Pan Jerk Chicken with Sweet Potatoes and Crispy Collard Greens	890	60	15	280	550	34	8	9	51
Glazed Chicken Breasts with Currant-Pistachio Couscous	740	31	4.5	125	1030	62	6	12	50
Lemon-Oregano Chicken with Farro Salad	650	29	6	135	1080	50	5	2	50
Halal-Cart Chicken and Rice	950	60	10	185	1250	61	2	3	40
Chicken Sausages and Apples with Smoky Cheese Grits	730	38	18	180	1790	51	5	16	45
Coconut-Braised Chicken with Plantains and Peppers	630	37	21	125	1140	38	4	16	42
Murgh Makhani (Indian Butter Chicken)	460	31	17	210	1110	13	1	8	34
Simple Rice Pilaf	320	9	5	25	510	54	0	1	6
Mexican Red Rice	340	11	1.5	0	970	55	0	2	6
Creamy Parmesan Polenta	190	5	3	15	730	27	2	0	6
San Bei Ji (Three-Cup Chicken)	390	20	2.5	135	1380	9	1	4	38

	Cal	Total Fat (g)	Sat Fat (g)	Chol (mg)	Socium (mg)	Carbs (g)	Fiber (g)	Total Sugar (g)	Protein (g)
chapter 1. never boring chicken continued									
Cashew Chicken	550	29	4	125	1600	22	2	9	47
Gai Pad Krapow (Spicy Thai Basil Chicken)	280	16	3	100	900	12	0	4	22
Chicken Piccata Meatballs	550	42	13	180	900	13	1	3	28
Skillet Orzo with Chicken Meatballs, Green Olives, and Feta	790	38	12	90	1770	76	1	8	42
Couscous Risotto with Chicken and Spinach	770	25	13	220	1620	65	2	5	68
Cheesy Green Chile, Chicken, and Bean Skillet	610	35	14	150	1180	34	4	6	40
chapter 2. beyond steaks and chops									
Seared Skirt Steak with Hominy and Tomatoes	680	44	14	185	1790	21	5	7	53
Moroccan Steak Tips with Spiced Couscous and Chickpeas	500	15	3	80	1610	53	7	12	38
Steak Tips with Creamy Summer Squash Orzo	770	35	17	130	1790	67	2	10	45
Sesame-Glazed Meatballs and Broccoli	630	36	9	205	1490	31	3	8	44
Pan-Roasted Broccoli	90	7	1	0	170	6	2	1	2
Sautéed Baby Bok Choy	60	4.5	0	0	75	3	1	1	1
Fastest, Easiest Mashed Potatoes	300	14	9	40	640	37	4	4	5
Boiled Carrots with Lemon and Chives	70	3	2	10	140	10	3	5	1
New York Strip Steaks with Crispy Potatoes and Parsley Sauce	720	48	8	90	1010	30	4	3	43
Hoisin-Glazed Rib-Eye Steaks with Baby Bok Choy	390	22	7	100	1270	11	2	6	37
Bourbon-Glazed Rib-Eye Steaks with Collard Greens Salad	780	53	13	150	1080	20	4	11	49
Ancho-Rubbed Flank Steak and Cilantro Rice with Avocado Sauce	650	29	8	115	1390	56	4	1	46
Stir-Fried Cumin Beef	350	24	4	75	700	6	1	3	25
Rice Bowls with Harissa Beef, Chickpeas, and Olives	760	31	8	75	1630	82	11	4	37
Rice and Lentils with Spiced Beef and Crispy Onions	630	32	9	80	970	52	6	4	31
Pork Medallions with Sautéed Asparagus and Peas	390	19	10	150	1240	11	3	3	42
Lemon and Herb Pork Chops with Cauliflower Puree	460	28	16	170	1230	8	3	3	41
Pan-Seared Pork Chops with Apples and Spinach	360	16	2.5	85	860	19	5	11	33
Pork Chops with Creamy Corn and Lima Beans	610	30	13	130	890	42	6	4	43
One-Pan Pork Tenderloin and Panzanella Salad	390	22	3.5	75	920	19	2	7	27
Pork Tenderloin with White Beans and Romesco	600	25	4	110	1770	42	10	4	51

	Cal	Total Fat (g)	Sat Fat (g)	Chol (mg)	Sodium (mg)	Carbs (g)	Fiber (g)	Total Sugar (g)	Protein (g)
chapter 2. beyond steaks and chops continued									
Jammy Skillet Sausages with Blackberries and Fennel	420	18	6	50	1400	35	6	24	30
Roasted Cabbage with Kielbasa and Pierogi	550	32	9	70	1920	46	5	7	23
Kimchi Bokkeumbap (Kimchi Fried Rice)	470	15	1.5	15	1030	69	2	4	14
Miso Pork and Eggplant Stir-Fry	550	37	11	80	1520	27	6	16	25
White Pizza with Peach and Prosciutto	430	22	9	50	1310	37	1	4	19
Smoky Peppers and Eggs with Chorizo and Garlic Toast	580	35	8	210	1690	46	5	11	21
Cilantro-Lime Lamb Chops with Cucumber-Pea Salad	600	36	12	115	880	20	5	10	48
One-Pot Lamb Meatballs with Eggplant and Chickpeas	710	36	13	130	1780	28	11	36	31
Spiced Lamb Patties with Roasted Cauliflower	640	58	16	85	1140	10	4	3	23
chapter 3. foolproof fish									
Salmon Cakes with Sugar Snap Pea Salad	770	49	9	85	1210	46	12	18	38
Spiced Crispy-Skinned Salmon with Tomato-Mango Salad	640	42	8	95	690	29	3	9	39
Pan-Seared Salmon with Braised Beans and Greens	660	38	7	95	1280	31	1	2	45
Salmon with Old Bay Butter and Confetti Grits	730	39	15	140	1210	49	3	9	43
Maple-Soy Salmon Bowls with Quinoa and Brussels Sprouts	1080	57	11	145	1360	76	9	29	66
Spicy Salmon Sushi Bowls	880	43	6	105	1490	76	7	8	44
Spiced Red Snapper with Creamy Tahini Sauce and Butter-Toasted Almonds	440	28	6	80	840	9	3	3	40
Roasted Asparagus	110	9	1.5	0	290	5	2	2	3
Roasted Butternut Squash	100	8	1	0	650	7	2	5	3
Broiled Smashed Zucchini	130	5	0.5	0	300	22	4	4	2
Fastest-Ever Baked Potatoes	180	0	0	0	10	41	3	1	5
Tilapia with Harissa Beurre Monté and Bulgur Salad	580	36	16	130	1150	33	6	4	35
Flounder with Herbed Asparagus Rice and Salsa Verde	530	31	4.5	65	1400	40	2	1	24
Black Cod with Charred Tomatoes, Stewy Beans, and Tarragon-Pistachio Pesto	660	47	8	85	1010	29	7	6	32
Seared Tilapia with Olive Vinaigrette and Warm Chickpea Salad	580	38	5	70	1530	25	7	2	36
Swordfish with Charred Orange and Radicchio Salad	520	29	5	110	710	28	6	19	37
Lemony Halibut with Roasted Fingerling Potatoes	360	9	1.5	85	710	33	5	3	35
One-Pan Cod and Green Rice	640	29	4.5	85	1680	58	1	2	38

	Cal	Total Fat (g)	Sat Fat (g)	Chol (mg)	Sodium (mg)	Carbs (g)	Fiber (g)	Total Sugar (g)	Protein (g)
chapter 3. foolproof fish continued									
Poached Halibut with Pearl Couscous and Spicy Tomato Zhoug	610	36	5	0	1120	61	2	4	12
Moroccan Fish Tagine	390	23	2.5	75	600	13	4	6	32
Chraime	290	12	1.5	90	900	14	5	6	30
Seared Tuna Steaks with Wilted Frisée and Mushroom Salad	450	22	3.5	65	770	12	2	7	46
Warm White Beans with Tuna, Fennel, and Herbs	570	26	4	15	1300	54	9	6	31
Tuna Quinoa Bowl with Tahini	540	30	4	20	950	40	7	5	32
Kedgeree	630	22	9	250	1940	78	5	4	28
Seared Scallops with Polenta, Bacon, and Poblano Chiles	580	35	15	105	1410	34	4	2	33
Shrimp with Black Bean Sauce	210	11	1.5	105	590	11	1	5	16
Seared Shrimp with Tomato, Lime, and Avocado	220	12	2	145	480	12	5	3	18
Fried Rice with Shrimp, Lime, and Peanuts	630	29	5	250	1420	65	5	13	26
Red Curry Shrimp with Coconut Rice and Cucumber Relish	640	27	16	180	1380	70	2	7	32
Mussels with White Wine and Parsley	600	26	7	140	1450	23	1	2	55
chapter 4. mostly vegetables and beans									
Roasted Cauliflower and Chickpeas with Romesco and Sumac Onions	420	32	4.5	0	1180	29	11	7	10
Braised Eggplant with Soy, Garlic, and Ginger	100	4.5	0.5	0	600	12	3	7	2
Roasted Mushrooms and Escarole with Couscous and Lemon Vinaigrette	490	22	3	0	980	61	13	9	14
Loaded Sweet Potato Wedges with Tempeh	520	28	4	0	710	59	12	15	13
Stuffed Delicata Squash	500	26	11	45	1150	60	11	8	14
Buttery Summer Squash with Caramelized Lemon and Burrata	330	29	17	80	840	11	2	4	14
Broccoli and Feta Frittata	360	25	10	585	940	8	2	4	26
Chickpea and Spinach Frittata with Cumin and Paprika	360	23	5	370	1220	21	8	2	21
Savory Dutch Baby with Portobellos, Roasted Red Peppers, Walnuts, and Feta	680	37	13	325	1100	62	3	13	25
Lavash Flatbreads with Romesco, Tomatoes, and Spinach	420	31	3.5	0	880	26	3	4	9
Corn, Tomato, and Arugula Pizza	470	27	13	70	850	43	1	8	17
Fregula with Chickpeas, Tomatoes, and Fennel	360	10	1.5	0	630	59	9	4	13
Risotto with Asparagus, Mushrooms, and Peas	600	23	12	50	1040	84	5	6	21

	Cal	Total Fat (g)	Sat Fat (g)	Chol (mg)	Sodium (mg)	Carbs (g)	Fiber (g)	Total Sugar (g)	Protein (g)
chapter 4. mostly vegetables and beans continued									
Spicy Polenta with White Beans and Kale	640	34	11	40	1850	61	11	5	22
Wild Mushroom Ragout with Farro	450	10	1	0	690	74	10	14	17
Easy Cuban Black Beans	260	8	0.5	0	790	44	1	4	12
Curried Lentils	250	8	1	0	390	32	12	4	14
Stewed Chickpeas and Spinach with Dill and Lemon	160	7	1	0	510	18	6	0	7
Easy White Bean Gratin	250	11	3	10	640	26	7	4	14
Ful Medames	580	25	3.5	95	1250	67	9	2	26
Palak Dal	400	13	7	30	920	50	13	2	23
Chana Masala	320	15	1	0	1100	37	11	4	12
Sicilian White Beans and Escarole	140	4.5	1	0	530	21	7	4	6
Calabrian Chile White Beans with Almond Romesco	430	25	4	10	1350	34	10	8	19
Cacio e Pepe Beans with Squash, Sage, and Walnuts	580	29	11	45	1070	61	14	5	22
East African Coconut Curry with Tofu and Squash	360	28	15	0	690	23	5	6	10
Chickpea Curry	300	17	8	0	1470	30	7	7	8
Chickpea Shakshuka	320	17	5	195	1460	30	8	12	16
chapter 5. always craveable noodles									
Mezzi Rigatoni with Spicy Gochujang Tomato Sauce	480	18	11	50	390	68	4	6	13
Cacio e Pepe	410	12	6	35	390	55	3	1	19
Pasta with Creamy Lemon-Sichuan Peppercorn Sauce	500	10	10	55	390	61	3	5	12
Chili Crisp Noodles	540	25	5	30	1610	53	2	13	22
San Francisco–Style Garlic Noodles	290	14	8	65	500	33	0	0	9
Liang Mian (Chilled Sesame Noodles)	520	16	2	5	1340	74	1	14	16
Mixed Green Salad with Miso-Honey Vinaigrette	260	25	3	0	230	7	0	4	1
Arugula Salad with Grapes, Fennel, and Blue Cheese	330	27	7	20	470	19	3	12	7
Zucchini Ribbon Salad	180	15	3.5	10	560	8	2	4	7
Pai Huang Gua (Sichuan Smashed Cucumbers)	50	2.5	0	0	650	4	2	3	2
Bucatini with Charred Zucchini, Mint, and Lemon	460	19	4.5	15	630	61	5	4	14
Viet-Cajun Garlic-Butter Rice Noodles with Corn and Shrimp	540	24	14	220	750	55	2	6	25
Rigatoni with Marinated Tomatoes and Burrata	490	23	7	25	730	60	4	4	17
Pasta with Burst Cherry Tomato Sauce and Fried Caper Crumbs	420	19	4.5	10	910	53	4	5	10

	Cal	Total Fat (g)	Sat Fat (g)	Chol (mg)	Sodium (mg)	Carbs (g)	Fiber (g)	Total Sugar (g)	Protein (g)
chapter 5. always craveable noodles continued									
Spaghetti al Tonno	430	12	1.5	20	840	59	3	3	22
Penne with Pancetta and Asparagus	440	16	8	40	500	58	4	3	17
Orecchiette with Navy Beans, Brussels Sprouts, and Bacon	450	13	4.5	25	880	67	8	4	17
Mushroom Yaki Udon	190	4	0.5	0	1170	54	3	8	10
Mapo Eggplant Pasta	690	36	10	80	1160	56	6	6	30
Creamy Pumpkin Ramen	600	28	15	70	1080	73	1	6	17
Pea and Pistachio Pesto Pasta	570	28	4	5	860	65	7	4	17
Ultracreamy Spaghetti with Zucchini	650	23	9	35	960	89	6	7	25
Creamy Broccoli Pasta with Crispy Panko	630	32	7	10	620	68	5	4	18
Tortellini with Corn and Basil Cream Sauce	500	27	15	95	780	51	1	5	17
Crispy Skillet Gnocchi with Spicy Cumin Lamb and Celery	510	40	12	60	980	25	1	3	14
Samosa Gnocchi Chaat	490	32	7	25	940	41	6	7	12
Gochujang-Tahini Noodles	460	11	1.5	0	1030	84	1	9	14
Lemony Shrimp with Orzo, Feta, and Olives	470	14	5	205	1980	49	1	6	32
Vegetarian Ramen with Shiitakes and Soft Eggs	530	18	3	185	1820	75	2	8	20
chapter 6. hearty soups and stews									
Chicken and Leek Soup with Parmesan Dumplings	520	20	9	185	1930	42	3	6	43
Spiced Chicken Soup with Squash and Navy Beans	300	7	1	50	1990	40	9	5	21
Curried Chicken Soup with Coconut and Kale	360	26	14	90	890	9	2	3	26
Carrot Ribbon, Chicken, and Coconut Curry Soup	440	29	14	100	850	23	4	11	25
Posole Verde	530	31	10	80	1780	38	10	14	26
Quick Beef and Vegetable Soup	370	18	7	75	1490	25	4	7	26
Corn Muffins	310	14	8	80	380	41	1	13	6
Drop Biscuits	160	8	5	25	230	18	1	0	2
Garlic and Herb Breadsticks	80	2.5	1.5	5	150	12	0	1	2
Pan-Grilled Flatbreads	360	13	4.5	15	660	54	0	7	9
Pork Meatball Soup with Wonton Noodles and Baby Bok Choy	560	30	10	140	1980	39	3	6	31
Spicy Tomato Soup with Tortellini and Sausage	420	21	10	65	1330	36	4	8	25
Thai-Style Hot and Sour Soup with Shrimp and Noodles	270	3	0	105	1810	41	3	9	20
Creamy Butternut and Fennel Soup	410	28	7	20	1080	33	7	9	13

	Cal	Total Fat (g)	Sat Fat (g)	Chol (mg)	Sodium (mg)	Carbs (g)	Fiber (g)	Total Sugar (g)	Protein (g)
chapter 6. hearty soups and stews continued									
Chilled Cucumber-Avocado Soup	290	22	5	20	1020	17	6	8	10
Red Lentil Soup with Warm Spices	400	13	7	30	1200	53	9	3	20
Pasta e Fagioli	450	13	3	15	1950	61	13	9	24
Quick Mediterranean Beef Stew	380	15	4.5	90	1000	13	3	5	40
Picadillo-Style Beef Chili	420	20	7	75	1900	31	2	6	26
Creamy Chickpea and Sweet Potato Stew	500	33	15	0	860	42	11	8	16
chapter 7. dinner-size salads									
Chicken and Arugula Salad with Cherries and Feta	570	36	8	100	560	21	2	8	39
Chicken Salad with Cabbage and Fish Sauce	350	8	2	90	1320	27	4	17	40
Charred Broccoli Caesar Salad with Chicken	680	47	8	115	1240	24	5	4	40
Quick Cooked Chicken	160	4.5	1	95	130	0	0	0	29
Sirloin Steak Tips	250	13	2.5	80	820	2	0	1	29
Crispy-Skinned Salmon Fillets	350	23	5	95	390	0	0	0	35
Pan-Seared Tofu	110	7	0	0	150	1	0	0	8
Hummus Bowls with Roasted Chicken and Cauliflower	660	40	6	135	1840	32	5	6	49
Orecchiette Salad with Roasted Vegetables, Chicken, and Jalapeño-Lime Dressing	480	27	2.5	60	990	34	3	3	28
Tomato Salad with Steak Tips	590	41	11	130	810	10	3	6	43
Pinto Bean, Ancho, and Steak Salad with Pickled Poblanos	720	40	14	130	1300	48	14	9	45
White Beans and Chorizo with Quick Marinated Tomatoes and Onion	570	41	10	35	1270	29	8	5	20
Bún Chả	600	27	9	80	1230	63	2	14	26
Napa Cabbage and Noodle Salad with Shrimp and Citrus	490	15	5	180	1010	63	3	9	42
Hearty Green Salad with Hot-Smoked Salmon	410	27	5	205	1810	20	3	14	24
Oil-Poached Tuna and Potato Salad	630	43	6	45	1010	28	3	4	32
Seared Scallops with Citrus and Avocado Salad	540	37	5	40	1320	32	12	13	25
Farro Salad with Peaches and Pickled Jalapeños	520	28	8	25	430	55	7	17	14
Three-Pea Salad with Burrata and Spicy Shallot–Pine Nut Crisp	780	53	13	40	1430	55	6	11	24
Crispy Coconut Rice and Pigeon Pea Salad with Tropical Fruit	530	20	9	0	1020	81	7	25	11
Tortellini Salad with Broccoli, Cannellini Beans, and Castelvetrano Olives	420	26	5	25	930	34	2	3	13

	Cal	Total Fat (g)	Sat Fat (g)	Chol (mg)	Sodium (mg)	Carbs (g)	Fiber (g)	Total Sugar (g)	Protein (g)
chapter 8. sandwiches and other handhelds									
Avocado Chicken Salad Sandwiches with Jicama and Banana Peppers	470	20	4.5	110	1430	33	8	6	38
Spicy Kimchi Fried Chicken Sandwiches	540	29	7	135	920	43	0	5	26
Chicken and Plantain Lettuce Wraps with Mafé Sauce	680	38	6	135	1340	43	6	20	48
Chicken Tinga Tacos	460	19	2.5	160	770	33	2	5	37
When Reuben Met Rachel Turkey Burgers	680	43	12	120	1430	38	2	8	34
Pork Meatball Banh Mi	640	39	11	120	1310	34	2	5	37
Philly-Style Sausage and Broccoli Rabe Subs with Portobellos	540	31	11	50	1130	44	4	7	22
Korean Sizzling Beef Lettuce Wraps	570	39	12	120	1520	18	2	14	35
Cast-Iron Pork Fajitas	540	22	5	110	1420	41	3	6	43
Smoked Mackerel Tartines with Dill Pickled Radishes	400	22	11	85	650	28	1	6	20
Crispy Fish Cake Sandwiches	710	42	5	60	1080	53	2	7	29
Honey-Sriracha Shrimp Lettuce Wraps	290	18	2.5	150	1160	15	1	11	17
Blackened Salmon Tacos with Slaw, Avocado, and Grapefruit	560	23	4.5	105	690	53	11	15	40
Raw Vegetable Wraps with Feta and Dill	790	48	15	50	1730	74	11	13	23
Chickpea Salad Sandwiches with Quick Pickles	560	32	6	290	1410	47	7	2	22
Tofu Katsu Sandwiches	550	25	3	95	1100	55	2	10	22
Chipotle Mushroom and Cauliflower Tacos	430	23	5	25	1320	49	4	17	10

conversions and equivalents

Some say cooking is a science and an art. We would say that geography has a hand in it too. Flours and sugars manufactured in the United Kingdom and elsewhere will feel and taste different from those manufactured in the United States. So we cannot promise that the loaf of bread you bake in Canada or England will taste the same as a loaf baked in the States, but we can offer guidelines for converting weights and measures. We also recommend that you rely on your instincts when making our recipes. Refer to the visual cues provided.

The recipes in this book were developed using standard U.S. measures following U.S. government guidelines. The charts below offer equivalents for U.S. and metric measures. All conversions are approximate and have been rounded up or down to the nearest whole number.

EXAMPLES

- 1 teaspoon = 4.9292 milliliters, rounded up to 5 milliliters
- 1 ounce = 28.3495 grams, rounded down to 28 grams

volume conversions

U.S.	Metric
1 teaspoon	5 milliliters
2 teaspoons	10 milliliters
1 tablespoon	15 milliliters
2 tablespoons	30 milliliters
1/4 cup	59 milliliters
1/3 cup	79 milliliters
1/2 cup	118 milliliters
3/4 cup	177 milliliters
1 cup	237 milliliters
1 1/4 cups	296 milliliters
1 1/2 cups	355 milliliters
2 cups (1 pint)	473 milliliters
2 1/2 cups	591 milliliters
3 cups	710 milliliters
4 cups (1 quart)	0.946 liter
1.06 quarts	1 liter
4 quarts (1 gallon)	3.8 liters

weight conversions

Ounces	Grams
1/2	14
3/4	21
1	28
1 1/2	43
2	57
2 1/2	71
3	85
3 1/2	99
4	113
4 1/2	128
5	142
6	170
7	198
8	227
9	255
10	283
12	340
16 (1 pound)	454

conversions for common baking ingredients

Because measuring by weight is far more accurate than measuring by volume, and thus more likely to achieve reliable results, in our recipes we provide ounce measures in addition to cup measures for many ingredients. Refer to the chart below to convert these measures into grams.

Ingredient	Ounces	Grams
flour		
1 cup all-purpose flour*	5	142
1 cup cake flour	4	113
1 cup whole-wheat flour	5½	156
sugar		
1 cup granulated (white) sugar	7	198
1 cup packed brown sugar (light or dark)	7	198
1 cup confectioners' sugar	4	113
cocoa powder		
1 cup cocoa powder	3	85
butter †		
4 tablespoons (½ stick, or ¼ cup)	2	57
8 tablespoons (1 stick, or ½ cup)	4	113
16 tablespoons (2 sticks, or 1 cup)	8	227

* U.S. all-purpose flour, the most frequently used flour in this book, does not contain leaveners, as some European flours do. These leavened flours are called self-rising or self-raising. If you are using self-rising flour, take this into consideration before adding leavening to a recipe.

† In the United States, butter is sold both salted and unsalted. We generally recommend unsalted butter. If you are using salted butter, take this into consideration before adding salt to a recipe.

oven temperature

Fahrenheit	Celsius	Gas Mark
225	105	¼
250	120	½
275	135	1
300	150	2
325	165	3
350	180	4
375	190	5
400	200	6
425	220	7
450	230	8
475	245	9

converting temperatures from an instant-read thermometer

We include doneness temperatures in many of the recipes in this book. We recommend an instant-read thermometer for the job. Refer to the table above to convert Fahrenheit degrees to Celsius. Or, for temperatures not represented in the chart, use this simple formula:

Subtract 32 degrees from the Fahrenheit reading, then divide the result by 1.8 to find the Celsius reading.

EXAMPLE

"Roast chicken until thighs register 175 degrees."

TO CONVERT

175°F − 32 = 143°

143° ÷ 1.8 = 79.44°C, rounded down to 79°C

index

Note: Page references in *italics* indicate photographs.

C

D

E

F

G

H

I

J

K

L

M

N

O

P

Q

R

S

T

V

W

Y

Z